W9-AMY-787

INFORMATION ECONOMY REPORT 2012

The Software Industry and Developing Countries

UNITED NATIONS
New York and Geneva 2012

NOTE

Within the UNCTAD Division on Technology and Logistics, the ICT Analysis Section carries out policy-oriented analytical work on the development implications of information and communication technologies (ICTs). It is responsible for the preparation of the *Information Economy Report*. The ICT Analysis Section promotes international dialogue on issues related to ICTs for development, and contributes to building developing countries' capacities to measure the information economy and to design and implement relevant policies and legal frameworks.

In this Report, the terms country/economy refer, as appropriate, to territories or areas. The designations employed and the presentation of the material do not imply the expression of any opinion whatsoever on the part of the Secretariat of the United Nations concerning the legal status of any country, territory, city or area or of its authorities, or concerning the delimitation of its frontiers or boundaries. In addition, the designations of country groups are intended solely for statistical or analytical convenience and do not necessarily express a judgement about the stage of development reached by a particular country or area in the development process. The major country groupings used in this Report follow the classification of the United Nations Statistical Office. These are:

Developed countries: the member countries of the Organization for Economic Cooperation and Development (OECD) (other than Mexico, the Republic of Korea and Turkey), plus the new European Union member countries that are not OECD members (Bulgaria, Cyprus, Latvia, Lithuania, Malta and Romania), plus Andorra, Israel, Liechtenstein, Monaco and San Marino. Countries with economies in transition: South-East Europe and the Commonwealth of Independent States. Developing economies: in general, all the economies that are not specified above. For statistical purposes, the data for China do not include those for Hong Kong Special Administrative Region (Hong Kong, China), Macao Special Administrative Region (Macao, China), or Taiwan Province of China.

Reference to companies and their activities should not be construed as an endorsement by UNCTAD of those companies or their activities.

The following symbols have been used in the tables:

Two dots (..) indicate that data are not available or are not separately reported. Rows in tables have been omitted in those cases where no data are available for any of the elements in the row;

A dash (–) indicates that the item is equal to zero or its value is negligible;

A blank in a table indicates that the item is not applicable, unless otherwise indicated;

A slash (/) between dates representing years, for example, 1994/95, indicates a financial year;

Use of an en dash (–) between dates representing years, for example, 1994–1995, signifies the full period involved, including the beginning and end years;

Reference to "dollars" ($) means United States dollars, unless otherwise indicated;

Annual rates of growth or change, unless otherwise stated, refer to annual compound rates;

Details and percentages in tables do not necessarily add up to the totals because of rounding.

The material contained in this study may be freely quoted with appropriate acknowledgement.

UNITED NATIONS PUBLICATION

UNCTAD/IER/2012

Sales No. E.12.IID.14

ISSN 2075-4396

ISBN 978-92-1-112857-4
e-ISBN 978-92-1-055890-7

Copyright © United Nations, 2012

All rights reserved. Printed in Switzerland

JUN 24 2013

PREFACE

Information and communications technologies continue to transform our society. In recent years we have seen dramatically improved access to mobile telephones, the Internet and broadband connectivity throughout the developing world. These trends are gradually helping to dismantle barriers towards the goal of an "information society for all" agreed by world leaders at the World Summit on the Information Society.

Such a society depends on software. The growing emphasis on ICTs in the delivery of government, healthcare, education and other goods and services demands customized applications. Countries therefore need the capacity to adopt, adapt and develop relevant software. Such capacity is also important to facilitate successful technology transfer.

The *Information Economy Report 2012* provides an in-depth analysis of software industry developments in developing countries. It underlines the importance of focusing not only on the export opportunities offered by the sector, but also on domestic needs. Using new data, it makes a fresh assessment of the software performance of different countries, highlights key drivers in the evolving software landscape, reviews selected country cases and proposes concrete recommendations to policy makers in developing countries. I commend the report to Governments and development partners working to create an information society for all.

BAN Ki-moon
Secretary-General
United Nations

ACKNOWLEDGEMENTS

The *Information Economy Report 2012* was prepared by a team comprising Torbjörn Fredriksson (team leader), Cécile Barayre, Scarlett Fondeur Gil, Suwan Jang, Diana Korka, Rémi Lang and Smita Lakhe under the overall guidance of Anne Miroux, Director of the Division on Technology and Logistics, and the supervision of Mongi Hamdi, Head of the Science, Technology and ICT Branch.

The *Information Economy Report 2012* benefited from major substantive inputs provided by Fouad Bajwa, KJ Joseph, Harsha Liyanage, Michael Minges, Lucas von Zallinger (Capgemini) and a joint survey with the World Information Technology and Services Alliance (WITSA) of national IT/software associations.

Additional inputs were contributed by Anna Abramova, Kwame Andah, Nathan Bartel, Olga Cavalli, Juliana Dib, Dirk Elias, Peter Haddawy, Arafat Hossein, Nnenna Nwakanma, Astrit Sulstarova and Chris Uwaje.

Useful comments on various parts of the text were made by experts attending a global seminar organized at the Federal Ministry for Economic Cooperation and Development (BMZ) in Bonn, Germany, in May 2012, including Susanne Dorasil, Bernd Friedrich, Helani Galpaya, Petra Hagemann, Anja Kiefer, Martin Labbe, Nicole Maldonado, Andreas Meiszner, Ola Pettersson, Thorsten Scherf, Balthas Seibold and David Souter. Valuable comments were also received at various stages of the production of the report from Dimo Calovski, Angel Gonzalez-Sanz, Yumiko Mochizuki, Thao Nguyen, Marta Perez Cusó, Christoph Spenneman, Susan Teltscher, Ian Walden and Dong Wu.

UNCTAD is grateful for the sharing of data by national statistical offices and the responses received to UNCTAD's annual survey questionnaire on information and communication technology (ICT) usage by enterprises and on the ICT sector. The sharing of data for this report by the Emerging Market Private Equity Association, Eurostat, Everest Group, the International Telecommunication Union, the Organization for Economic Cooperation and Development, WITSA/IHS Global Insight Inc. and the World Bank is also highly appreciated.

The cover was done by Sophie Combette. Desktop publishing was done by Nathalie Loriot, graphics were carried out by Philippe Terrigeol and the *Information Economy Report 2012* was edited by Maritza Ascencios and John Rogers.

Financial support from the Government of Finland is gratefully acknowledged.

CONTENTS

Boxes

Box figure

Tables

Figures

LIST OF ABBREVIATIONS

3G	third generation (refers to mobile phones)
A4D	Android for Development
ACE	Africa Coast to Europe
AFRICOMM	International Conference on e-Infrastructure and e-Services for Developing Countries
AGEXPORT	Guatemalan Exporters Association
AGPL	Affero General Public License
AHTI	Asociación Hondureña de Tecnologías de Información
AICOS	Assistive Information and Communication Solutions
APIs	application program interfaces
APKIT	Association of Computer and Information Technology Producers (Russia)
app	application software
ASEAN	Association of Southeast Asian Nations
ASSESPRO	Association of Brazilian Information Technology Companies
AVOIR	African Virtual Open Initiatives and Resources
B2B	business-to-business
BASIS	Bangladeshi Software and Information Services Association
BASSCOM	Bulgarian Association of Software Companies
BIND	Berkeley Internet Name Domain
BNDES	Brazilian Development Bank
BPO	business process outsourcing
BRIC	Brazil, Russia, India and China
BSA	Business Software Association
BSD	Berkeley Software Distribution
BMZ	German Federal Ministry for Economic Cooperation and Development
CAD/CAM	computer-aided design and computer-aided manufacturing
CMM	Capability Maturity Model
CMMI	Capability Maturity Model Integration
COBIT	Control Objectives for Information and Related Technologies
COMESA	Common Market for Eastern and Southern Africa
CRM	client relationship management
CSC	Common Services Centres
CSIS	Center for Strategic and International Studies
DNS	Domain Name System
DVD	Digital Versatile Disc
EASSy	Eastern Africa Submarine Cable System
EFTA	European Free Trade Association
EITO	European Information Technology Observatory
EMPEA	Emerging Market Private Equity Association
ESI	European Software Institute
ETS	Educational Testing Service
FDI	foreign direct investment
FENAINFO	National Federation of Information Technology Companies (Brazil)
FINEP	Financiadora de Estudos e Projetos (Brazil)
FONSOFT	Trust Fund for the Promotion of the Software Industry (Argentina)
FOSS	free and open source software

FOSSFA	Free Software and Open Source Foundation for Africa
FSF	Free Software Foundation
GB	gigabyte
GDP	gross domestic product
GIZ	Gesellschaft für Internationale Zusammenarbeit (Germany)
GLO-1	Globacom Limited submarine communications cable
GNU	GNU is not Unix
GPL	General Public License
HSPA	High Speed Packet Access
HTML	HyperText Markup Language
HTML5	Fifth revision of the HTML standard
ICT	information and communication technology
ICTA	Information and Communication Technology Agency (Sri Lanka)
IDC	International Data Corporation
IEC	International Electrotechnical Commission
IFI	international financial institutions
IMAP	International Network of Mergers and Acquisition Partners
IMF	International Monetary Fund
IPR	intellectual property rights
ISIC	International Standard Industrial Classification of All Economic Activities
ISO	International Organization for Standardization
ISPON	Institute of Software Practitioners of Nigeria
ISTQB	International Software Testing Qualifications Board
IT	information technology
ITES	information technology enabled services
ITIL	Information Technology Infrastructure Library
ITU	International Telecommunication Union
LAMP	Linux, Apache, MySQL, PHP
LPI	Linux Professional Institute
LDC	least developed country
LGPL	Lesser General Public License
MASIT	Macedonian Chamber of Information and Communication Technology
MERCOSUR	Southern Common Market
MIIT	Ministry of Industry and Information Technology (China)
MIT	Massachusetts Institute of Technology
mLab	mobile applications laboratory
MPL	Mozilla Public License
MPS.br	Brazilian Software Process Improvement Program
MySQL	My Structured Query Language
NACE	General Industrial Classification of Economic Activities within the European Communities
NAICS	North American Industry Classification System
NASSCOM	National Association of Software and Services Companies (India)
NGO	non-governmental organization
NIS	national innovation system
NITDA	National Information Technology Development Agency (Nigeria)
OECD	Organization for Economic Cooperation and Development
PC	personal computer
PHP	Hypertext Pre-processor

PRAM	Poverty Reduction and Agriculture Management
R&D	research and development
RUP	Rational Unified Process
RUSSOFT	Russian Software Developers Association
SaaS	software as a service
SEBRAE	Brazilian Service of Support for Micro and Small Enterprises
SECC	Software Engineering Competence Center (Egypt)
SEI	Software Engineering Institute
SEO	search engine optimization
SLASSCOM	Sri Lanka Association for Software and Service Companies
SME	small and medium-sized enterprise
SMS	short message service
SOFEX	Comisión de Software de Exportación (Guatemala)
SOFTEX	Association for the Promotion of Brazilian Software Excellence
SRDI	Soil Resource Development Institute (of Bangladesh)
SUSE	Software und System Entwicklung
TCP	Transmission Control Protocol
TEAMS	The East African Marine System
TNC	transnational corporation
UNCITRAL	United Nations Commission on International Trade Law
UNCTAD	United Nations Conference on Trade and Development
UNESCO	United Nations Educational, Scientific and Cultural Organization
UNU-IIST	United Nations University International Institute for Software Technology
UNU-MERIT	United Nations University Maastricht Economic and Social Research Institute on Innovation and Technology
WACS	West Africa Cable System
WITSA	World Information Technology and Services Alliance
WSIS	World Summit on the Information Society
WTO	World Trade Organization

OVERVIEW

The spread of information and communication technologies (ICTs) continues to facilitate technological change in the globalizing economy. Recent editions of the *Information Economy Report* have documented how the rapid diffusion of mobile telephony and improved international broadband connectivity, including in the least developed countries (LDCs), as well as the introduction of new services and applications, are facilitating more inclusive development. This not only has implications for enterprise development but it also expands the scope for leveraging ICTs in such development areas as health, education, governance, the private sector and more.

In order, however, to ensure that this improved access to ICTs brings about the desired benefits, the devices and services provided have to respond effectively to the needs and capabilities of users. In many instances, this in turn necessitates access to relevant technological capabilities within the domestic economy. This applies in particular to the area of software, which critically influences the functionality of goods and services offered by both the private and public sectors. Against this background, the *Information Economy Report 2012* puts the focus on the role of software in developing countries.

To facilitate structural transformation and technological advancement, it is necessary for countries to build domestic capabilities to allow individuals, firms and organizations to engage in learning processes. In this context, Governments should seek to adopt policies that help expand the opportunities for such learning, especially in new industries that offer wide learning opportunities. The software industry is such an industry. As a general-purpose technology, software has wide application throughout the economy and society. It is also characterized by relatively low capital barriers to entry and its relevance is likely to remain high in the future.

Developing software capabilities is important for several reasons. Software consists of a set of instructions that enable different hardware (computers, mobile phones, smart phones and tablets, and the like) to perform the operations required. In this sense, it can be seen as the "brain" of ICT devices. Software can help firms to manage their resources better, access relevant information, lower the costs of doing business

and reduce time to market. Greater emphasis on ICTs in the delivery of government, health care, education and other services is also raising the need for capabilities to develop customized software applications. Different ICTs are increasingly permeating societies in countries of all levels of development. In this context, developing the technological capabilities to adopt and adapt existing software solutions, and eventually to innovate, becomes more relevant.

Consequently, countries increasingly need a certain capacity to understand, manipulate and adapt software. Other things being equal, locally based software expertise is better positioned to understand domestic needs and therefore to develop relevant and innovative applications and content. Countries with well-developed software industries are better placed to implement their own tailored solutions. Furthermore, close interaction between domestic producers and users generates learning opportunities and gains in terms of productivity and operational efficiency, and thereby contributes to market expansion and diversification. Software industries also tend to generate high-end, direct and indirect employment, especially for skilled youth.

The opportunities of software and service activities for developing countries – thanks to the low capital entry requirements as well as the sector's high-value, high-growth nature and high-technology, knowledge-rich profile – are well recognized. However, in many developing countries, it is only recently that sufficient demand for ICT applications and software has emerged to warrant a more systematic treatment of the software area. Thanks to changes in the ICT landscape, there is today more scope even for small-scale developers in developing countries to participate in software development and production.

The expanding use of mobile phones is creating new domestic demand for mobile applications and services geared towards improving access to domestic news and entertainment, government services, patient care, market information services and mobile money transfers. Having the software developed locally enhances the chances of it being adapted to the specific needs of the domestic users (for example, taking cultural and language considerations into account). Improved broadband Internet access allows developers in developing countries to engage in software projects and export their services. Meanwhile, novel software production modes – such as distributed peer-production over the Internet – are leading to the creation of new business models based on local software service provision and adaptation.

As a framework for its analysis, the *Information Economy Report 2012* introduces the concept of the national software system. It emphasizes that actions and interactions of domestic software producers and users are greatly influenced by the quality and affordability of ICT infrastructure, access to relevant human resources and capital, the legal framework, and enabling business infrastructure, as well as by the links with software networks in the rest of the world. Overall, the competitiveness of the system is affected by the national vision, strategy and government policies which should nurture software capabilities and the software system as a whole. Governments play a central role in the system. They are important users of software (notably through e-government and public procurement activities) and they strongly influence the enabling factors of the system.

Available data suggest that there is considerable room for developing countries to make better use of the software potential. According to estimates from the World Information Technology and Service Alliance (WITSA)/IHS Global Insight, spending on computer software and services (excluding software embedded in devices) amounted to an estimated $1.2 trillion in 2011. Most of this (four fifths) is accounted for by developed countries. The remaining share is mainly accounted for by developing countries in East, South and South-East Asia, while the combined spending in the rest of the developing world corresponded to only 4 per cent. Developed regions also spend relatively more on software and services as a share of their overall ICT spending. For example, in North America, computer software and services made up 43 per cent of ICT spending compared with only 11 per cent in Latin America. Low ratios in developing regions can be seen as a sign of limited software use, hindering the passage to the information society. At the same time, a low level of income does not in itself have to be a barrier to the development of software capabilities and use.

Expanding the availability of local software capabilities can help to generate employment in the software industry as well as in industries for which embedded software development is important. Such jobs can help absorb the growing number of tertiary students graduating each year in developing countries. New areas of software development may also help create a critical mass of local capabilities to develop software solutions in traditional application fields for the business and government sectors, which in many countries are still underserved.

Capability needs vary. For developing countries with nascent software sectors, catching up on the advances of other countries by technological learning will initially involve a considerable adoption of software techniques developed abroad. A common starting point in low-income countries is to focus on services such as reselling, installation, customization and training linked to imported, foreign packaged software. This can help local enterprises to obtain knowledge about that particular software before seeking to move up to the next level by becoming a producer of their own software. Producing software and IT services for export requires greater capabilities. Building capabilities requires a continuous learning process during which new competencies and skills are acquired by interacting with clients, peers and through various networks.

There are significant differences between developing countries in terms of the market orientation of software production. In a number of low and middle-income countries, computer software and IT service exports exceed the value of spending on domestic computer software and services (for example, Costa Rica, India, Jamaica, the Philippines, Sri Lanka and Uruguay). In some of these (for example, Sri Lanka and Uruguay), software spending is very small relative to the size of the economy, suggesting that domestic software needs might be crowded out by demand from foreign markets. In India and the Philippines, computer software has become an important part of the local economy and they have joined Argentina and Malaysia as countries where both exports and the domestic computer software industry have reached relatively high levels. In many other developing countries, software is important in the domestic economy but exports are low. Such a pattern applies, for example, to Brazil, the Republic of Korea and South Africa, suggesting that there is significant scope for an expansion of exports.

The mix of local sales and export sales has implications for the development impact of software production. Many governments see exports of software and IT services as a way to generate foreign exchange, reduce trade deficits, induce job creation and transfer technology. They can also accelerate the integration into global value chains and contribute to economic diversification. Moreover, globalization of the software industry and greater reliance on peer-to-peer production imply greater scope for developers and software enterprises in developing countries to engage in exporting activities linked to outsourcing and crowdsourcing of software services.

From the perspective of harnessing the value of software in local economic development, however, it is important that software services and capabilities are available to support the needs that exist locally in the public and private sectors. As noted above, domestic use of software can be instrumental in improving the competitiveness of enterprises and the welfare of society. The domestic market is potentially an important base for enterprises to develop relevant skills and innovative products. Indirect effects on society may be expected to be larger when software is locally developed for domestic enterprises and institutions.

The performance of China is striking in this respect. According to Chinese official statistics, software production rose from $7 billion in 2000 to $285 billion in 2011. As much as 90 per cent of this is produced for the domestic market. Much of the local production is either embedded in the manufacturing of ICT and other goods (which are often subsequently exported from China to the world market), or developed to meet rapidly growing ICT use in the domestic economy. The development of indigenous e-commerce platforms (Alibaba and Taobao), web platforms for social networking (Renren) and local search engines (Baidu) has contributed to the demand for locally adapted software applications. The building of software capabilities, goods and services has been supported by government policies and institutions, including publicly financed research into Chinese language software, translation engines and security systems.

Governments should take an active part in fostering software capabilities, taking all relevant aspects of the national software system into account. Intentionally or unintentionally, they influence the evolution of the system. Governments are important buyers of software. They determine the educational curricula for the production of software engineers as well as the availability of affordable ICT infrastructure. They shape legal and regulatory frameworks that influence the extent to which ICTs are taken up and used productively in the economy and society. The *Information*

Economy Report 2012 offers several policy recommendations.

The experience of countries that have managed successfully to strengthen their software capabilities and industries suggests that the development of a national strategy, based on consultations with all relevant stakeholders, is a useful starting point. It should be well integrated in the overall national ICT strategy and adapted to the specific situation of each country. For most developing countries, focus should be on nurturing capabilities that are required to meet domestic software needs. For countries that have reached a certain level of maturity in the software field, it becomes more relevant to explore software also as a source of export revenues.

For governments to be able to design and implement relevant measures to strengthen the sector, a careful assessment of the system should be undertaken at an early stage of the process. Such an analysis helps to identify critical underlying challenges, such as capacity and skill gaps, regulatory shortcomings and other barriers to the sector's evolution. The UNCTAD–WITSA Survey of National IT/Software Associations found that the most frequently mentioned barriers for the growth and development of the software and IT services industry were lack of venture capital, shortages of qualified human resources and too little government procurement.

In terms of policy areas to consider, attention should be given to developing adequate ICT infrastructure, generating relevant skills from universities and specialized training institutes, making the business and legal frameworks conducive to the strengthening of software capabilities and production, and facilitating interaction among domestic producers and users as well as with international networks.

The availability of an educated workforce and students enrolled in computer-related education fundamentally affects the potential of the system. With a view to making available a pool of skilled manpower, curricula of regular education systems and professional training facilities need to be adapted to the skill requirements of software producers and users. This necessitates close dialogue with private-sector stakeholders, universities and key software users. Particular focus should be given to skill development around new models of networking, community building and international knowledge-sharing. At the same time, it needs to be generic, flexible and adaptable, rather than targeted at certain programmes or tools.

As technologies and markets are in constant flux, software enterprises tend to look for employees with the ability to learn new things on the job as projects evolve.

Many countries have set up technology parks, innovation hubs and incubators with the aim of making it easier for enterprises to get started, interact, innovate and expand. Such facilities are of particular value when weak basic infrastructure represents a barrier. Co-location of software skills and enterprises can spur innovation and cross-fertilization between enterprises and the developer community. By facilitating the creation of informal networks such structures can facilitate transfers of tacit knowledge among different stakeholders, including the local developer community. Relevant initiatives may include meetings that bring developers together to develop solutions around specific software platforms or for certain development concerns (clean water, disaster risk reduction, open government) as well as various technology conferences and workshops.

Governments should also build on the rising demand for mobile applications (apps). This domain is particularly relevant in low-income countries in which the current use of computers remains limited while mobile phone use is booming. Ensuring that there is a market place for local developers to sell their output is essential if such development work is to be sustainable. Governments can help catalyse activities by incentivizing mobile operators to develop mobile apps markets and create new demand by identifying their own needs for new mobile apps. Mobile app stores should facilitate the participation of developers in developing countries. Governments should ease the remaining restrictions on on-line payments, as these can represent a barrier for local developers to participate in software-development activities.

Governments should consider public procurement related to their e-government needs as tools to spur demand for software development. In this context, adequate attention should be given to the role of open standards, open innovation and free and open source software (FOSS) whenever it offers a competitive solution. Strategic advantages of FOSS include the empowerment of micro- and small software enterprises to innovate freely, the lowering of the cost of ownership for new software development, a reduction of errors and greater security. The way in which FOSS promotes grassroots creativity, innovation,

leadership and teamwork is a key value added. The process of learning about and adapting software enables users to become creators of knowledge rather than mere passive consumers of proprietary technologies. Technological trends, especially with regard to cloud computing, mobile applications and big data, are further accentuating the reliance on FOSS. There is still large regional variation in the intensity of FOSS policy activity. Europe is the most active region, accounting for close to half of all known related policy initiatives. Among developing regions, Asia is the front-runner, followed by Latin America and Africa.

In the spirit of the World Summit on the Information Society, development partners should consider expanding their assistance to developing countries in the software area. Examples cited in this report offer a base of support activities on which to build in the areas of training, application development, strengthening of legal and regulatory frameworks, supporting IT/software associations and clusters, meetings of developers, development of small and medium-sized software enterprises, and more. Development partners can also contribute by using software enterprises and developers in developing countries for the development of software services and applications needed in their projects.

Some of the world's leading producers of software products and services are based in the South, and there is considerable experience in developing countries with public procurement and use of software, skills development and promotion of new business models. In other locations, the software industry is still nascent. This combination of diversity and excellence makes the software area attractive for South–South cooperation. Through its three pillars, UNCTAD could offer a platform for developing countries to discuss how to use South–South cooperation with a view to bridging the digital divide, developing software capabilities and harnessing the software and ICT sector for development. Such discussions may help to avoid a lopsided approach by which many developing countries become mere passive adopters of software technology.

Supachai Panitchpakdi
Secretary-General, UNCTAD

SOFTWARE FOR DEVELOPMENT

1

Software has become a linchpin of the information society. As a cross-cutting technology with multiplier effects on other industries, its application has implications for companies of all sizes, Governments and individuals. Domestic software capabilities are therefore increasingly important for countries to create an inclusive information society. Software production and development can contribute to structural transformation, learning and innovation, job creation and export revenues. It is also an enabling factor for social and environmental development. Recent changes in information and communication technologies (ICTs) have expanded the scope for nurturing local capabilities among individuals and firms and for low-income countries to take part in software production and development.

Against this background, the *Information Economy Report 2012* puts the spotlight on the role of software in developing countries. Building on earlier UNCTAD work on the role of the ICT sector and the software industry in particular (see, for example, UNCTAD 2002, 2003a, 2011a), it examines prospects for developing and transition economies to develop relevant capabilities and eventually a competitive national software system. The analysis is undertaken in light of the significant changes characterizing the global landscape, with greater emphasis on mobile applications, cloud computing and open source software. These trends are accentuating the relevance for Governments and their partners to integrate software in their strategies to develop the information society.

A. THE GROWING RELEVANCE OF SOFTWARE FOR DEVELOPMENT

The spread of ICTs continues to facilitate technological change in the globalizing economy. Recent editions of the *Information Economy Report* have documented how the rapid diffusion of mobile telephony and improved international broadband connectivity, including in least developed countries (LDCs), as well as the introduction of new services and applications, are facilitating more inclusive development (UNCTAD, 2010, 2011a). It has implications for enterprise development and also expands the scope for leveraging ICTs in such development areas as health, education, governance and more.

The new ICT landscape is providing both opportunities and risk to developing countries. On the one hand, effective implementation of ICTs in the private and public sector may offer opportunities for leapfrogging into new technologies and for making economies more competitive. At the same time, failure to develop the required domestic capabilities to seize such opportunities may instead hamper the prospects for a country to catch up with others in the field, resulting in increasing economic inequalities and digital divides.

Against this background, many developing countries are actively looking for ways to speed up the transition towards a more inclusive information society. This implies, inter alia, facilitating widespread use of relevant ICT applications in all parts of society, and fostering a productive domestic ICT sector that can help to make such use sustainable and generating opportunities for income generation, job creation, export revenues and innovation (UNCTAD, 2011a). In order to make sure that improved access to ICT infrastructure and services generates the desired benefits, they need to be adapted in such a way that they respond effectively to the needs and reflect the ability of the users.

The ability of a country to adopt, adapt and develop appropriate technological solutions and applications depends on the strength of its domestic capabilities. This applies in particular to the area of software, as this concerns a general-purpose technology with relevance to a wide range of economic and social development fields. As ICTs permeate societies in countries at all levels of development, developing the technological capabilities to adopt and adapt existing software solutions, and eventually to innovate, becomes increasingly important. In the case of enterprises, software can help to manage

resources better, access relevant information, lower the costs of doing business and improve the ability to bring outputs to markets. In the public sector, greater emphasis on ICTs in the delivery of government, health care, education and other services is accentuating the need for capabilities to develop customized applications. And for development partners, effective adaptation of software to the relevant context represents a key ingredient for ensuring that ICT-enabled development projects have the desired impact (box I.1).

Software consists of the set of instructions that enable different hardware to perform the required operations. In this sense, it constitutes the "brain" of ICT devices. Today, it represents a critical component in the production of almost all goods and services. In cars, telecommunications, consumer electronics, medical devices and robotics it is embedded to provide the desired functionality (Stryszowski, 2009). Because software is embedded in many final goods, equipment and productive processes, a capacity to understand, manipulate and adapt software is necessary for countries to be able to successfully absorb new technologies in many different areas. Companies aspiring to participate in international supply chains and to make their business processes competitive similarly need access to competitive software solutions. Without a relevant set of domestic capabilities to adopt, adapt and develop relevant software and applications (reflecting the mix of ICTs that are used in an economy), countries will find it increasingly difficult to participate in the learning processes that are essential for the development of the information society.

The software sector in itself is also an area that holds potential for technological upgrading in low-income countries. In some developing countries, such as India, Argentina, Brazil, China, Costa Rica and South Africa, the software sector has grown significantly in recent years, generating new job opportunities, innovation and export revenue (see chapters II and III). As the entry barriers are relatively low in this sector, and with the growing trend towards the outsourcing of various software-related activities, software production is potentially of interest for countries at low levels of development. This was already recognized a decade ago by UNCTAD (UNCTAD, 2002, p. 34):

> Computer software and services activities hold vast opportunities for developing countries primarily due to low capital entry requirements as well as the industry's high value, high growth nature and the high technology, knowledge-rich profile of software activities. Above

Box I.1.   Software for sustainable development: the case of UNU-IIST

The United Nations University International Institute for Software Technology (UNU-IIST) located in Macau, China, runs several programmes aimed at addressing global challenges of sustainable development with the help of ICTs. The institute has found that tailored software that directly addresses the most pressing needs and relevant content in local languages is an essential ingredient. In one of its programmes, UNU-IIST is developing software and local content in partnership with Governments and non-governmental organizations (NGOs) in order to make their poverty reduction initiatives more effective.

In the Lao People's Democratic Republic, one of the poorest countries in Asia, the weak capacity of local staff is a key constraint to effectively realizing the Government's poverty-reduction strategy. Moreover, rural development initiatives with a capacity-building component are often driven by the immediate needs of the particular project or programme rather than by the longer-term needs of the country. As a result, local staff often lack the necessary breadth of knowledge and skills to make them effective problem solvers.

In 2007, the Ministry of Agriculture and Forestry, in collaboration with the Wetlands Alliance, developed a new approach to staff development. They piloted an innovative bachelor's degree programme in Poverty Reduction and Agriculture Management (PRAM) to provide skills at the grass roots level. The programme provides students with a broader base of skills and competencies for poverty reduction. However, an insufficient supply of qualified teachers and the remoteness of the poorest districts made it difficult to scale up the project to serve a greater proportion of the Ministry's 5,000 extension workers.

Although access to ICTs – including third generation (3G) Internet connectivity – is increasingly emerging in rural areas of the Lao People's Democratic Republic, appropriate software and local content are needed to unlock the latent capacity of the infrastructure. To address this challenge, UNU-IIST entered into a strategic partnership with the Ministry. This partnership led to the creation of the PRAM Knowledge Sharing Network, which enables extension officers to record and communicate local knowledge concerning poverty reduction projects in a peer-to-peer learning framework. Beyond this, the network provides a direct communication channel between the district and ministerial levels, enabling more informed national level poverty reduction policies. Extension workers can easily access government material (such as text, photos and video clips) and post questions which are answered by ministry staff or external experts.

The system was designed with the full participation of agencies at the national, provincial and district levels. Thanks to this participatory process, only two months after the software was delivered it was used by district agriculture and forestry offices, technical services and village development centres in 15 districts of the seven southern provinces of the country. Moreover, the process strengthened local ownership and helped to identify valuable future functionalities, such as the aggregation of the information gathered at the local level so as to better enable provincial and central offices to monitor the effectiveness of poverty reduction programmes, and to support disaster reporting and response.

The methodology and some of the solutions developed in the Lao People's Democratic Republic should have widespread applicability and UNU-IIST is also considering supporting capacity-building activities in Cambodia, the Republic of the Union of Myanmar and Thailand. Beyond this, the institute is exploring support for other areas of poverty-reduction initiatives, such as helping development agencies to identify where relevant local competency exists, developing more effective and participatory systems of monitoring and evaluation, incorporating voices and agendas of local communities and enabling early warning of natural disasters.

In carrying out this project, UNU-IIST is keenly aware of the need to produce sustainable solutions. While UNU-IIST has so far been responsible for the technical aspects of building and maintaining the software, the participatory design approach provides an excellent mechanism to build local capacity as an integral part of the development process. At the same time, UNU-IIST seeks to build upon widely supported open source and cloud services platforms and to design software in easily extendable ways. It also organizes summer schools and workshops related to software development and it is about to launch formal degree programmes targeting the needs of developing countries.[a]

For software to help address issues in developing countries, it must be fundamentally needs-driven and participatory. This requires a strong presence of developers in the developing world to provide a kind of living laboratory for creating and testing new methods. Against this background, UNU-IIST is now planning to establish a formal institutional presence in the Lao People's Democratic Republic. This will allow students from several countries in the region to participate in UNU-IIST degree programmes and provide opportunities for students and visiting scholars to carry out research in the living laboratory.

Source: UNU-IIST.

[a] The first such programme is a PhD in ICT for sustainable development, offered as a double degree with the University of Pisa. Masters programmes in e-governance and in health informatics are planned for the coming year.

all, although developing countries face barriers in the establishment of the industry ..., they hold a number of notable locational advantages...the industry provides almost unique and unparalleled opportunities for the wider development and growth of developing countries, which should not be ignored.

Since then, the ICT landscape has been radically transformed in several ways, with implications for developing countries. In some respects, the scope has expanded for nurturing local capabilities, and for individuals and firms, including those in countries at lower levels of development, to take part in software production and development.

First, from its initial focus on software applications for personal computers (PCs) and other computers, the Internet has become the crucial platform for software development, delivery and use. The Internet is what mostly defines how software is designed and how it creates value. It has also dramatically added to the innovative potential of software for productive and social activities. Web 2.0 is often used to describe a new generation of web-based services and social media that allow people to interact, collaborate and share information. This has become possible thanks to greater bandwidth and computing power. An important feature of Web 2.0 is the increased amount of user-generated content.

Second, the expanded use of mobile phones throughout the developing world is accentuating the demand for new applications, content and services. Greater access to mobiles in developing countries is creating local demand for short message service (SMS)-based as well as more sophisticated mobile applications that are adapted to local contexts. This trend has already given rise to a highly dynamic industry for the development of mobile applications for smartphones and other mobile devices, with growing involvement of developers in developing countries (see chapters II and III).

Third, many developing countries that were previously suffering from poor international broadband connectivity have in the past few years become linked to one or several international fibre-optic cables. In sub-Saharan Africa, for example, six new major interregional undersea cables have become operational since 2009 and another four are scheduled to be launched in the next two years.[1] Whereas broadband divides remain wide, with LDCs in particular lagging far behind developed countries,[2] such improved connectivity is enabling programmers in more countries to engage in software projects and increasing the demand for web-based applications.

Fourth, related to the improved broadband Internet access, cloud-based services are expanding fast. By providing computing resources on demand via a computer network, cloud computing allows clients to use applications without actually having them installed locally. It is closely related to the concept of software as a service (SaaS), which is making it less costly for users to benefit from software applications. Cloud computing will have a substantial impact on business models in the information technology (IT) industry in terms of pricing, licensing and maintenance. As a consequence, software companies from developing and transition economies may have to adjust their business and service delivery models to this trend.

Fifth, new production modes for software, such as distributed peer-production over the Internet, are leading to new business models based on local software service provision and adaptation (ict@innovation, 2010). Opportunities for the internationalization of software value chains are expanding thanks to the introduction of new tools, platforms and technology for collaboration and crowdsourcing (that is, the outsourcing of tasks and activities that would normally be undertaken by employees or those within a particular social group to a wider community of people who respond to opportunities online). This approach differs from the traditional outsourcing of services, which typically involves larger-scale work and transactions between enterprises. As shown in chapter II, software developers from a large number of developing countries are already delivering work over the Internet directly to clients by freelancing (UNCTAD, 2011a), harnessing the power of distributed peer-production and servicing (see also section I.E).

Finally, there is growing recognition of the value of free and open source software (FOSS) (see chapter IV). This trend has several implications for the development of local software capabilities, including the reduction of the market power of proprietary software producers and an increase in the relevance of methodologies and technologies supporting collaborative software development. For software enterprises from developing and transition economies, greater emphasis on FOSS can promote domestic market development and local innovation. Rather than purchasing software licences and services abroad, local software development, sales and services keep resources within the local economy, reduce dependencies, and provide opportunities for income generation and employment. There may also be greater opportunities for developing innovative and cost-effective solutions that are customized to the specific needs of the domestic market.

While these new trends imply better opportunities for developing countries, their ability to meet domestic needs for software and to supply software services or products to international markets depends on the strength of their domestic capabilities. As in other technological areas, in order to benefit fully from inflows of software knowledge and technology, a certain level of absorptive capacity is required.[3] If such capabilities are insufficiently nurtured, a country will have to depend primarily on imported solutions, as in the case of Nigeria (box I.2). Successful technology adoption and diffusion require significant technological efforts (Lall, 2001, 2005) and absorptive capacity (Cohen and Levinthal, 1989). Moreover, with innovation processes becoming increasingly open, countries that achieve a minimum level of innovative and learning capacity stand a greater chance of linking up to international knowledge and innovation systems.

To summarize, improved access to ICTs in the economy and society, especially with respect to countries with low levels of income, is making the nurturing of domestic software capabilities more pertinent. At the same time, changes in the ICT landscape are also enabling software developers in the developing world to participate more actively in the production process, to meet domestic needs as well as to contribute to international projects. Depending on the level of maturity of the domestic software industry and developer community, developing

---

Box I.2. The new software strategy of Nigeria

The software industry was for a long time given limited attention by policymakers in Nigeria. As a result, the country became heavily dependent on foreign software, which accounts for more than 90 per cent of all software used in Nigeria.[a] The new Federal Ministry for Communication Technology is intending to change this situation. The draft national ICT policy notes, among other things, that "Nigeria can benefit tremendously from developing its own domestic software industry to cater for both domestic and export markets".[b] Tailored applications are needed to make governance and government services more efficient, boost business productivity, facilitate better communication and to address various educational and health-care objectives.

There is limited recent data on the composition of the Nigerian software market. A survey conducted in 2004 estimated that there were more than 100 active firms in the industry, most of them small and virtually all privately owned (Soriyan and Heeks, 2004). The industry was mainly servicing the domestic private sector with installation, customization and training services related to imported software packages. The picture has not changed much since then.[c] The young Nigerian software industry is largely organized through the private sector and professional initiatives such as the Institute of Software Practitioners of Nigeria (ISPON) and the Nigeria Computer Society.

The new Ministry recognizes the importance of nurturing a capable local software industry to respond to emerging challenges and opportunities. The Minister of Communications Technology, Ms. Omobola Johnson, has engaged ICT stakeholders in a round table to discuss the Government's new ICT vision, mission and strategies for implementation. Software development is one of the four strategic pillars of this new vision and a national software policy is being prepared through the National Information Technology Development Agency (NITDA) (www.nitda.gov.ng).

A key priority is to build significant software engineering and developer capacities at education and industry levels. This will among other things involve the modernization of IT curricula and the strengthening of software skills among lecturers. Software engineering and technology skills are needed for the development of more effective methods of governance, education, information exchange and communication, agriculture, management and use of natural resources, health care, and many other development objectives. An IT Innovation Fund has been established as an incentive to the IT industry and the Government is also in the process of setting up IT parks in strategic areas.

The Government's new vision is welcomed by the software-developer community. In 2011, NITDA announced a prize award for software excellence for the National Software Innovation Cup initiated by ISPON.[4] The National Software Competition seeks to uncover indigenous software development talent and make the software developers ready for entrepreneurship and global competitiveness in ICT (see www.softwareclubnigeria.org). A National Software Conference and various round tables have also been organized by ISPON to promote indigenous software development and support services. There are also plans by ISPON to facilitate the future participation of developers in various software technology competitions, such as the United Nations Youth Summit Awards. The Institute has also established software development clubs in about 30 tertiary institutions under the platform of the National Association of Computer Science Students.

Source: UNCTAD, based on information provided by ISPON.

[a] See draft national ICT policy, http://www.commtech.gov.ng/downloads/National_ICT_Policy_DRAFT_090112.pdf.

[b] Ibid.

[c] ITEdgenews.com, 2012.

countries may also see opportunities in leveraging software skills to promote economic diversification, job creation, innovation and export revenue generation.

B. SOFTWARE DEFINITIONS AND OPPORTUNITIES FOR DEVELOPING COUNTRIES

1. Software definitions

When analysing the role of software used in various devices, it is important to distinguish between various kinds of software. A starting point is to separate software products from software services (figure I.1).[5] Software products can in turn be divided into application software (programs that do the work users are directly interested in) and system software (programs that support application software). The former comprises productivity-enhancing software, such as word processing, spreadsheets and database management, as well as vertical – or industry-specific – application software (for example, tailored to the banking and finance, entertainment or public sectors). Other vertical market software that is of high relevance to developing countries includes that for medicine (diagnosis, therapy, management), education, engineering and mass computation (for instance, for meteorological purposes). Application software is often sold as packaged or off-the-shelf products.

Figure I.1. Categories of software

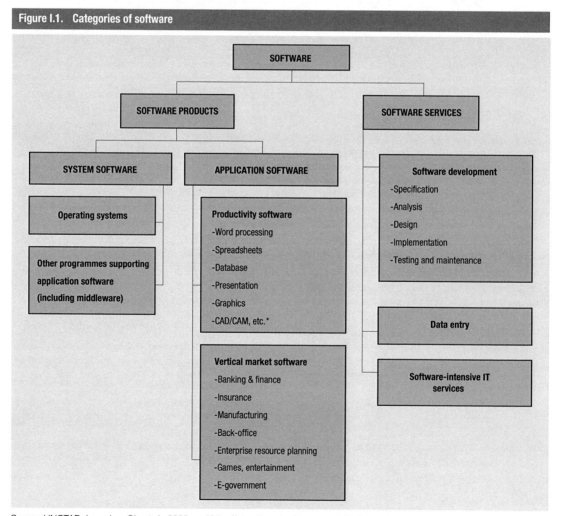

Source: UNCTAD, based on Ojo et al., 2008, and http://searchsoa.techtarget.com/definition/software.

* Computer-aided design and computer-aided manufacturing.

Meanwhile, system software includes operating systems of servers, desktop computers and mobile devices, as well as other programmes needed to run application software.

Software services include all services related to the traditional software development lifecycle, including specification and analysis, design and implementation, testing and maintenance. They can also be said to encompass related activities of data entry and software-intensive IT services (Ojo et al., 2008). Whereas it is common to see a sharp differentiation between software and IT services, it is becoming increasingly difficult to maintain. The two segments are often closely integrated, blurring the boundaries between them. Many IT companies are also active in both categories.[6] It should be noted that business processoutsourcing (BPO) and other ICT-enabled services are not included in the definition of software and IT services.

2. The software value chain

The scope for value creation depends on the nature and market orientation of production, as depicted in figure I.2. Where are the most important software production opportunities for countries at different levels of development? For most developing countries, producing data entry and software services for the domestic market is the natural entry point, with the lowest entry barrier (Heeks, 1999). Nascent software industries often focus on services such as reselling, installation, customization and training linked to imported, foreign packaged software. A key hurdle to expanding local software activities and moving up the value chain has traditionally been a lack of technological capabilities combined with limited use of ICTs and demand for software applications in the private and public sector.[7]

Producing software and IT services for export requires greater capabilities. Relatively few developing and transition economies have successfully managed to enter this market. The most prominent exception is India, which has emerged as a leading exporter of software services. Many other developing and transition economies that have built domestic software capabilities are actively seeking to promote the internationalization of their software industries. The

Figure I.2. Software value chain

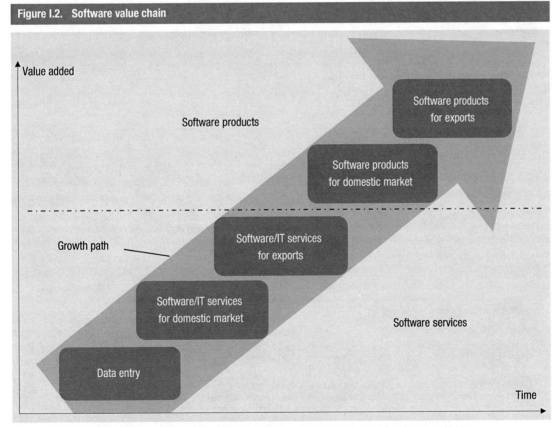

Source: UNCTAD, adapted from Germany, Federal Ministry for Economic Cooperation and Development, 2011a.

introduction of new platforms for online work (such as oDesk and Elance, see chapter II) is lowering the threshold for export-oriented service production as it enables individual programmers and developers to participate in international projects.

The production of application packages involves high barriers to entry and intense competition. As few places are insulated from foreign competition, domestic firms have to compete with imported proprietary software, often developed and disseminated with the backing of sizeable budgets for research and development, advertising, sales and marketing. On the one hand, as such packages are often expensive to buy there should logically be an opportunity for local companies to develop cheaper solutions if they have the necessary expertise. On the other hand, however, due to their high cost, such packages are often copied and distributed at low or no cost, reducing the demand for domestically developed alternative solutions. Widespread use of unlicensed, proprietary software may

in this way hamper the opportunities for developing a domestic software industry. The main opportunity to move into software products typically lies in the development of applications tailored to local conditions (for example, business culture, legal framework and languages). The greatest potential development gain from software is also likely to materialize through its contribution to enhanced efficiency of productive activities (box I.3), public services and engagement of citizens.

The kind of capabilities needed differs depending on the stage of the value chain. They also vary across different segments of the software industry. For firms in developing countries with nascent software sectors, the process of technological learning required to close the gap with more advanced countries will initially involve a considerable amount of adoption of software techniques developed abroad. A common starting point in low-income countries is for enterprises to start by becoming the local representative of a foreign software vendor and obtain knowledge about that

---

Box I.3. Locally developed software to improve farmers' access to information in Bangladesh

The Katalyst programme aims to contribute to increased income for men and women by strengthening the competitiveness of different sectors.[a] It focuses on 17 sectors with high growth potential in terms of income, productivity, profitability and/or exports. In recent projects, having access to local software expertise has been of great significance.

In one of its projects, Katalyst partnered with the Soil Resource Development Institute (SRDI), an agency under the Ministry of Agriculture, to develop an ICT-based service that would improve the access of farmers to recommendations on how to use fertilizers in different locations and for different crops. Knowledge of the precise dosage of fertilizer is important and highly demanded as it influences the cost of input and the yield. The service required the development of software that could analyse a large set of data on soil samples on which to base the recommendations.

Katalyst formed a coalition with Grameenphone and Banglalink, the top two mobile network operators in the country, to develop a mobile-based fertilizer information service, leveraging existing networks of the private partners.[b] A local IT company, eGeneration, was asked to develop the required software application, reflecting the local context and the specific needs of the agricultural community. The new service was launched in July 2009 and has since shown positive results. Users have experienced two main benefits: reduced costs for using fertilizers (in some cases up to 25 per cent) and higher crop yields (in some cases as much as 15 per cent). Based on the success of the software, Katalyst has initiated a process of developing a similar software and service to address irrigation-related information needs of farmers.

The fact that the software was locally developed was important. It helped to keep costs down and to adapt the service to the local users' needs and capabilities. For example, the user interface is completely in the Bangla language, the data used as input were provided by the SRDI and the software is hosted on the server of a local company, Ensii. The software is owned by the Government, which has decided to integrate the new service in its Agriculture Information and Communication Centres and Union Information and Service Centres. The experience underscores the value of using public–private partnerships to develop software projects. It also demonstrates the importance of having access to local expertise to develop tailored solutions at low cost.

Source: UNCTAD, based on information provided by Katalyst.

[a] Katalyst is funded by the Swiss Agency for Development and Cooperation, UKaid, the Canadian International Development Agency and the Embassy of the Kingdom of the Netherlands. It is implemented under the Bangladesh Ministry of Commerce by Swisscontact and GIZ International Services.

[b] Grameenphone already had more than 500 community information centres or telecentres across the country which could allow farmers to access the service for a small fee. Banglalink added the fertilizer recommendation service to those it already offered via its agriculture helpline known as Krishi Jigyasha 7676.

particular software. Building capabilities over time requires an on-going learning process during which new competencies and skills are acquired, typically by interacting with clients, peers and through various networks.

C. NATIONAL SOFTWARE SYSTEMS

The ability to generate the software capabilities required to produce the output demanded by users is intrinsically influenced by the environment in which software producers and users operate. As economies and societies become more dependent on ICT and other products with high software content, user-centred functionality requirements become particularly important (Stryszowski, 2009). Building on previous research, this section introduces a conceptual framework for understanding software production and development, identifies the various actors involved, the interactions between them and the institutional environment surrounding them. It draws on analytical concepts, benchmarking frameworks, competitive indexes and rating systems that have been developed by academic experts and consulting companies as well as donor organizations, to analyse and assess the software performance of countries.

A useful framework for assessing the role of policies in facilitating innovation is the national innovation system (NIS) (Nelson, 1993; Lundvall, 1992). Production and innovation activities of the industry itself are an important, but not the only, component of the NIS. The system approach emphasizes that innovation and technology development result from interactions between enterprises, universities, research institutes, and government agencies. An understanding of the NIS can help policymakers identify ways to enhance innovative performance and assist in pinpointing mismatches within the system, both among institutions and in relation to government policies. Proper institutions are crucial to the effective functioning of an NIS (North, 1990; Metcalfe, 1995; Edquist, 1997). The innovation systems approach has also been applied at the sectoral level (see, for example, Malerba, 2005 and Joseph, 2010).

Inspired by research related to innovation systems and industrial clusters (Porter, 1998), other scholars have proposed conceptual models to analyse software industries specifically, notably with a focus on export capabilities. The Software Export Success Model is one of the most comprehensive approaches

(Heeks and Nicholson, 2004). It identifies five key factors: demand for software, national software vision and strategy, international software linkages and trust, national software industry characteristics, and national software-related infrastructure (which includes human resources, research and development (R&D) and telecommunications).[8] An extended version is the so-called Oval Model, which places more emphasis on human capital and access to capital, de-emphasizes some other factors, such as piracy and trust, and adds new factors, including quality of life (Carmel, 2003). The German Agency for International Cooperation (Gesellschaft für Internationale Zusammenarbeit – GIZ) took the model further and elaborated the IT Industry Capability Model. This comprises seven software-capability dimensions including state institutions, ICT infrastructure, demand, structural characteristics of the industry, company capabilities, academia and support institutions, and international linkage and branding (Germany, Federal Ministry for Economic Cooperation and Development, 2011a).[9]

A third strand of research refers to ICT ecosystems, a living, breeding and evolving environment, much like the complex dynamics and interplay of biological organisms (Fransman, 2010). Accordingly, the "interacting organisms" in the ecosystem are firms and users of technology products and services. The nature of their interactions continually changes as learning and adaptation take place. The interactions are in turn embedded in a broader network consisting of institutions and other non-firm entities, such as universities and government research and policy-making institutions that influence the ecosystem. In addition, there are technical aspects of the ecosystem, such as platforms, architectures and networks.[10]

Among the above-mentioned concepts and frameworks, there is broad agreement that certain factors influence the performance of a domestic software industry. They include the national vision, government policies and institutions, ICT and business infrastructure, work-force skills, incentives for entrepreneurship and risk-taking, access to venture capital, public procurement and international linkages. In addition, all models emphasize the importance of effective interaction among the key actors.

Drawing on the frameworks and models mentioned above and reflecting recent changes in the ICT landscape, the *Information Economy Report 2012* introduces the concept of a "national software system". It allows for a holistic analysis of the software industry in countries at varying levels of development. At its core stands the notion that the software capabilities and performance of a country are determined by a system of interconnected resources, capabilities and stakeholders. As illustrated in figure I.3, the national software system identifies four actors involved in the development, production and use of software:

(a) The software industry;

(b) Software users (individuals, private companies and Government);

(c) The software-developer community (not least to account for the growing importance of freelancing, distributed peer production of software and application development);

(d) Universities and research centres.

The actions, interactions and output of these four groups of actors are greatly influenced by the surrounding enabling environment, which is in turn determined by the quality and affordability of ICT infrastructure, adequate business infrastructure (including technology parks), access to relevant human resources and capital, the legal and regulatory frameworks, as well as by the links with various software networks in the rest of the world. Overall, the competitiveness of the system is affected by the national vision, strategy and government policies to nurture software capabilities and the software system as a whole.

Governments are an integral part of the system and influence its performance in multiple ways. In addition to being domestic buyers of software and related applications, they determine curricula for the education of new software engineers, influence the availability of affordable ICT infrastructure, determine relevant legal and regulatory frameworks, and coordinate the development of a national vision and strategy. A key role for the Government is to create an enabling environment and to ensure that the role of the software industry is adequately integrated into broader ICT policies and development strategies. The chances of fostering a competitive national software system that can contribute to national development are likely to be higher if all relevant stakeholders coordinate their activities and collaborate towards a common vision and goal. Close interaction between the Government and other stakeholders is also required for the system to be able to adapt to changing technology and market trends that characterize the software industry.

The trend among software companies to rely on open systems of innovation is accentuating the importance

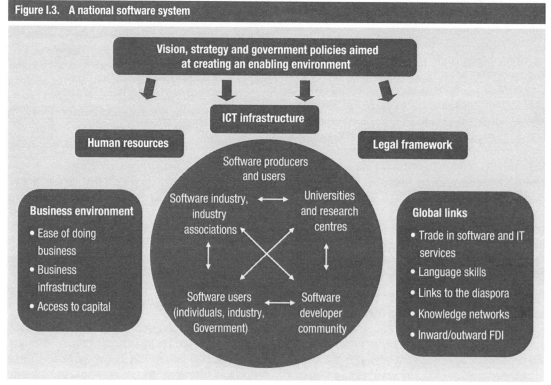

Figure I.3. A national software system

Vision, strategy and government policies aimed at creating an enabling environment

ICT infrastructure

Human resources

Legal framework

Software producers and users

Software industry, industry associations ←→ Universities and research centres

Software users (individuals, industry, Government) ←→ Software developer community

Business environment

• Ease of doing business

• Business infrastructure

• Access to capital

Global links

• Trade in software and IT services

• Language skills

• Links to the diaspora

• Knowledge networks

• Inward/outward FDI

Source: UNCTAD.

of networks and interaction (Chesbrough, 2003, 2005; OECD, 2008). When advancing their knowledge and technology, firms use external as well as internal ideas and internal as well as external paths to market. The central idea is that, in a world of widely distributed knowledge, companies cannot afford to rely entirely on their own research, but instead have to buy, develop collaboratively or license processes, research or inventions from external sources (other companies, research institutions, freelance experts, customers or other non-formal innovation networks). Open software systems are gradually evolving as innovation environments that rely on decentralization, building of open peer-production networks and comingling of local and global resources.

This trend is linked to the growing reliance on FOSS (see chapter IV). It is the freedom to create, study, use, remix and redistribute without having to pay a licence fee that defines the level of freedom to innovate and, thereby, the innovation potential in resource-poor environments. The core of open innovation is the ability of the outside innovator to think and act freely, as enabled by the global building of a knowledge commons around distributed peer production and the guarantee of open licences (Seibold, 2010, p. 89). Elements of openness emerge in a system when it incorporates and sustains interoperability, collaborative development, transparency and the freedom to innovate. Opening up and merging local and global software knowledge and skills can create the basis for an open software system. Opening up to unbiased, collaborative and redistributable innovation can generate various benefits for Governments, end users and industry. Ultimately, this can translate into economic efficiency, innovation and growth (Berkman Center for Internet & Society, 2005, p. 9).

D. DESCRIBING THE MAIN COMPONENTS OF THE NATIONAL SOFTWARE SYSTEM

1. Producers and users of software

(a) The software industry

The software industry encompasses software companies at the micro-level and software industry associations on the meso-level. At the micro-level, an important determinant of the competitiveness of a national software system is the size and capabilities of the industry, which may comprise large transnational corporations (TNCs), small and medium size enterprises (SMEs) as well as microenterprises. In most developing and transition economies, the sector is dominated by small and young enterprises. For example, in Guatemala, Honduras and the former Yugoslav Republic of Macedonia, the average size of software enterprises is 20 employees or less.[11] Small size often correlates with a lack of resources needed for the successful penetration of export markets.

Concerning structural characteristics, the level of specialization and differentiation among software companies in terms of technologies and vertical specialization (target industries, for example, the financial industry) and horizontal specialization (functional areas, for example client relationship management (CRM) applications) vary considerably. The same applies to the technical profiles of software companies with regard to operating systems and platforms, programming languages, development tools and database technologies, as well as management capabilities, all relevant for their ability to meet customer requirements in domestic and/or export markets and to innovate. Innovation capabilities in the national software system are of central importance given the short product life cycle of software and its potential for facilitating innovation in other sectors.[12] Innovation capabilities are also critical for moving up the computer software and services value chain.

For countries at early stages of development, the immediate concern may be to strengthen the capabilities of software enterprises to ensure an adequate supply of support services to domestic users in the public and private sectors. In the context of developing countries, it is useful to consider the following types of enterprises (Rizk and El-Kassas, 2010; Roeding et al., 1999): software resellers and support providers; producers of own software products; software service providers; IT and business consulting firms; other IT service providers (table I.1). As can be seen, most types of companies belong to the services area. In many developing countries, in particular LDCs, most domestic software enterprises belong to the category of resellers and support provides.

It is common for local software companies to start by representing a foreign vendor as a local reseller of products and support, and then seek to move up to the next level by becoming a producer of their own software. In Nigeria, for example, some of the leading

Table I.1.   Types of software enterprises in developing countries

Type of enterprise	Description
Producers of own software products	Can be separated into three subcategories: producers of standardized business products, R&D-based products and embedded systems products
Software resellers and support providers	Typically act as agents or resellers for other software suppliers, such as proprietary packaged software. Support can range from installation and maintenance of the software to sophisticated consultancy and customization work.
Software service providers	Develop software for others by offering consultants or development services
IT and business consulting firms	Tend to focus on the customization of training and consulting on enterprise-level software solutions, be localized and relatively small in size
IT service providers	Include Internet service providers and application service providers. Their role increases with a growing reliance on web-based and cloud-based software applications. These companies may offer access to their networks, systems and applications.

Source: Rizk and El-Kassas, 2010.

software companies started as agents for foreign enterprises. They were able to translate the experience from working with the foreign suppliers into software sales, implementation and value-added activities, and eventually found a niche for themselves in the market. SystemSpecs, for example, started by providing support services for a British company (SunSystems). After five years, it was able to launch its own human resource management software, which it now also exports to other countries (Bamiro, 2007).

The way in which the software industry is organized at the meso-level plays an important role. Industry associations and various informal networks (such as technical online communities) allow for rapid interchange of information and knowledge between companies and serve as a platform to pool resources and capabilities to promote the software industry (Carmel, 2003, p. 7). The case studies presented in chapter III support this argument.

(b) Universities and research institutes

Universities and research institutes are important actors in the development and production of software in a country. Not only does the competitiveness of the industry depend to a large extent on the quality and quantity of graduates produced by universities in relevant subjects (see below), it is also important to ensure effective collaboration between universities and research centres, on the one hand, and the software industry on the other, in the design and implementation of projects related to software development.

(c) The software-developer community

In earlier approaches to analysing the software potential of countries, the software-developer community

was typically not singled out as a separate category. In view of recent changes in the ICT landscape – the trend towards outsourcing of micro-work, growing demand for mobile and web applications, new peer-to-peer production methods and greater reliance on community-developed open source software – this community is playing a more important role within the system. Building openness into polices and technologies can result in greater opportunities for developing countries to transform into equitable and sustainable knowledge societies (Smith and Elder, 2010). It is decisive to what degree such openness is geared towards enabling software developers to freely innovate on top of others' open innovation (Seibold, 2010) and to engage into collaborative, continuous and open learning processes.

In developing and transition economies, software-developer communities offer various advantages. First, they provide local software companies with an additional resource pool, from which developers can be hired when there is increased demand. This is particularly valuable in the software industry, which tends to be cyclical and project based. Second, the digital nature of software and the possibility of developing software remotely in distributed teams make outsourcing/crowdsourcing to software-developer communities an attractive option for potential clients. This also means that software-developer communities can become a generator of software export revenues.[13] Third, developer communities promote knowledge generation and sharing within the IT industry and represent a source for innovation. This is especially true in the case of regional and global software-developer groups, such as the Linux Developer Network, Mozilla Developer Network and various groups on social media, such as Linkedin and Facebook.

(d) Software users

Software users are included in the national software system to reflect the role of domestic demand. Domestic demand can be differentiated into two main subsegments: private sector (from individuals and enterprises) and public sector demand.

In most developing and transition economies, certain industries tend to figure more frequently than others among the main users of software products and services, such as the financial, telecommunications, manufacturing, health and tourism industries (MASIT, 2011; SOFEX, 2011; AHTI, 2011). Furthermore, in Africa, firms from the financial and telecommunications industry are among the main buyers of software and IT services. For example, the financial sector is currently investing in cloud computing and mobile money-related applications both to reduce costs and to enable business innovation (Forrester, 2012a). In countries with a competitive manufacturing sector, such as Brazil, China, Mexico and the Republic of Korea, much of the software produced locally is embedded in the manufactured goods that are subsequently sold domestically or in export markets (see chapter III). Meanwhile, in countries that are well endowed with natural resources, the extractive industries are often major buyers of software. Foreign affiliates of TNCs tend to account for a major share of private-sector domestic demand for software products and services in developing countries.

In many developing and transition economies, the public sector represents a key part of domestic software demand. Its procurement of software products and services is often linked to tenders for large-scale e-government projects.[14] Beyond being an important creator of domestic demand, the public sector can also play a catalytic role in spurring innovation through public procurement related to e-government, e-health and e-learning.

2. Enabling factors in the national software system

(a) Access to ICT infrastructure

A competitive ICT infrastructure is an essential condition for the national software system. Particularly important is the broadband infrastructure, allowing for sufficient connectivity and Internet access at internationally competitive prices. Programmers need computers and access to the Internet. Good network capability is becoming indispensable as applications move to the cloud and for participating in global software activities. Infrastructure is also essential for the development of local software markets by linking applications and content with users through national backbone networks. In view of the rapidly increasing importance of mobile technologies and applications in many developing countries, mobile broadband is a key infrastructure element.

(b) Access to skilled human resources

Almost all facets of software development require some degree of knowledge imparted through the formal education systems or by specialized training institutions. The availability of an educated workforce and students enrolled in computer-related education fundamentally affects the potential of the system. As emphasized by an earlier study (Tessler et al., 2002, p. 12), "there is no more important element of a country's efforts to increase software capacity than the development of its corps of software professionals".[15] Similarly, in an UNCTAD–World Information Technology and Services Alliance (WITSA) survey, limited access to qualified human resources was an often cited barrier to the growth and development of the software and IT services industry (chapter V).

The kind of skills that software enterprises, or other enterprises that are conducting in-house software development, are looking for varies considerably depending on the nature of work involved and on the stage in the software value chain. It is important for programmers to have a solid knowledge of coding, but they also need to be able to understand requirements and specificities of the domain for which the software is adapted and developed (Vijayabaskar and Suresh Babu, 2009). Partly for this reason, it is important to develop local capabilities that have an understanding of the specific context in which the software is produced. In view of the rapid pace of change in the software field, firms are often searching for programmers with the ability to learn new skills on the job. Such skills go beyond the pure technical aspects and concern also project management and other general business skills. The size and capabilities of a country's human resources are a function of three determinants – the education system (notably universities), the system for professional, industry-based education and training, and in-house training organized by software enterprises themselves.

(c) Legal framework

The legal and regulatory environment needs to be conducive to software industry growth. While this factor potentially involves a wide range of legal issues, particular attention can be given to intellectual property rights, regulations on payment transactions and legislation affecting trust among ICT users.

The system for intellectual property rights is often seen as a relevant element of the overall business and legal framework influencing the software industry. The main purpose of protecting intellectual property is to give incentives to invest resources in bringing new products (open source and proprietary software) to market. Encouraging local firms to develop new solutions has the advantage of promoting indigenous innovation and its commercialization, as well as more sustainable employment. The appropriate level of intellectual property protection depends, however, on a country's level of development, status of domestic software sector capabilities and capacity to enforce intellectual property law and provide legal remedies. For the local industry to benefit from such protection, it needs the relevant capabilities to produce what the market demands (see also chapter V).

Enabling the development of transactional applications is an important aspect of the legal and regulatory framework. It is particularly relevant for expanding the scope of software into electronic or mobile commerce and interactive online applications for business and Government. The legitimization of online financial transactions is necessary for small software developers in order to receive payments from abroad (UNCTAD, 2011a). For example, software developers in the freelance industry of Bangladesh have lobbied the Government to allow PayPal transactions, since it is a common method for paying freelancers because of its convenience and low charges for small transaction amounts.[16]

More generally, laws and regulations that help to build trust among users of different ICTs, for example for the purpose of e-commerce, e-government or other electronic applications, facilitate use of ICTs and, indirectly, raise the demand for relevant software applications.

(d) An enabling business environment

Small companies and start-ups are highly prevalent in the software industry and need an enabling business environment to survive, innovate and thrive. An enabling business environment is a broad category that involves such dimensions as the relative ease of starting and running a business, and the availability of dedicated business infrastructure to support software and technology development. This environment should also ensure access to capital. In many developing and transition economies, access to capital is a concern for software companies (particularly for SMEs) due to deficiencies in the banking system or strict collateral requirements. The financing situation is often aggravated by the absence of venture capital and public financing schemes such as loans or grants (chapter V).

(e) Global links

The production of software is increasingly internationalized, with expanding international trade, investment, production and development networks. Today, even small companies or individual developers in developing countries can export to clients abroad or participate in peer-to-peer learning networks. Such international interaction can provide critical learning experience and linkages that can help strengthen the capabilities to develop software for local needs. It is important for a national software system to ensure access to imported knowledge and software as well as to export markets. Such access can be enabled through interaction with the diaspora, migration, access to international knowledge networks and foreign direct investment (FDI) flows. Governments and other stakeholders can take various measures to strengthen such global links. International links are greatly facilitated by language capabilities, especially English. A contributing factor to the success of countries such as India, Israel, the Philippines and Sri Lanka in software and IT services exports is their English language skills.

3. Vision, strategy and government policies

Within the national software system, the Government plays a crucial role in terms of facilitating the development of a national vision and strategy, developing sectoral policies, generating public demand as well as creating a supportive business environment. The actions of the Government provide the basic framework in which the producers and users in the national software system behave and interact. In most countries that have successfully managed to nurture domestic software capabilities, active Government involvement was instrumental, especially at the early stages of the industry's development. This applies to the United States of America as well as to diverse countries such as India, Ireland and Israel (Heeks, 1999; Carmel, 2003; Tessler et al., 2002). Effective strategy development and government policy implementation requires a collaborative approach, involving all relevant stakeholders (chapter V).

E. ROADMAP TO THE REPORT

This chapter has emphasized the importance for developing countries to build software capabilities so that the information society can take hold and to allow for ICT services and applications to be adapted to the specific needs and circumstances in each country. First, countries with well-developed capabilities are better equipped to implement their own customized solutions and less dependent on outside expertise. Second, local software expertise is, other things being equal, in a stronger position to understand local needs and therefore to develop relevant and innovative applications and content. Third, close interaction between local developers and users generates learning opportunities and potential development gains in terms of productivity and operational efficiency for users across the economy. This in turn increases the potential for market expansion and diversification. Finally, the software sector in itself offers opportunities for technological upgrading, creation of high-end direct and indirect employment, not least for country's youth, the generation of income and export revenues, as well as

innovation. The conceptual framework presented in this chapter serves as a basis for the rest of the report.

Chapter II reviews recent trends with regards to the global software landscape and considers the position of different countries from various perspectives. While recognizing data limitations, it describes the main forms of software activities and highlights different software user categories with a view to identifying opportunities for developing countries at varying levels of software capabilities. It also compares the performance of countries with their level of development and software spending.

Chapter III presents selected country case studies on the role of the software industry, distinguishing between countries with a strong export-orientation and those that are mainly supplying software products and services for the domestic market. Chapter IV examines how the role of FOSS is evolving in different parts of the world and for various kinds of applications. It discusses how FOSS can help develop stronger local software capabilities in developing countries and considers to what extent FOSS is currently reflected in national policies and strategies.

Chapter V identifies and discusses key policies needed to enable national software systems. It presents the results of the UNCTAD–WITSA Survey of IT/Software Associations, including key barriers to the software growth in different countries. The analysis gives particular attention to policy measures that can help strengthen the performance of a national software system in key areas identified in this chapter. Chapter VI presents the overall conclusions and a set of policy recommendations.

NOTES

1. The East African Marine System (TEAMS), Seacom, EASSy, MainOne, WACS and GLO-1 undersea fibre-optic cables are in commercial deployment. ACE, SAex, WASACE and BRICS are scheduled for launch in 2012–2014. See African Undersea Cables at http://manypossibilities.net/african-undersea-cables/.

2. In 2010, an average person in a developed economy was 294 times more likely to have access to fixed broadband than one living in an LDC (UNCTAD, 2011a). In 2010, about a quarter of people in developed countries enjoyed fixed broadband access, and more than half had mobile broadband. In developing countries, the corresponding figures were estimated at 4.4 per cent and 5.4 per cent, respectively (Broadband Commission for Digital Development, 2011).

3. For a recent review see Fu et al., 2011.

4. Formed in 1999, ISPON has as objective the creation of an enabling environment for local content developers to thrive locally and also internationally. See www.ispon.org.

5. See http://searchsoa.techtarget.com/definition/software.

6. In the former Yugoslav Republic of Macedonia, for example, more than 70 per cent of the IT companies provide both software and IT services (see the former Yugoslav Republic of Macedonian ICT Chamber of Commerce at www.masit.org.mk).

7. As a consequence, the domestic market alone is often not able to absorb innovative software solutions and does not provide sufficient demand to induce growth effects.

8. This model has been applied to several software-exporting nations, including the Islamic Republic of Iran (Nicholson and Sahay, 2003), Ukraine (Gengler, 2003) and Indonesia (Bruell, 2003).

9. Other related examples include AT Kearney's Global Services Location Index (www.atkearney.com) and Mc Kinsey & Company's Location Readiness Index for the World Bank to help countries identify their areas of relative strengths and weaknesses in terms of IT services and ICT-enabled services (Sudan, et al., 2010).

10. Some scholars have presented dedicated software ecosystems (Oh, 2011), comprising four components: software companies (producing IT services, packaged software and embedded software), software user companies, universities and governments.

11. See MASIT, 2010, p. 34, AGEXPORT: http://www.export.com.gt, SOFEX, 2011 and AHTI, 2011.

12. See http://www.unece.org/fileadmin/DAM/ceci/ppt_presentations/2008/ic/Stryszowski.pdf.

13. It should be noted that this new form of online work remains little studied. There may be possible downsides with such models of distributed work. Some advantages of larger-scale cooperation may be lost, particularly for more sophisticated undertakings, and more research is needed on how the value is distributed in a crowdsource-based business model. Concerns may arise with regard to low levels of pay, work ethics and working conditions.

14. In the former Yugoslav Republic of Macedonia, for example, the government and education sectors both represented greater demand than the financial sector (MASIT, 2010).

15. The shortage of qualified human resources (skills shortage) has also been identified by software companies as a major challenge in various country studies (SOFEX, 2011; Bulgarian Association of Software Companies (BASSCOM), 2011; MASIT, 2011).

16. See http://my.news.yahoo.com/freelancers-bangladesh-long-paypal-095003371.html.

SOFTWARE TRENDS

2

The global software landscape is rapidly evolving, reflecting increased internationalization and technological change. Developing countries display strikingly different software growth paths, with some being predominantly export oriented while others are producing software mainly to meet domestic needs. Meanwhile, new demand for mobile applications at both national and international levels is generating opportunities for production, innovation and learning. In addition, improved broadband connectivity and the introduction of on-line platforms for micro-work are expanding the scope for developing countries to engage in international software projects. Chapter II examines various ways of measuring the software industry and reviews potential indicators regarding its status and performance in different countries. It concludes by discussing recent demand-side trends that are having an impact on the software landscape.

A. MEASURING THE SOFTWARE INDUSTRY

1. Software in the world economy

Estimates of the size of the global software industry vary greatly, reflecting different definitions and measurement methods. This section reviews existing data sources for measuring the computer software and IT services sector and draws on both official and market research figures to derive an estimate for the global software sector, with information especially on spending, employment, investment and trade.

(a) Classifications

Prior to the fourth revision of the International Standard Industrial Classification of All Economic Activities (ISIC Rev.4) there was no specific statistical category assigned to the ICT sector, let alone the computer software and services industry. With ISIC Rev.4, information and communication were identified as a separate industry with computer software and related computer services as a subcategory (division 62: computer programming, consultancy and related activities; division 63: information service activities (table II.1).

In Europe, the General Industrial Classification of Economic Activities within the European Communities (NACE) Rev.2 was created based on ISIC Rev.4 and adapted to European circumstances. Thus, Eurostat now compiles data using the same divisions as ISIC Rev.4, such as those cited in table II.1, covering output and employment.[1] Meanwhile, the North American Industry Classification System (NAICS) includes computer software and related services within the "Information and Cultural" industries.[2] This system consists of three main categories: software publishers; data processing, hosting and related services; Internet publishing and broadcasting and web search portals.

Although an international classification exists for computer software and services, little international official data are available outside of Europe and North America. In some cases, national statistical offices have carried out, or are contemplating, one-off special ICT satellite sector accounts (for example, Chile and South Africa).[3] In other countries (for example, India and Singapore), sector ministries or regulators compile ICT-sector statistics, including computer software and services revenue, using their own methodologies.

Given the lack of official data from official government sources, market consultancy information on the sector is often used by policy makers. This chapter draws heavily on information on computer software and information services spending, as reported by WITSA using data provided by IHS Global Insight Inc. (WITSA, 2010) (box II.1). This data set measures what different economic sectors spend on computer software and services rather than the value added that would be captured in the national accounts. As the WITSA data pertain to spending only, other sources are used to complement the picture. This has the inherent drawback that the various sources sometime differ in definitions, country coverage and geographic groupings. Furthermore, computer software and services data do not capture embedded software, or applications that are increasingly included in a growing number of microprocessor-driven devices used in products from automobiles to televisions. The embedded

Table II.1. Computer and information services in ISIC Rev.4
Section J: Information and communication

| Division: 62 – Computer programming, consultancy and related activities
Breakdown:
This Division is divided into the following Groups:
• 620 - Computer programming, consultancy and related activities

Explanatory note
This division includes the following activities of providing expertise in the field of information technologies: writing, modifying, testing and supporting software; planning and designing computer systems that integrate computer hardware, software and communication technologies; on-site management and operation of clients' computer systems and/or data processing facilities; and other professional and technical computer-related activities. | Division: 63 – Information service activities
Breakdown:
This Division is divided into the following Groups:
• 631 - Data processing, hosting and related activities; web portals
• 639 - Other information service activities

Explanatory note
This division includes the activities of web search portals, data processing and hosting activities, as well as other activities that primarily supply information |

Source: United Nations, http://unstats.un.org/unsd/cr/registry/regcs.asp?Cl=27&Lg=1&Co=J.

Box II.1.   Data compiled by WITSA on ICT-sector spending

Four groups of services and goods are identified by WITSA within the ICT sector:

- Computer software: includes the value of purchased or leased packaged software such as operating systems, database systems, programming tools and applications. It excludes expenditures for internal software development and outsourced custom software development.
- Computer services: includes the value of outsourced services – domestic or offshore – such as IT consulting, computer systems integration, outsourced custom software development, outsourced web design, network systems, network systems integration, office automation, facilities management, web hosting, and data processing services.
- Computer hardware: includes the value of purchased or leased computers, storage devices, memory upgrades, printers, monitors, scanners, input–output devices, terminals, other peripherals, and bundled operating systems.
- Communications: includes the value of voice and data communications services, and equipment.

Source: WITSA.

---

software value is instead counted statistically as part of the hardware value of the equipment it is used in. This can cause discrepancies in the data of large ICT hardware manufacturing economies, where national statistics may derive a value for the embedded software that is not captured in international data sets (see also chapter III).

Trade in computer software and services is relatively well defined internationally within the commercial services segment of the balance of payments.[4] The computer and information services category can be further broken down into computer services (hardware- and software-related services and data-processing services), news agency services (provision of news, photographs and feature articles to the media), and other information provision services (database services and web search portals). In this area, international data sets are available with time series. Note that not all software-related trade is recorded, and that much

software is indirectly exported when embedded in manufactured goods.

(b)   Size of the software and IT services market

According to WITSA and IHS Global Insight, the spending on computer software and services (excluding software embedded in devices) amounted to an estimated $1.2 trillion in 2011, or almost one third of global ICT spending that year (figure II.1).[5] This share has remained fairly stable since 2005. Similarly, the proportion of computer software and services in overall ICT spending has hovered around 30 per cent. Spending on computer software and services amounts to about 2 per cent of gross domestic product (GDP). The sector has shown solid growth albeit with a decline in 2009 due to the global financial crisis. However, even then computer software proved more resilient than other ICT-sector segments (Mickoleit et al., 2009).

Figure II.1   Global computer and software spending and distribution with ICT spending

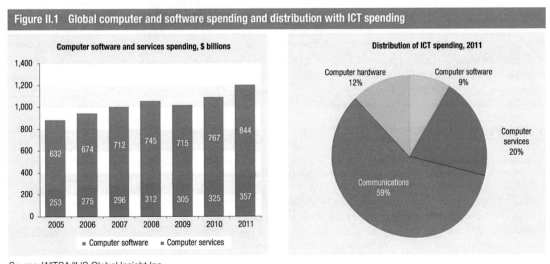

Source: WITSA/IHS Global Insight Inc.
Note: Data for 2011 are estimates.

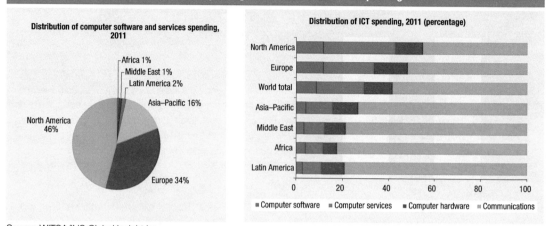

Figure II.2   Global computer and software spending and distribution with ICT spending

Source: WITSA/IHS Global Insight Inc.
Note: Regions correspond to those used in the source data (see annex table II.1).

Developed countries account for the vast share of the expenditure. North America and Europe generated four fifths of the total in 2011 (figure II.2, left). The remaining share is mainly accounted for by East, South and South-East Asia, while spending in the developing regions of Africa, Latin America and the Middle East corresponded to only 4 per cent, well below their share of world GDP (10 per cent). This suggests significant scope for increasing the size of the computer software and IT services use in developing countries. Growth is indeed much higher in these economies. For example, according to data from the European Information Technology Observatory (EITO), between 2008 and 2012 software markets grew by about 40 per cent or more in China, India, the Russian Federation and in Latin America and the Caribbean, whereas the equivalent growth rates in North America and Europe were only about 15 per cent. Furthermore, IT services grew faster outside developed countries, especially in India and China (EITO, 2011).

Developed regions also spend relatively more on computer software and services as a share of their overall ICT spending. For example, in North America, computer software and services accounted for 43 per cent of ICT spending compared with only 11 per cent in Latin America (figure II.2, right). In none of the developing countries for which data are available was the share of software and services above the world average. Low ratios in developing regions can be seen as another sign of little software use, hindering their passage to the information society.

Some analysts attribute part of the lower ratio of software to overall ICT spending to a high incidence of piracy in many developing countries (box II.2). Other explanations may be that smaller countries with few companies large enough to need or afford servers will tend to have a lower software to hardware spending ratio, and that more developed countries have a higher level of software configuration (and therefore greater need for IT services) per hardware unit (IDC, 2009).

Box II.2.   Packaged software and the use of unlicensed software

According to the Business Software Association, the global unlicensed ("pirated") PC software rate was 42 per cent in 2010, valued at $59 billion. This would imply that a little over two fifths of all computer software spending is on unlicensed packaged PC software. The total (potential) value of packaged software (licensed sales plus estimated unlicensed value) was $140 billion in 2010. The use of unlicensed as well as open source software creates some uncertainty regarding the size of the computer software market. Developed countries account for the bulk of packaged software spending. While developing regions appear to have a higher rate of unlicensed to licensed packaged software, in absolute value, developed countries account for 40 per cent of all unlicensed software.

Source: UNCTAD, based on Business Software Association and IDC, 2011.

(c) Software and IT services employment

Boosting software employment not only helps to build up the software sector itself, it also has downstream multiplying effects. Moreover, jobs in software and IT services can help attract skilled young people and reduce the brain drain.

According to the most recent data (covering countries representing 95 per cent of computer software and services spending in 2011), an estimated 10 million people are employed in the global computer software and services sector. National shares of this sector range from 0.1 per cent to 2.2 per cent of total employment (figure II.3). Most countries in which computer software and services represent a low employment share are developing countries, indicating scope for potential expansion. The developing countries with the highest proportion of employment in this sector and for which data are available are Costa Rica (0.8 per cent), South Africa (0.7 per cent) and India (0.6 per cent).

In the European Union, computer software and IT services employment has remained flat at about 1.5 per cent of total employment on average for the past few years, with a workforce of about 3.3 million people in

2010. Data compiled by UNCTAD for 21 non-European Union countries indicate that about 7 million people are employed in the computer software and IT services sector in these countries. The bulk of these employees (64 per cent) are in the BRIC group of countries (Brazil, Russian Federation, India and China) and another 27 per cent are in Japan and the United States of America. The computer software and services share in total ICT-sector employment varies from more than 80 per cent in Japan to less than 5 per cent in Cameroon and Oman (figure II.4). On average, computer software and services account for just over half of all ICT-sector employment in these countries. It should be noted that very few low-income countries report ICT-sector employment data.

In addition to the direct employment created, the computer software industry generates significant indirect employment in areas such as retailing, software integration, training and maintenance. For example, a 2006 study on the Chinese ICT sector found that every $1 spent in the software industry generated $2.25 in additional economic activity, including over 0.5 million software-related jobs (Gantz, 2006). Data from India indicate that the IT and business process outsourcing (BPO) sector employed some 2.5 million

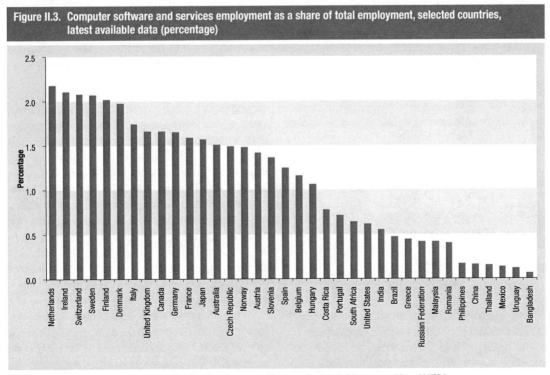

Figure II.3. Computer software and services employment as a share of total employment, selected countries, latest available data (percentage)

Source: UNCTAD, based on international and national sources. Total employment data sourced from WITSA.

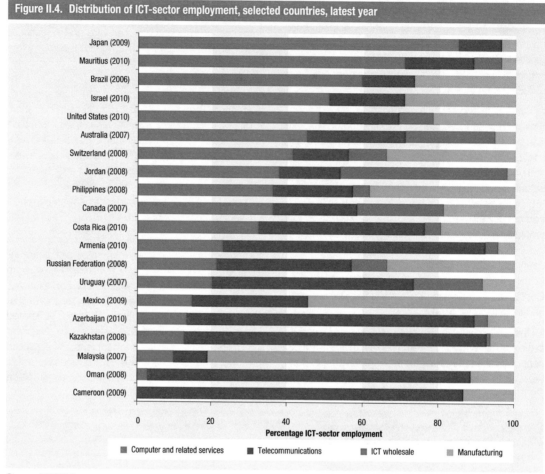

Figure II.4. Distribution of ICT-sector employment, selected countries, latest year

Percentage ICT-sector employment

■ Computer and related services   ■ Telecommunications   ■ ICT wholesale   ▨ Manufacturing

Source: UNCTAD.

people in 2011 with indirect employment attributed to this sector estimated at 9 million (from the Indian Ministry of Information Technology, various years). In South Africa, while software represented only 12 per cent of total ICT spending, it accounted for as much as 47 per cent of ICT-industry employment (Walker, 2009). Some software labour is not captured in official employment statistics, such as so-called free-lancer programmers and micro-workers (see also section II.C.4).

(d) Trade and offshoring related to computer and information services

Exports of computer and information services stood at an estimated $215 billion in 2010, recovering from a dip caused by the global financial crisis in 2009 (figure II.5, left). They have almost doubled since 2005 reflecting strong growth in outsourcing, now repre-

senting about 5.7 per cent of all commercial services. In value terms, Ireland is the leading exporter, both in absolute terms and relative to GDP. The country's computer software and services exports almost quintupled between 2000 and 2010, from $7 billion to $37 billion, and appear to have been relatively unaffected by the global financial crisis. Computer and information service exports accounted for 16 per cent of the Irish GDP in 2010 (figure II.5, right). In Costa Rica, India and the Philippines, computer and information services account for 1–2 per cent of GDP. The European Union, United States of America and Japan are the top three importers while the BRIC countries are among the top ten.[7] The main developing country exporters (in absolute terms) of computer and information services among exporters are all Asian and include China, India, the Philippines and Singapore (figure II.6).

Figure II.5. Computer and information services exports, 2005–2010, and top ten exporters as a percentage of GDP, 2010

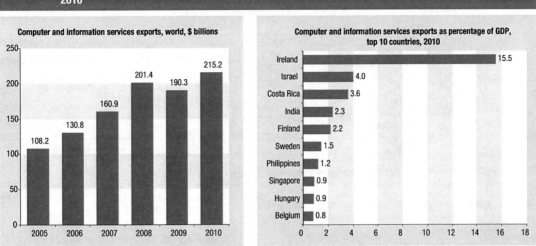

Source: UNCTAD, adapted from World Trade Organization (WTO) Statistics database.

Figure II.6. Computer and information services exports, 2010 or latest, top twenty exporters by value (millions of dollars)

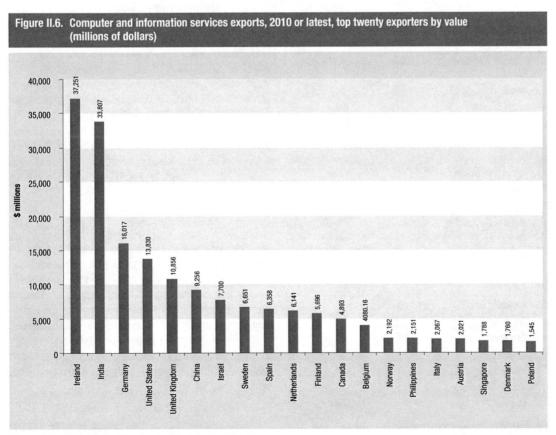

Source: UNCTAD, adapted from the WTO statistics database.

Figure II.7. Global market for IT services offshoring, by destination, 2011 (percentage)

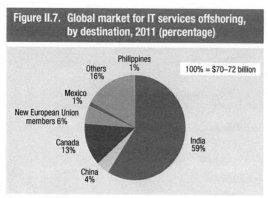

100% = $70–72 billion

Philippines 1%
Others 16%
Mexico 1%
New European Union members 6%
Canada 13%
China 4%
India 59%

Source: UNCTAD, based on information from the Everest Research Institute.

Table II.2. Greenfield FDI projects in software and IT services, by destination, 2007–2011 (number of projects)

Destination region/economy	Number of projects
World	7 553
Developed countries	4 419
Developing countries	2 956
Africa	228
South Africa	72
Egypt	29
Morocco	27
Tunisia	26
Kenya	11
Asia and Oceania	2 043
India	541
China	422
Singapore	255
United Arab Emirates	172
Hong Kong (China)	164
Malaysia	96
Republic of Korea	71
Philippines	46
Viet Nam	45
Latin America and the Caribbean	685
Brazil	200
Mexico	146
Argentina	92
Colombia	63
Chile	57
Transition economies	178
Russian Federation	71
Ukraine	24

Source: UNCTAD, based on information from the Financial Times Ltd. *fDi Markets* (www.fDimarkets.com).

In terms of IT service offshoring, the total market was estimated at between $70 billion and $72 billion in 2011. Of this total, software and engineering services accounted for about $17 billion and IT services for the rest. India has reinforced its position as the preferred choice for IT services offshoring, with a market share of about 59 per cent, according to data from the Everest Research Institute (figure II.7). Canada accounted for approximately 13 per cent and new European Union members for about 6 per cent. China, Mexico and the Philippines were also each responsible for at least 1 per cent of the overall market. The category indicated as others in the figure include countries such as Argentina, Brazil, Chile and Costa Rica in Latin America, Thailand and Sri Lanka in Asia, and Egypt and South Africa on the African continent.

(e) Foreign direct investment projects in software

The software and IT services industry is becoming increasingly internationalized, and foreign direct investment (FDI) is playing an important role in this process. There is limited information on the value of FDI flows into the industry, but data exist on the number of greenfield FDI projects that have been announced. Table II.2 shows the geographical distribution of such projects over the period 2007–2011. While the majority of the projects were undertaken in developed countries, developing economies attracted 39 per cent. The top five developing country recipients – India, China, Singapore, Brazil and the United Arab Emirates – accounted for more than half of all greenfield projects in developing countries. In Africa, such projects mainly went to South Africa and countries in North Africa.

(f) Access to venture capital

Venture capital is a promising, growing but largely untapped source of investment in the software industry of developing countries. Between 2008 and 2011, the amount of private equity capital (of which venture capital accounts for a major share) invested in developing and transition economies in computer software and IT rose from $450 million to $1.5 billion (figure II.8). In terms of geographical distribution, however, such projects were highly concentrated to a few locations, notably the BRIC countries (table II.3).

In the United States of America, the software industry is the largest recipient of venture capital, attracting some $1.8 billion in the last quarter of 2011 alone (figure II.9).

Figure II.8. Private equity investment in computer software and IT, developing and transition economies, 2008–2011 (millions of dollars)

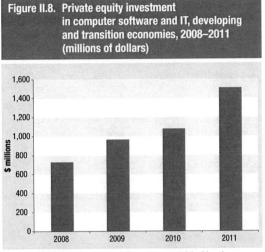

Source: UNCTAD, based on information provided by the Emerging Market Private Equity Association (EMPEA).

Note: The data underestimate the total value of investments as the investment value is not known for several deals concluded during the period.

Table II.3. Private equity investment projects in software and IT services in developing and transition economies, by destination, 2008–2011 (number of projects and millions of dollars)

Economy	Number of projects	Value of projects
India*	83	1 661
China*	79	916
Russian Federation*	20	482
Brazil*	10	541
South Africa*	6	30
Singapore*	4	4
Viet Nam*	4	60
Argentina	4	43
United Arab Emirates*	4	98
Uruguay	3	14
Malaysia*	2	4
Turkey*	2	2
Egypt	2	N/A
Kuwait*	2	20
Nigeria	2	12
Taiwan Province of China	1	4
Ukraine	1	N/A
Chile	1	52
Mexico	1	N/A
Morocco	1	N/A
Kenya	1	2

Source: UNCTAD, based on information from EMPEA, May 2012.

* The investment value is not known for all projects included.

Figure II.9. Venture capital in the United States of America, fourth quarter 2011, by recipient industry (millions of dollars)

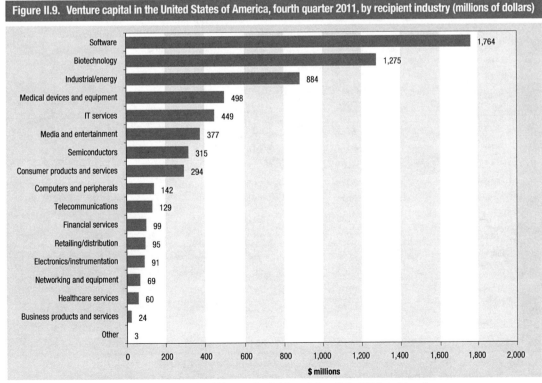

Source: UNCTAD, based on data from the National Venture Capital Association, United States of America.

In addition, significant venture capital is invested in related industries such as IT services. Similar findings emerge from Argentina, where software and computer services accounted for the largest share of venture capital in 2008, with start-up companies attracting over three quarters of the total investment (UNESCO, 2010).

(g) Largest software firms

The world's top 100 software firms by revenue reported sales of over $235 billion in 2010, up 7 per cent from 2009.[8] The data indicate the high level of concentration in the industry; the top 10 companies accounted for over 60 per cent of this revenue with Microsoft hav-

ing by far the largest share. Its software revenues exceeded $54 billion in 2010, representing more than one fifth of the world total and twice as much as those of the second largest company, IBM (table II.4).

The corporate list is dominated by enterprises based in developed countries, and especially from the United States of America. In 2010, 15 of the world's top 25 software firms were based in that country, as were 63 of the top 100 software firms. However, the trend is that software companies from other countries are gaining ground. In 2008, the United States of America had as many as 74 entries on the list.[9] In 2010, Japan saw 10 entries in the top 100, France six and

	Company	Software revenue (millions of dollars)	Growth over 2009	Software revenue as a share of total revenue (percentage)	Headquarters
Table II.4. Top 25 software companies, by revenue, 2010 (millions of dollars and percentage)					
1	Microsoft	54 270	11	81	United States
2	IBM	22 485	5	23	United States
3	Oracle	20 958	13	69	United States
4	SAP	12 558	11	75	Germany
5	Ericsson	7 274	-4	24	Sweden
6	HP	6 669	8	5	United States
7	Symantec	5 636	1	94	United States
8	Nintendo	5 456	-20	40	Japan
9	Activision Blizzard	4 447	4	100	United States
10	EMC	4 356	10	26	United States
11	Nokia Siemens Networks	4 229	-6.60	25	Finland
12	CA	4 136	3.10	93	United States
13	Electronic Arts	3 413	-8.40	100	United States
14	Adobe	3 177	13.60	83	United States
15	Alcatel-Lucent	2 561	-4.60	12	France
16	Cisco	2 383	11.50	6	United States
17	Sony	2 083	8.80	2	Japan
18	Hitachi	1 939	22.00	2	Japan
19	Dassault	1 885	19.00	90	France
20	BMC	1 843	4.80	93	United States
21	SunGard	1 762	-11.70	35	United States
22	Autodesk	1 701	9.20	88	United States
23	Konami	1 643	3.10	53	Japan
24	Salesforce.com	1 523	27.90	94	United States
25	Sage	1 485	-4.60	67	United Kingdom

Source: Software Top 100, http://www.softwaretop100.org/global-software-top-100-edition-2011.

Note: Software revenues are defined as revenues coming from sale of licences, maintenance, subscription and support. Revenues from custom software development are excluded.

the United Kingdom four. Only a few companies from developing economies feature in the top 100 list and none are included among the top 25. There are, however, signs of fast growth among enterprises in Brazil, China, the Russian Federation and the Republic of Korea (see also chapter III).

It is noteworthy that many of the companies in this list are not purely software firms. The fact that software is a significant revenue source for many firms in which software does not represent the primary focus attests to the importance of software across diverse business activities. Software specialization varies among the top companies. Several produce operating system and productivity software, in some cases for their branded hardware (for example, HP and IBM). Others specialize in enterprise applications such as database and accounting systems (Oracle, SAP). Ericsson, Nokia Siemens Networks and Alcatel-Lucent are telecom equipment manufacturers. Security (Symantec), games (Activision Blizzard, Nintendo), cloud computing (EMC) and consumer electronics (Sony, Hitachi) are other categories represented.

Despite being the developing world's leading computer software and services exporter, no Indian firm featured among the top 100 computer software companies. This is because Indian companies are focusing primarily on custom software development for multiple clients rather than on developing their own branded software products. In listings of IT services companies, however, India is well represented, with Tata Consultancy, Wipro and Infosys among the top 15 in the world.[10]

B. MEASURING THE SOFTWARE PERFORMANCE OF COUNTRIES

Using available data, this section explores linkages between computer software and services spending and the overall economy, and its relation to economic development and domestic versus export sales.

1. Software in the national economy

One way of evaluating a country's software performance is to compare the share of computer software and services spending within total ICT spending (figure II.10, left) with its share of the overall economy (figure II.10, right). In developing and transition economies that display a ratio above average, computer software and services have assumed relatively high importance. South Africa and Thailand are the only developing countries ranked top in both categories. The bottom four countries are the same in both charts.

The impact of software production and development on the domestic economy depends partly on the mix of local and export sales. Indirect effects on society may be expected to be greater if software is developed for and applied by domestic enterprises and public institutions (Kumar and Joseph, 2005). In order to interpret whether there is excessive reliance on software exports, the export share in low- and middle-income countries is

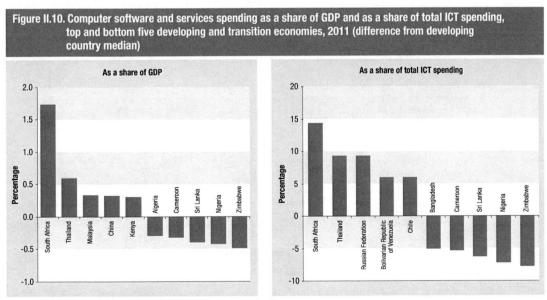

Figure II.10. Computer software and services spending as a share of GDP and as a share of total ICT spending, top and bottom five developing and transition economies, 2011 (difference from developing country median)

Source: UNCTAD, based on data from WITSA/IHS Global Insight Inc.

contrasted below with the sector's share of the overall economy (figure II.11). The ratio of computer software and IT services exports to computer software and services spending can be seen as a measure of software export intensity. Meanwhile, computer and IT services spending as a percentage of GDP is a measure of the sector's importance to the economy:

- If both values are low, it suggests that the computer software and IT services sector is undeveloped (figure II.11, quadrant A);
- If the export intensity is high but the share of the economy is low, then domestic demand is unfulfilled (quadrant B);
- If the share of GDP is high, but the export intensity is low, there may be scope for increased exports (quadrant C);
- If both show high values, then exports are less likely to be detracting from domestic demand for software (quadrant D).

A number of developing countries have computer software and IT services exports that exceed do-

mestic computer software and services spending (for example, Costa Rica, India, Jamaica, the Philippines, Sri Lanka and Uruguay). In some of them (for example, Sri Lanka and Uruguay),[27] software spending is small relative to the size of the economy, possibly suggesting that domestic software is being crowded out. In India and the Philippines, computer software has also become an important part of the local economy. They have joined Argentina and Malaysia as countries where both exports and the domestic computer software industry have relatively high values. Most economies in quadrant C (where software is important in the economy but export intensity is low) are upper-middle-income economies. In these cases, which include Brazil, China and South Africa, there appears to be significant scope to increase software exports.

There are noteworthy regional contrasts. In Latin America, Costa Rica and Uruguay have focused on exports whereas in Brazil the large local market is more significant. In North Africa, Morocco is emerging as a key export player, Tunisia displays a significant domestic

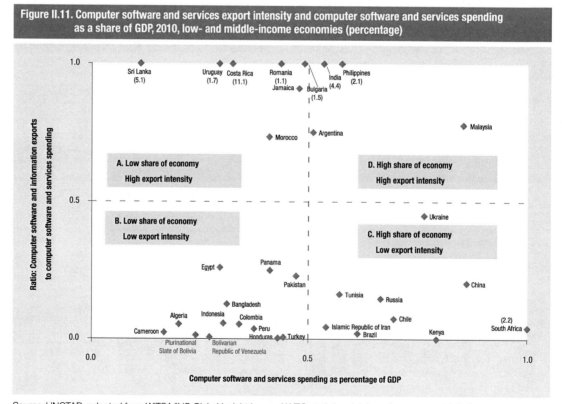

Figure II.11. Computer software and services export intensity and computer software and services spending as a share of GDP, 2010, low- and middle-income economies (percentage)

Source: UNCTAD, adapted from WITSA/IHS Global Insight Inc. and WTO statistics database (see annex table II.2).
Note: The ratio of exports to computer software and services spending and computer software and services as a percentage of GDP has been capped at 1 to enhance readability of the figure.

market, while there appears to be scope for an expansion of the software industry in Algeria and Egypt.

2. Contrasting software spending with demand

Contrasting the availability of computer software and IT services (measured in terms of spending as a percentage of GDP) with a proxy for demand (Internet users as a percentage of the population) yields the relationship shown in figure II.12 (left). The difference between the actual and expected share of spending (derived from the percentage of Internet users) indicates whether countries are performing above or below that which could be expected in view of their level of Internet penetration.

The top and bottom five among developing countries in terms of the difference between actual and expected spending are shown in the right panel of figure II.12. South Africa and Thailand most exceed the expected level of computer software spending, confirming earlier observations made in this chapter (box II.3).[12] In other words, these countries spend a relatively large amount on software and services compared with other countries reporting similar levels of Internet use. Bangladesh and India also perform better than expected. This can be attributed to relatively low domestic demand (reflected by low levels of Internet use) and a strong focus on exports. The burgeoning domestic market of Kenya, triggered by

rapid mobile growth and innovation in areas such as mobile money, is boosting computer software and IT services spending. Among those performing below expectation, three Latin American nations have, along with Morocco, emphasized software exports despite indication of domestic market potential (reflected by relatively high Internet penetration rates). Nigeria appears to have an unbalanced domestic market with computer software and IT services spending dominated by consumer and natural resources to the detriment of other sectors such as government, financial services and education.

To summarize, developing and transition economies display different patterns in terms of the market orientation of their software sector. A few countries have considerably larger exports of software and IT services than the amount spent on software in the domestic economy. Meanwhile, others are characterized by substantial spending on software and IT services but relatively low levels of exports. Among this latter category are both large economies, such as Brazil, China, the Russian Federation and South Africa, and smaller economies, such as Chile, Kenya and Tunisia. This section has also highlighted noticeable variation in software spending when compared with the ICT maturity in a country, as proxied by Internet use. Bangladesh and Kenya both belong to those countries that are now devoting relatively more spending on software compared with other countries with similar levels of Internet use.

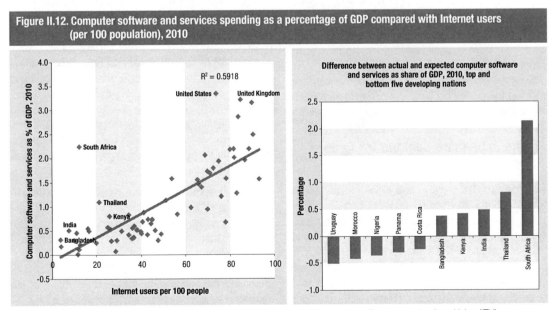

Figure II.12. Computer software and services spending as a percentage of GDP compared with Internet users (per 100 population), 2010

Source: UNCTAD, based on data from WITSA/IHS Global Insight Inc., and International Telecommunications Union (ITU).

Box II.3.   Software performance in South Africa and Thailand

South Africa and Thailand have consistently ranked high in the various computer software performance measures used in this chapter. Common factors for both countries include experience, a well-developed infrastructure and a geographic location characterized by upper-middle-income status surrounded by lower- and middle-income nations. Though both countries export software, it is not the main focus of the industry.

The performance of South Africa can be attributed to a large and mature ICT sector and conscious efforts to apply and adapt technology to the domestic market. It has a long experience in this area. For example, the Computer Society of South Africa is the second oldest such organization in the world. With the largest economy on the African continent, South Africa also has the biggest ICT sector with the presence of many leading ICT TNCs. The telecom market is relatively developed with over 100 mobile subscriptions per 100 inhabitants, several domestic Internet exchanges and growing undersea fibre-optic connectivity. In 2012, smartphone penetration exceeded 23 per cent. Specific areas where South Africa is strong include system integration and applications development in industries such as mining, finance and mobile communications. Labour shortages remain an issue although there are high-level educational faculties such as the Johannesburg Centre for Software Engineering at the University of the Witwatersrand and emerging technological hubs.

The software industry of Thailand benefits from an educated workforce and a growing domestic market. The country is interconnected by numerous submarine fibre-optic cables and has extensive data-centre capacity. It is also emerging as an animation and gaming software centre. Software, animation, and data centres are identified as key industries in the country's ICT master plan. The Government supports an enabling environment through targeted policies aimed at critical infrastructure, training and internships, and access to financing.

Source: UNCTAD, adapted from South Africa Department of Trade and Industry, The South African Software Development Industry (http://www.suedafrika-wirtschaft.org/index.php?&pageID=45), (South Africa Department of Communications, 2012) and Thailand Board of Investment, Thailand Software Industry (http://www.boi.go.th/index.php?page=opp_software).

C. DEMAND DRIVERS OF SOFTWARE

The shape of the software industry is influenced by various changes in the market and in the technological landscape. Current demand drivers of software industry development of particular relevance to developing countries include mobile communications and social networking growth as well as cloud computing and demand for national content. The growth of freelancing and crowdsourcing services is also highlighted below.

1. The expanding demand for mobile applications

According to ITU, there were 6 billion mobile cellular subscriptions in the world in 2011. Subscriptions per 100 people reached 86 globally and 84 in the developing world (figure II.13, left).[13] This is a huge potential base of demand for software as mobile users move beyond simple voice services. Progress has also been remarkable among the LDCs, where penetration rose between 2006 and 2011 from 9 to 41 subscriptions per 100 inhabitants.

The number of users of mobile data services is significant and growing. China alone counted for over 350 million mobile Internet users in 2011, whereas in Kenya, 99 per cent of Internet subscriptions come from mobile phones.[14] Mobile data use is also becoming significant in other developing countries (figure II.13, right). Apart from the large base of mobile owners in the world, demand for mobile software and applications is driven by two other factors: the expansion of mobile broadband networks and the emergence of smartphones and tablet devices. In 2011, global sales of smartphones exceeded those of PCs for the first time (figure II.14, left) and, although penetration is still relatively low, smartphones are rapidly being taken up in developing countries (figure II.14, right).

The mobile applications (apps) industry, a recent development, is estimated to have generated a worldwide revenue of $15 billion–$20 billion in 2011.[15] It has been calculated that the app economy in the United States of America alone may have employed some 466,000 people in 2011 – up from zero in 2007 (Mandel, 2012). Following the success of Apple's App Store, many operating system vendors, ICT manufacturers, mobile operators and others have taken the initiative to launch

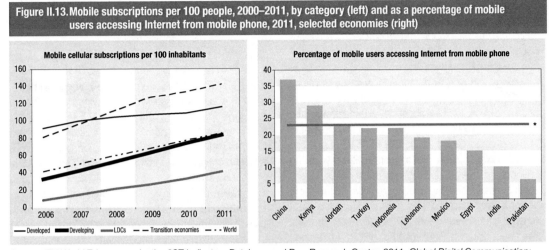

Figure II.13. Mobile subscriptions per 100 people, 2000–2011, by category (left) and as a percentage of mobile users accessing Internet from mobile phone, 2011, selected economies (right)

Source: ITU World Telecommunication/ICT Indicators Database and Pew Research Center, 2011, *Global Digital Communication: Texting, Social Networking Popular Worldwide* (http://www.pewglobal.org/2011/12/20/global-digital-communication-texting-social-networking-popular-worldwide/).

* = Based on 21 developed and developing countries accounting for 60 per cent of global mobile subscriptions.

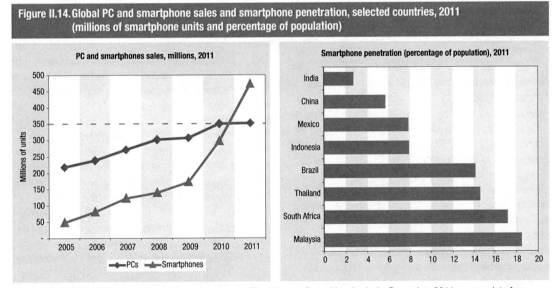

Figure II.14. Global PC and smartphone sales and smartphone penetration, selected countries, 2011 (millions of smartphone units and percentage of population)

Source: UNCTAD, based on information from Gartner and TomiAhonen Consulting Analysis, December 2011, on raw data from Google/Ipsos, and on data from the *Netsize Guide*, and *TomiAhonen Almanac 2011*.

their own app stores. As of April 2012, more than a million apps had been created, including 600,000 for Apple, 400,000 for Android and about 70,000 for the new Windows phone – and many more are in the pipeline.[16]

Notwithstanding the uncertainty regarding precision of the numbers, it is clear that this segment of the software industry is currently expanding at high speed. One study predicts that the market will grow to about $38 billion by 2014 (AT Kearney, 2011). Within the mobile apps market, mobile enterprise applications are expected to be the next growth driver as employees become more mobile (IMAP, 2010). This trend, which is particularly relevant for developing and transition economies, might be amplified by the introduction of HyperText Markup Language 5 (HTML5), which is able to support different features, is platform-independent and more robust in regions with limited mobile coverage and low connectivity.

From a developing country's perspective, it is worth noting that technical barriers to entry tend to be relatively low in the case of mobile apps development. Many micro and small enterprises as well as freelance developers in developing countries are participating in this industry, serving both local and international markets (World Bank, 2012). For example, according to the online work platform, oDesk, mobile apps development was the seventh most requested freelance job in September 2011 (see also II.C.4).[17] As developers cannot assume that users have a specific platform, applications are being developed for multiple devices, such as mobiles, smartphones, tablets and laptops, using various software platforms (World Bank, 2012). This work involves various types of software, such as SMS (low-end phones), Java and Hypertext Pre-processor (PHP) (mid-range devices) and Apple iOS, Blackberry, Windows and Android (smartphones).

2. Social networking

More than four out of five web surfers, representing around 1.2 billion users around the world, use social networking sites.[18] In October 2011, social networking ranked as the most popular Internet use accounting for almost a fifth of all time spent online. Social networks are increasingly globalized. The share of Facebook users—the most frequently used social networking site—from outside the United States of America is growing rapidly. In 2009, 65 per cent of Facebook's daily active users came from outside North America, whereas by December 2011 this figure had risen to almost three quarters of its 483 million daily active users.[19] The mobile version is particularly popular in developing countries. More than three quarters of all Facebook users in Botswana, Brunei Darussalam, Malawi, Namibia, Nigeria, Papua New Guinea and South Africa use the mobile version.[20] In addition, local social networking sites are also gaining in popularity in countries such as China and the Russian Federation.

Social networking creates opportunities for developing linked applications including games, music and social causes. For example, the Facebook programmer's platform allows developers to create apps that link into the social network's application interface. More than 2.5 million websites have been linked to Facebook and its users install some 20 million apps every day. It is estimated that the new Facebook app economy has created between 183,000 and 236,000 jobs for programmers in the United States of America alone with an employment value of between $12 billion and $16 billion.[21]

3. Cloud computing

A related trend is the increasing reliance on cloud-based applications, such as SaaS. Simply put, cloud computing provides computer processing and storage over a network as an alternative to purchasing packaged or customized software. Growing demand from companies for cloud computing and SaaS models is mainly fuelled by the need for cost efficiency and flexibility as well as by the standardization benefits from resource sharing. Spending of companies on SaaS is projected to reach $33 billion in 2012, representing an increase of 57 per cent compared with 2011 (Forrester, 2012b, p. 9). Some observers expect growth to be fuelled by organizations taking their data centres towards hybrid public and private cloud infrastructure. This will generate new demand for the software industry to create infrastructure as well as application services.[22]

Developing and transition economies are following this key trend. According to Capgemini, Brazil and China are among the fastest adopters of the cloud infrastructure (Capgemini, 2011, p. 39). In these countries, large enterprises are setting up "private clouds" as part of their IT modernization efforts. Smaller companies are starting to use public cloud infrastructure and services to gain a competitive advantage without having to build large data centres, and host and maintain their IT systems. The same study found that about 37 per cent of Chinese companies are planning to migrate 11–25 per cent of their applications to the cloud in the next year, and a further 40 per cent are making such arrangements. Similar trends are visible among African organizations, particularly in the retail, telecom and media industry. In these cases, cloud-based applications for e-mail, servers and networks are the top three uses by services companies (Forrester, 2012a, p. 12). As fixed broadband is generally poorly developed in Africa, mobile access to cloud-based services plays an important role.

4. Local content

Local content is taking an increasingly prominent place on the Internet. The proportion of non-English speakers on the Internet is rising fast. In 2010, a market research firm estimated that only one quarter (536 million) of nearly two billion Internet users were native English speakers (Bruegge, 2011). Thus, there is growing demand for programmers to support and develop local content and applications such as online national media and web site hosting. This trend also relates to traditional business and government software applications. Even off-the-shelf packaged software needs to be adapted to the idiosyncrasies of each country's business and legal framework. Another trend is that more content is user generated, particularly via social media. While such content may not require advanced computing knowledge, development of sophisticated portals and software will require local skills. Open access, open data and open education provide unprecedented opportunities for lowering the costs of skill acquisition and software development.

5. Software freelancing

Online work, also commonly referred to as crowdsourcing or remote, contract or freelance work, is fast becoming a prominent feature in global software development. It offers a new potential source of employment for the growing number of graduates from schools in developing countries. It also helps develop entrepreneurial skills since freelancers have to be proactive in marketing themselves. Freelancing is not an employment panacea in itself but does represent one possible outlet for youth employment. Given that the work is typically done over the Internet, it also provides more location flexibility. However, for the local software-developer community to participate effectively, broadband Internet needs to be widely available, accessible and affordable. A significant number of software developers from developing countries are already engaged in such activities. In Bangladesh, for example, some 10,000 freelance programmers are reportedly earning around $15 million per year. Their income is equivalent to one fourth of the country's total software exports.[23]

As this is a recent phenomenon, only piecemeal, quantitative evidence is available (UNCTAD, 2011a). The online work market is growing at record pace, up more than 100 per cent from 2010 and is expected to surpass $1 billion during 2012.[24] Formal statistical systems generally fail to capture such work and there are no official data on its actual contribution to software development. A brief look at two platforms for on-line work – oDesk.com and Elance.com – may offer a better understanding of the phenomenon (box II.4).

D. CONCLUSIONS

International statistical classifications of the ICT sector – including computer software and services – have improved in recent years. The sector is now a specific category within the international industrial classification used for national accounts. Computer software and services are also identified in balance of payments statistics as a separate category. Most developed countries compile detailed and timely data on the sector. However, few developing countries have moved to use these classifications. As a result, official ICT sector data are typically sparse or not up to date. This impedes the analysis of the role of the ICT sector in these economies. Greater effort is needed to compile relevant ICT-sector statistics on value added, revenue, number of establishments and employment in developing nations. Information is particularly scarce for low-income countries.

Box II.4.   Two platforms for online work

oDesk offers a global job marketplace targeted at businesses that intend to hire remote workers. Launched in November 2004, it has emerged as one of the world's leading global job marketplaces. It enables employers to hire, manage and pay online workers from around the world, creating opportunities for software development and knowledge worker talent. Since 2007, oDesk has experienced an annual growth rate of more than 100 per cent. Currently, contractors are together earning more than $300 million per year through this platform. As from February 2012, workers had generated $25 million in revenue, and worked 2.5 million hours related to 138,351 different jobs.

On Elance.com, more than 2 million jobs had been posted by the end of the first quarter of 2012, with cumulative earnings surpassing $500 million. The number of businesses hiring and the number of professionals working online continue to grow. In 2011, Elance had 550,000 active contractors and 130,000 active clients. Elance online workers resided in over 150 countries, whereas clients were also located in more than 150 countries. The top category on the Elance platform in the first quarter of 2012 was IT-related work, led by PHP and HTML. Demand for mobile app development also continued, with 17,000 app jobs posted in the quarter, with the fastest growth noted for Android.[25]

Source: UNCTAD, based on information from www.odesk.com and www.elance.com.
[a] See Crunch Base oDesk.com profile at http://www.crunchbase.com/company/odesk.

Available data from private sources on ICT spending suggest that the computer software and services segment has grown steadily in the past few years, with a brief dip in 2009 following the financial crisis. Likewise, packaged PC software and exports of computer software and services have also expanded. These data suggest that many developing countries allocate a disproportionately high share of their ICT spending on hardware and communications rather than on software and related services. This constrains their ability to fully exploit ICTs for the benefit of their economies and societies. Although there is some uncertainty about software to hardware spending due to piracy and use of open source software, the ratio remains low.

Expanding the local software industry can be an attractive option to generate employment that can help absorb the growing number of tertiary students graduating each year in developing nations. New demand for software skills related to mobile apps, social networking and freelancing is particularly relevant in this context. These new areas of software development may, furthermore, help create a critical mass of local capabilities to develop software solutions in traditional application fields for the business and government sectors of many developing countries, which are segments still underserved in many countries. Governments should forge links between academia and the business sector, create an appropriate enabling environment and more local software demand.

Existing data point to a weak link between the relative size of the computer software and services sector and per capita income in developing nations. This suggests that a low level of income is not an a priori barrier to the development of the software industry. Several growth trajectories can be chosen for countries to achieve local capabilities that can serve both domestic needs and export markets. In chapter III, selected case studies are presented to illustrate different strategies that have been followed in this regard.

NOTES

1   National Accounts detailed breakdowns (by industry, by product, by consumption purpose) in the National Accounts database at http://epp.eurostat.ec.europa.eu/portal/page/portal/national_accounts/data/database.

2   Canada and the United States of America compile relevant information on their computer services sector such as the number of firms, employees, revenue and value added. See http://stds.statcan.gc.ca/naics-scian/2002/cs-rc-eng.asp?criteria=51.

3   See http://www.statssa.gov.za/publications/D0407/D04072011.pdf.

4   See International Monetary Fund (IMF), Balance of Payments and International Investment Position Manual, http://www.imf.org/external/pubs/ft/bop/2007/pdf/bpm6.pdf.

5   This is similar to the figures reported by other consultancies. For example Gartner stated that enterprise software and IT services spending was $1.1 trillion in 2011. See: "Gartner Says Worldwide IT Spending to Grow 3.7 Percent in 2012." Press Release. January 5, 2012. http://www.gartner.com/it/page.jsp?id=1888514.

6   Eurostat Annual National Accounts database, see http://epp.eurostat.ec.europa.eu/portal/page/portal/national_accounts/data/database

7   Brazil and the Russian Federation run a deficit in this trade category.

8   These data are derived from the software sales of companies regardless of whether computer software is their main business activity. Thus the compilation differs from others that focus on pure software companies.

9   See http://www.softwaretop100.org/highlights-analysis.

10   See, for example, http://www.businessweek.com/interactive_reports/it100_2010.html?chan=technology_special+report+--+tech+100_special+report+--+tech+100.

11   By comparison, only five developed countries report software exports that exceed total spending on software and services: Bulgaria, Finland, Ireland, Israel and Romania (see annex table II.2).

12   In the case of South Africa, computer software spending greatly exceeds expectations based on the size of the Internet market. One reason is that Internet use is relatively low in the country, illustrating the wide digital divide.

13   See http://www.itu.int/ITU-D/ict/facts/2011/material/ICTFactsFigures2011.pdf

14   See http://www.apira.org/data/upload/The29thStatisticalReportonInternetDevelopmentinChina_P9G97q.pdf and http://www.cck.go.ke/resc/downloads/SECTOR_STATISTICS_REPORT_Q2_2011-12.pdf.

15   For the lower estimate, see http://www.reuters.com/article/2011/01/26/us-mobile-apps-idUSTRE70P2MB20110126; for the higher estimate, see http://www.appnationconference.com/appnation3/AN3_USAppEconomy_2011-2015.pdf.

16   See "Microsoft is writing checks to fill out its app store", The New York Times, 5 April 2012.

17   See https://www.odesk.com/oconomy/report/2011/9/.

18   See comScore, 2012. "It's a social world: Top 10 Need-to-Knows About Social Networking and Where It's Headed", www.comscore.com.

19   Facebook Inc. 2012. Form S-1 Registration Statement Under The Securities Act of 1933.

20   See http://www.jeffbullas.com/2012/05/18/facebook-approaches-500-million-mobile-users-infographic/.

21   See http://www.rhsmith.umd.edu/digits/pdfs_docs/research/2011/AppEconomyImpact091911.pdf.

22   See http://about.datamonitor.com/media/archives/5727.

23   See http://my.news.yahoo.com/freelancers-bangladesh-long-paypal-095003371.html.

24   See http://techcrunch.com/2011/11/09/odesk-online-work-market-will-grow-to-1-billion-by-2012/.

25   See https://www.elance.com/q/node/685.

SOFTWARE MARKET ORIENTATION – SELECTED CASES

3

The preceding chapter showed that countries have followed different paths with regard to the role of software in their economies. Special attention was given to the market orientation, that is, the extent to which the software industry is mainly servicing domestic or export markets. This chapter looks at the experience of selected countries in which the software sector plays an important role in the economy but which demonstrate markedly different market focuses.

The chapter is divided into four sections. The first discusses why the market orientation matters. The second section focuses on two countries with a strong export orientation of their software industry: India and Sri Lanka. The third section examines the experience of four countries in which software is still primarily produced for domestic market needs: the Republic of Korea, Brazil, China and the Russian Federation. Most of these economies have relatively large and dynamic domestic markets. The final section draws lessons from the case studies.

A. WHY THE MARKET ORIENTATION MATTERS

As highlighted in chapter I (figure I.2), the scope for value creation in a national software system depends in part on the nature and market orientation of production. For most developing countries, producing software services for the domestic market is typically the natural entry point, as it is associated with the lowest barriers and requires the lowest level of capabilities. From their entry into the software market, countries can then move along different paths. Depending on the circumstances, local software enterprises may move towards developing software services for the export market or towards deepening the range of software services and products offered domestically.

From the perspective of harnessing the value of software in local economic development – and given that it is a general purpose technology with potential application in virtually all sectors of society – it is of particular importance to ensure that software services and capabilities are available to support the needs that exist locally in the public and private sector. Domestic use of software can be instrumental in improving the competitiveness of enterprises and the welfare of society. The social marginal benefit of a dollar worth of ICT (including software) consumed locally is likely to be higher than that of a dollar worth of ICT (including software) that is exported (Kumar and Joseph, 2005). The domestic market is also potentially an important base to develop relevant skills and innovative products. Focusing too heavily on exports implies a danger of transforming the software production into an enclave industry with little exchange with other domestic sectors. As noted by one expert (Heeks, 1999, p. 6):

> Putting your brightest software stars to work on applications that boost the growth of foreign firms and foreign economies incurs a large opportunity cost when applications to meet the many pressing domestic needs are consequently sidelined.

At the same time, in developing countries characterized by low disposable incomes, an underdeveloped IT infrastructure and limited ICT use in the public and private sectors, local software producers may find it hard to survive by relying only on a nascent domestic market. Exports can in this case represent a way to generate revenue growth and to access know-how and technology. The demand for software and IT services (particularly outsourcing/offshoring) is growing at the global level and many developing and transition economies offer attractive labour costs, relevant human resources and improved connectivity. Export markets may include the major developed countries (North America, Europe and Japan) as well as regional markets.[1] By developing software for international clients, domestic companies can become exposed to the latest technologies and management methods. International clients may place different demands, forcing suppliers to meet international standards and to innovate.

For a Government, exports of software and IT services can be seen as an attractive option to generate foreign exchange, reduce trade deficits, induce job creation and transfer technology. Moreover, software exports can accelerate the integration into global value chains and contribute to economic diversification.

Countries may, therefore, seek to strike a balance between export sales and software development for domestic consumption. Where domestic demand is constrained by weak purchasing power, active government policies are particularly important to create markets for domestic software production. For countries at an early stage of development of their software capabilities, it might be a valid option to pursue import substitution by fostering open standards and public procurement policies that encourage the participation of local companies (chapter V).

B. COUNTRIES WITH EXPORT-ORIENTED SOFTWARE INDUSTRIES

India and Sri Lanka were found in chapter II to have very high export orientation in their software industries. These two countries share certain features but differ in several other respects. They are located in the same region, have a significant English-speaking population and are among the preferred locations for offshoring of software and IT services. At the same time, India has a much larger domestic market and its software spending as a share of GDP is considerably higher than that of Sri Lanka.

1. India – a global leader in software services exports

India is one of few low-income countries that have managed to build significant software capabilities on a large scale. Its unprecedented growth in the exports of software and services has been an inspiration for many other developing countries (Schware, 1992; Arora et al., 2001; Joseph and Harilal, 2001; Kumar and Joseph, 2005). The export success has been the outcome of a national software system built up over many years, with the active involvement of the Government, universities, technology institutes and the private sector – not least through the National Association of Software and Services Companies (NASSCOM) (Joseph, 2006; Kumar and Joseph, 2005; Balakrishnan, 2006). Despite its proven capabilities, domestic spending on software and IT services is still relatively low in India compared with the other BRIC countries (chapter II), indicating a potential for further strengthening of the impact of the software industry on the country's economy.

(a) Trends in the software and IT services industry

Software and IT services represent an important part of the Indian economy. By 2007/08, the share of the software sector in the country's GDP had reached 5.4 per cent, up from less than 2 per cent at the beginning of the decade (India, Ministry of Finance, 2012). According to NASSCOM, direct employment in the software industry (including BPO) was estimated at 600,000 in 2011, up from 160,000 in 1996 (NASSCOM, various years). The indirect employment generated has been estimated at about four times the direct employment. The sector is creating job opportunities for qualified young graduates (especially those with an engineering degree).

Whereas the influx of foreign TNCs, such as Citicorp Overseas Software in Bombay in 1985 and Texas Instruments in Bangalore in 1986, had an important demonstrative effect both on other foreign companies and Indian investors, the production and exports of software in India is today mainly the result of domestic enterprises (NASSCOM, 2012).[2] The comparative advantage of Indian firms has traditionally been in the on-site export of services such as customized software development in low-level design, coding and maintenance (Arora et al., 2001; Kattuman and Iyer, 2001). In 1999, revenue per employee ($16,000) was only about one tenth of that in Israel and one fourth of that in Ireland.

This picture has changed, with increased internationalization and professionalism of Indian software enterprises. As of December 2010, 58 Indian companies were certified according to the highest level (5) of Capability Maturity Model Integration (CMMI), the most complex and challenging quality certification in the software industry (see chapter V).[3] Moreover,

according to NASSCOM, over 400 new software product companies have been founded in India since 2001.[4] These firms focus on five customer segments:

(i) Products and platforms for the IT and BPO sector (for example, Stelae Technologies);

(ii) Products and platforms for domestic e-government projects (for example, ABM OrangeScape);

(iii) SaaS solutions for SMEs (for example, ImpelCRM and Zoho);

(iv) Mobile value-added services solutions for Indian consumers (for example, Netcore, Apalaya);

(v) Online solutions for small office and home office customers in the United States of America (for example, Fusion Charts, DeskAway).

The production of software products and engineering services increased from $2.9 billion in 2003/04 to $9.6 billion in 2008/09, 25 per cent of which was sold domestically.

Another indication of the upgrading of the software industry in India is the establishment of software-related R&D. Of the 160 R&D centres identified in one study (Ilavarasan, 2011), two thirds were in the software product development domain, 15 per cent in engineering services and 20 per cent related to embedded software systems. More firms are entering into high-end consulting, embedded-software development, engineering and R&D services with the development of domain expertise and exports of packaged software. Moreover, the Internet has emerged as a major platform for lead generation and product delivery, providing smaller firms better opportunities to reach out to the market at lower cost.[5]

(b) Market orientation implications

During the past 20 years, production of software and BPO services in India surged from $200 million to reach $75 billion in 2010/11 (Electronics and Computer Software Export Promotion Council, various years) – a remarkable growth by any standard. Export sales rose particularly fast, from $110 million in 1990/91 to nearly $58 billion in 2010/11. As a result, the share of domestic sales has gradually fallen from 47 per cent in 1990 to about 20 per cent today.

The data from the Electronics and Computer Software Export Promotion Council – an autonomous body under the Indian Ministry of Information Technology

Table III.1.   Domestic sales and exports of software services, software products and engineering and design services in India, 2005–2011 (billions of dollars and percentage)

Year	Domestic software sales ($ billion)	Share of:		Exports of software ($ billion)	Share of:	
		Software services (percentage)	Software products and engineering R&D (percentage)		Software services (percentage)	Software products and engineering R&D (percentage)
2005	4.2	83.3	16.7	13.1	76.3	23.7
2006	5.8	77.1	22.9	17.3	76.9	23.1
2007	7.1	77.6	22.4	22.0	77.5	22.5
2008	10.1	77.9	22.1	30.5	72.8	27.2
2009	10.9	75.4	24.6	35.4	72.9	27.1
2010	12.0	75.4	24.6	37.3	73.2	26.8
2011	14.5	75.9	24.1	44.8	74.6	25.4

Source: NASSCOM (various years).

– do not distinguish between BPO and software. However, disaggregated information is available from NASSCOM since 2005 (table III.1). According to this source, total production of software and services in India rose from $17.3 billion to $59.3 billion, and exports from $14 billion in 2005 to $45 billion in 2011.[6] During this period, the share of exports consistently exceeded 75 per cent. Moreover, in both domestic and export markets, software services accounted for about three quarters of all software-related sales in 2011. In the domestic market, the share of soft-

ware products, engineering and design has risen from 17 per cent in 2005 to about 24 per cent, which is similar to the share of products in export sales.

The software industry has contributed significantly towards the strengthening of the external balance and the generation of foreign exchange for India. Exporters have seen rising profits and their clients abroad have benefited from improved competitiveness and efficiency. Today, the country exports software and IT services to over 170 countries and economies India,

Table III.2.   Changes in direction of India's computer software and BPO services exports 2005/06 and 2010/11 (millions of dollars and percentage)

Destination	2005/06		2010/11	
	Value ($ million)	Share of total (percentage)	Value ($ million)	Share of total (percentage)
North America	14 727.81	62.10	32 265.14	56.00
European Union	6 098.94	25.71	17 954.35	31.16
South and South-East Asia	632.48	2.67	1 843.72	3.20
East Asia	722.84	3.05	749.12	1.30
Middle East	564.72	2.38	1 728.49	3.00
Europe (Non-European Union)	496.95	2.10	633.89	1.10
Australia and other Oceania	293.65	1.24	979.59	1.70
Africa	96.00	0.40	691.40	1.20
Latin America and the Caribbean	79.06	0.33	576.16	1.00
Transition economies	5.65	0.02	194.47	0.34
Total	23 718.09	100.00	57 616.33	100.00

Source: Electronics and Computer Software Export Promotion Council (various years).

Ministry of Communications and Information Technology, various years). As of 2010/2011, North America and Europe still received about 87 per cent of India's exports of software and BPO services (table III.2). The share of developing countries rose somewhat between 2005/06 and 2010/11.

At the same time, there can be opportunity costs of software exports. For example, while the best talents and capabilities of India have been producing software services for exports, software used domestically has been largely imported (Kumar and Joseph, 2005). Inadequate attention to the domestic market by the industry may also have stunted the diffusion of IT technology. For instance, the availability of software in local languages would have facilitated more widespread use of IT in India. While different domestic sectors as a result may have missed the opportunity for software-based productivity improvement, Indian software companies' contribution to the performance of their foreign clients has been significant. A fiscal incentive regime that supports exports over domestic software production may also have created disincentives for firms to produce for the domestic market (Vijayabaskar and Suresh Babu, 2009).

Most of the export-oriented software companies in India have operated as "export enclaves" with few linkages to the domestic economy (D'Costa, 2003). Such a set up hampers knowledge spillovers to other sectors. Moreover, the bulk of the work has also been of a highly customized nature, serving the needs of clients in North America and Europe, with limited application domestically. Given high salaries and other

benefits, there has also been movement of personnel from domestic market-oriented firms in other skill-intensive sectors to export-oriented software firms (Kumar, 2001; Joseph and Harilal, 2001).

Information provided in table III.1 indicates that domestic sales of software services, products, and engineering and design services have recently begun to increase, growing from $4.2 billion to $14.5 billion between 2005 and 2011. This sector has become one of the fastest growing segments in the Indian domestic IT market, driven by localized strategies designed by various service providers (India, Ministry of Communications and Information Technology, various years). This trend may be further accentuated by recent software projects in the domestic economy (table III.3).

(c) Policy developments

The observed performance of the Indian software system has been facilitated by proactive state intervention over many years.[7] Key policy initiatives have included the development of the higher education system in engineering and technical disciplines, the creation of an institutional infrastructure for science and technology policy making and implementation, the setting up of centres of excellence and numerous other institutions for technology development along with the private sector. In addition, software technology parks have been helpful for software exports and the different regional governments and industry associations have also played their parts. The patterns of clustering of related activity in and around Bangalore suggests

Table III.3. Selected domestic software deals in India in 2010		
Software firm	**Client**	**Project details**
TechProcess	Indian Overseas Bank	Online payment services to customers and expansion of the market reach of its associated web merchants
Wipro	Janalakshmi Financial Services	Implementation of public cloud client relationship management solutions (CRM) to support new retail liability business
HCL Technologies	National Power Corporation	$100 million project for implementing smart grid solutions in the power sector
Spanco Ltd.	Maharashtra State Electricity Distribution Co.	Rs 950 million ($17 million) project on power distribution
Consortium led by Wipro	Andhra Pradesh State Government	Health care system for public hospitals
SAP	Indian Navy	Online financial information system
ORG Informatics	BSNL Ltd.	Rs 140 Million ($2.5 million) project for satcom network for the Indian Air Force

Source: NASSCOM News line, January 2011.

that public-funded technological infrastructure has crowded in the investments from the private sector in skill intensive activities such as software development (Kumar and Joseph, 2006).

Until the early 2000s, the focus in India was on fostering a software industry as a foreign exchange earner. Major initiatives during this period included the building up of IT personnel, the computer policy of 1984 and the software policy of 1986, the establishment of software technology parks and the National Task Force on IT and Software Development. Various initiatives by the central Government were complemented by state government IT policies, beginning with the State of Karnataka. The focus of most of the states in the early years was to use fiscal incentives to attract investment into the IT sector.

More recently, however, there has been a gradual shift in policy towards domestic needs for software development, manifested in various e-governance initiatives by the central and state Governments. More emphasis has been given to the harnessing of ICTs for improving efficiency, competitiveness and social welfare. The Information Technology Act (2000) improved the legal infrastructure for electronic commerce. In 2006, a national e-governance plan was approved, with a vision to provide public services to citizens at affordable cost. To facilitate the plan, a state-wide area network was envisaged with a significant software component. By 2010, this network was operational in all 23 states and union territories. The Government has also approved a scheme to support the establishment of 100,000 Common Services Centres (CSCs) in 600,000 villages, involving the development of a software–hardware platform to allow public and private stakeholders to align their social and commercial goals in rural areas. At the end of 2010, more than 87,000 CSCs had been set up (India, Ministry of Communications and Information Technology, various years).

Various e-government projects have also been launched, raising the demand for software applications. A major initiative involves the setting up of the Unique Identification Authority to issue identification numbers (*Aadhaar*) for all Indian citizens.[8] The project is generating domestic demand for various software, hardware and communication services. For example, Mindtree Ltd. was entrusted with the task of application software development.[9] Software companies involved in the implementation of biometric solutions include Mahindra Satyam and Accenture Services.

Meanwhile, firms such as Sagem Morpho Security, Linkwell Telesystems, Totem International, Sai Infosystem, HCL Infosystems, Geodesic and ID Solutions are engaged in the supply of biometric authentication systems.

The draft ICT policy issued by the Government in October 2011, provided for a greater emphasis on the domestic market.[10] It explicitly calls for the deployment of ICT in all sectors of the economy and finds that "emerging technologies such as Mobile Technology, Localization, Virtualization, and Cloud Computing provide Indian IT/ITES industry a major opportunity to become partners in value creation and drive transformation domestically". Fiscal incentives to promote IT adoption by SMEs are also expected to boost the domestic market for software. At the time of drafting this report, it was still too early to assess the impact of this new policy.

2. Sri Lanka – strong export bias with opportunities in mobile apps

Software production in Sri Lanka has witnessed rapid growth during the past decade and the country has one of the most export-oriented software industries in the world. Only Costa Rica and Ireland report a higher ratio of software exports to software spending (annex table II.2). At the same time, Sri Lanka is among the developing countries with the lowest level of software spending in relation to both GDP and overall spending on ICTs (chapter II). Today, new opportunities are also emerging in the domestic market as the move from a PC-driven software culture to one linked to mobile phones, broadband and smart devices, is creating new demand for applications.

(a) Trends in the software and IT services industry

The software industry is among the most progressive growth areas in Sri Lanka and offers high value added. Compared with other South Asian countries, such as Bangladesh and Nepal, Sri Lanka's software industry is more closely aligned with the Indian situation, but on a much smaller scale (Sung, 2011). In 2010, software and IT services were the fifth largest export revenue creator behind apparel, tea, rubber and tourism. More than 80 per cent of all IT exports are related to software products and services (Sri Lanka Export Development Board, 2010). The Sri Lanka Association for Software and Service Companies (SLASSCOM)

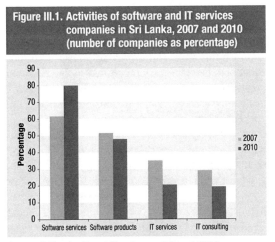

Figure III.1. Activities of software and IT services companies in Sri Lanka, 2007 and 2010 (number of companies as percentage)

Source: Sri Lanka Export Development Board, 2010.

predicts that the industry will generate $700 million in revenues by 2015.[11]

In the 1990s, Sri Lankan software companies were mainly providing sales, installation and maintenance services related to imported proprietary software. At the beginning of the new century, more local companies were established to sell in both domestic and international markets. Their products typically targeted the financial and insurance industry, as well as human resource systems for the telecommunication and airline industries. Some managed to win projects in competition with international companies.[12]

In 2010, there were 147 companies in the sector (Sri Lanka Export Development Board, 2010), 90 per cent of which had begun their operations in the past dec-

ade and more than half of them had less than 50 employees. The 18 per cent of the companies that had more than 100 employees contributed 76 per cent of the export revenues in 2010. Although software services represent the most common activity among these firms, a relatively high proportion of them also produce software products (figure III.1). On average, a company offers at least two service lines, and 80 per cent offer software products and services. Of the 147 companies, 60 per centwere Sri Lankan owned, 29 per centforeign owned and 11 per centwere joint ventures. Most (81 per cent) of the total revenue was generated by foreign affiliates and joint ventures (Sri Lanka Export Development Board, 2010). Software SMEs are mostly locally owned, while most of the large companies are joint ventures or foreign owned (Sri Lanka Export Development Board, 2007, 2008).

(b) Market orientation implications

The emphasis by industry leaders, policy makers and the mass media in Sri Lanka is still on promoting software and IT services as an export industry. Whereas the Government has had a strong ICT commitment, as outlined in the eSriLanka strategy, it does not have a dedicated policy for the software industry.[13] However, *Mahinda Chintana*, the political vision adopted by the Ministry of Finance and Planning in 2010, and the close collaboration between the Government and software industry organizations, have contributed to integrating software into the country's emerging knowledge economy (Sri Lanka Ministry of Finance and Planning, 2010).

Box III.1.   Sri Lanka: e-government and digital literacy boosting demand for software

Among a plethora of government ICT programmes, an e-government programme implemented by the Information and Communication Technology Agency (ICTA) has led over 92 per cent of all government agencies to provide their services online, creating about 290 websites and online application services (World Bank, 2010).

The implementation of School Net (http://www.schoolnet.lk) in 2006 by the Ministry of Education delivered a wide area network connecting schools and other educational institutions which provided computer labs and Internet connectivity. As of 2010, about 1,500 schools which had hardly ever been exposed to computers before were linked up via School Net. The required software for these projects were developed by local software companies.

The Nenasala programme (http://www.nanasala.lk/) implemented by ICTA installed over 600 rural telecentres all over the country, making computers and the Internet available to rural communities for the first time. Over 1,500 rural students (aged 13–25) have received ICT education from the Sarvodaya-Fusion (http://www.fusion.lk/), a not-for-profit social enterprise, through 53 rural telecentres during the period 2009–2011. The development programmes have improved computer literacy across diverse age groups. Computer literacy among people aged 5–69 increased from 16 per centto 20 per centbetween 2006 and 2009, with progress observed in both urban and rural sectors (Sri Lanka Department of Census and Statistics, 2009).

Source: UNCTAD.

The domestic market for software and IT services is small, estimated to be worth only $48 million in 2011.[14] However, the industry has contributed expertise, products and services to meeting the domestic software development needs of some government projects, such as the eSriLanka programme and the School Net project. Various programmes promoting e-government and digital literacy are also indirectly stimulating local demand for software, with opportunities for the industry to provide tailored solutions (box III.1).

The demand for software is partly curbed by relatively low levels of ICT use, with household PC penetration at 12.5 per centin 2009/10 (Sri Lanka Department of Census and Statistics, 2011). Moreover, in 2011, there were only about two fixed-broadband subscriptions per 100 inhabitants and about 15 users per 100 inhabitants.[15] By contrast, mobile broadband is experiencing rapid growth,[16] with five licensed mobile operators competing in the market.[17] Innovative models, such as prepaid mobile broadband, have enabled wide uptake of wireless broadband (Galpaya, 2011). Some 70 per cent of the population has a mobile phone and almost half use their handset to access the Internet.[18]

Increased ICT use among the youth is also creating potential demand for software applications in Sri Lanka.[19] In 2012, there were about 1.3 million Facebook accounts in Sri Lanka. Although global websites (such as Facebook, Google, YouTube and Wikipedia) have the greatest number of visits, according to the Alexa.com,[20] several local sites, including GossipLankaNews.com and Elakiri.com, are among the top 20 most popular ones, nurturing demand for domestic software solutions. Rising computer penetration, mobile broadband and Internet penetration, especially among the youth, are stimulating a new community of Internet users and thereby new demand for software. For example, the crowdsourcing platform, oDesk, reports about 300,000 hours of contributions by Sri Lankan software programmers.[21] There are also opportunities in the mobile apps area where a thriving developer community is emerging. In 2008, Sri Lanka featured among the global top ten countries in the Google Summer of Code.[22]

(c) Emerging opportunities in the mobile applications area

Low-cost phones combined with competitive broadband packages are contributing to rapid growth in

Table III.4. Most popular locally developed apps in Sri Lanka in the Android App Market, March 2012

	App	Category	User rating	Installs	Description	Developer/ publisher
1	SETT Sinhala/ Tamil web browser	Communication	197	10 000–50 000	The only Sinhala/Tamil-enabled web browser for Android.	Bhasha Inc.
2	SETT Hindi web browser	Communication	149	10 000–50 000	Renders Hindi Unicode within the app.	Bhasha Inc.
3	Tamil SMS	Social	46	10 000–50 000	It allows users to send SMS in Tamil with a simple keypad typing mechanism.	Microimage Mobile Media
4	Sinhala Tamil– English Dictionary	Books and reference	125	5 000–10 000	First English to Sinhala/ Sinhala to English dictionary on Android Market.	Sachith Dassanayake
5	Sinhala Dictionary Offline	Books and reference	111	5 000–10 000	Offline English to Sinhala/ Sinhala to English dictionary for Android 2.1 and above.	Sachith Dassanayake
6	Sri Lanka Radio Live	Entertainment	25	5 000–10 000	Free simple radio with over 10 live radio stations.	Manoj Prasanna Handapangoda
7	Helakuru Sinhala Keyboard + IME	Tools	54	1 000–5 000	First phonetic Sinhala keyboard and IME for mobiles.	Bhasha Inc.
8	Sri Lanka Train Schedule	Travel and local	49	1 000–5 000	Access to train schedules, delay information and ticket prices.	Dilshya
9	Bhasha Puvath	News and magazines	44	1 000–5 000	Multichannel trilingual (Sinhala, Tamil, English) Sri Lankan news reader.	Bhasha Inc.
10	Lankadeepa	News and magazines	36	1 000–5 000	Sinhala breaking news website updated 24/7 on Android mobiles.	Wijeya Newspapers Ltd.

Source: Android Market, see https://market.android.com/, March 2012.

smartphone penetration, especially those running on Android.[23] Rising demand among Android phone users is leading domestic firms, such as newspapers (Puwath), travel agencies (Kangaroo Cabs) and sports ventures (Live Cricket Scores) to develop new apps.[24] Locally developed apps published in the local language are gaining in popularity, indicating a rising home-grown demand (table III.4). While most of them target the general public with news, entertainment and practical information, there are also apps supporting social and community development.

For example, the SETT Singhala/Tamil Web Browser targets the local community and enables web browsing in local languages. It has been downloaded more than 10,000 times from the Android Market. Before its introduction, people who were not English literate had difficulties understanding how to interact with

---

Box III.2.   The emerging Android ecosystem in Sri Lanka

Etisalat is the third largest mobile operator in Sri Lanka, owned by Etisalat United Arab Emirates. In view of declining average voice revenue per user, Etisalat is investing in the smart device market to boost data revenue. The company's App Zone and Book Hub today form a central part of the emerging Android-based market place and business ecosystem (box figure III.1). In order to generate locally relevant apps, Etisalat is involving both individual app developers (or small start-up firms) (C and D in box figure III.1) and the software industry (E and G in box figure III.1).

When Etisalat enters into business partnerships with app developers, the latter earn 70 per cent of the revenue from app sales through the App Zone. Following this business model, some developers reportedly generate about Rs 200,000 ($200) per month. As of February 2012, about 20 developers were actively engaged with Etisalat to develop Android apps. For example, Etisalat has signed a contract with the leading book publisher in the country, M.D. Gunasena Company Ltd. (non-IT company to provide content, I in box figure III.1), and Microimage Pvt Ltd.[e] (E in box figure III.1), a software company that has already developed apps for the Android market place. This partnership plans to produce local-language e-books.

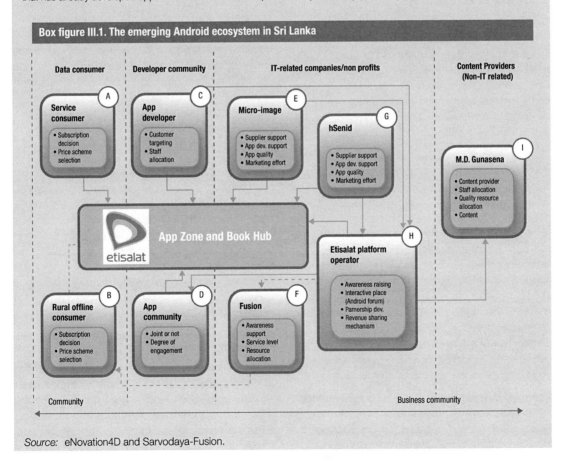

Box figure III.1. The emerging Android ecosystem in Sri Lanka

Source: eNovation4D and Sarvodaya-Fusion.

Box III.2. The emerging Android ecosystem in Sri Lanka (continued)

In order to engage the developer community, in 2011 Etisalat launched a series of Android Forums.[b] They put app developers in contact with subject experts and local champions and helped to create income-generating and learning opportunities, especially for young people. A forum held in February 2012 attracted 1,000 participants.[c] Etisalat is also engaging with non-profit-sector parties such as Sarvodaya-Fusion (F in box figure III.1) to raise awareness in grassroots communities (B in box figure III.1) not yet familiar with smart devices. Bringing together the lessons learned by the SmartVillage project of Sarvodaya-Fusion (box III.2), it aims to introduce other devices such as tablets and locally relevant apps into rural villages.[d]

As of March 2012, the App Zone had generated 120 apps. Out of its 4 million mobile phone subscribers, the top-rated Yalu app had been used by 1.8 million subscribers.[e] For local software companies, this emerging ecosystem provides a platform to build software products for the domestic market, which may subsequently be leveraged for customers abroad.

Source: UNCTAD.

[a]   See http://www.mimobimedia.com/Press/bookstore.html.

[b]   See http://blog.theandroidking.com/2011/11/first-ever-android-forum-in-sri-lanka.html.

[c]   See blog post by a participant, http://technomaha.wordpress.com/category/android/android-forums-sri-lanka/.

[d]   See http://fusionsmartvillage.blogspot.com/.

[e]   Analytics from http://apps.appzone.lk/#app_97 March, 2012.

smart devices. The developer of the app, a university student from a rural village (Payagala) in southern Sri Lanka,[25] has since January 2011 developed another six apps for the Android market.

The possibility of combining their own ideas with the latest technology, producing immediate outcomes in the local communities and affiliated business opportunities, is exciting to the younger generation. Refresh Colombo is a community of 80–100 enthusiasts who come together every month to share ideas and meet like-minded individuals.[26] There are plans to replicate this community in other parts of the country.

Although Google's Android Market is a large global app market place, it is not yet optimized to support small or individual local developers in Sri Lanka. For instance, at the time of preparing this report, it was not possible for developers in Sri Lanka to sell local apps in the Android Market (due to restrictions made by Google). Instead, developers had to offer their apps for free or generate revenue through third-party advertising. A new market place and ecosystem for mobile apps is, however, emerging in Sri Lanka. It involves the country's third largest mobile network operator, the community of app developers, social enterprises and clients. This new market offers a way to partly compensate the difficulties local developers experience in entering the global app market (box III.2).

Electronic payment gateways represent a bottleneck for the future growth of the Android ecosystem in Sri Lanka. These gateways, which are operated by local banks (for example, Sampath Bank and HSBC),

are not set up to support young entrepreneurs such as web and app developers. Moreover, international payment gateways, such as PayPal, are not yet available for in-bound payments. As noted above, local developers are not allowed to sell their apps in the Android Market.[27] Setting up a payment gateway, therefore, remains a challenge. The absence of plug and play models, extensive bank regulations and security problems have so far hindered the transformation of the efforts of individual/small software developers into commercial success stories.

(d) Concluding observations

The software industry in Sri Lanka continues to expand and contribute to the country's economic development. Looking at its diversity in terms of services and products, company numbers and export markets, the industry is likely to see sustained growth. Awareness-raising and advocacy activities by software associations such as SLASSCOM, and their interactions with key government institutions, can help sustain the industry's capacity in terms of work force quantity and quality, and to respond to fast-changing demand from export markets.

Government-led rural infrastructure development programmes and improved connectivity are also creating domestic demand for software. At the same time, there does not seem as yet to be a clear strategy from the industry's side to build upon the expanding opportunities in the domestic market. Emerging trends related to mobile apps offer opportunities to encourage the participation of individual developers and small software companies with passion and drive to serve local demands. It is too early to draw conclusions about its potential impact on the current PC- and Internet-driven software industry. Overall, however, it is a new field that the currently export-oriented software industry may explore to boost a mobile-centric, locally-oriented business dimension.

C. COUNTRIES WITH SOFTWARE INDUSTRIES ORIENTATED TO- WARDS THE DOMESTIC MARKET

In this section, four brief case studies demonstrate economies in which the domestic market accounts for the bulk of software and IT services sales. In contrast to the examples of India and Sri Lanka, these countries are characterized by an important element of embedded software production in various non-IT industries. At the same time, they are seeking to internationalize the software industry and promote exports. The four cases examined are the Republic of Korea, Brazil, China and the Russian Federation.

1. Republic of Korea – leveraging software to meet domestic needs

(a) A new strategy to boost software production and exports

The Republic of Korea is among the world's leading ICT nations. It has one of the largest ICT sectors per unit of GDP (UNCTAD, 2011a) and was the fifth largest exporter of ICT goods in 2010.[28] At the same time, the country is less prominent in terms of software production and exports. In 2007, the Korean software industry was estimated to have revenues of $21 billion (Oh, 2011) and in 2011 spending on software and IT services was estimated to be worth about $12 billion, or about 13 per cent of all ICT spending that year (annex table II.2). In addition, Korean exports of software and IT services remain limited.

The software industry is making important contributions to the Korean economy, especially in the form of embedded software. In 2009, this segment accounted for almost 59 per cent of all software production in the country, compared with only about 13 per centglobally.[29] Two Korean companies were included in the list

of the world's top software enterprises in 2010 (NC Soft and Nexon Corporation).[30] At the same time, such a vertical structure of software production may hamper specialization, economies of scale and open innovation. Moreover, other parts of the economy rely considerably on imported software.[31]

The Government regards the improvement of the software industry as a key priority. It sees a vibrant software industry not only as important in itself but also for the competitiveness of the economy as a whole. In 2010, the Government outlined a new strategy entitled the Software Korea Quantum Jump Strategy.[32] Among the targets set were to increase software exports from about $6 billion (including embedded software) in 2008 to $15 billion by 2013 and to more than double software employment from 140,000 to 300,000. Various policies and strategies were identified to achieve these and other targets.

In the area of embedded software, the main thrust of the strategy is to foster collaboration between manufacturing industries, system semiconductor companies and embedded software companies, and to utilize national defence R&D as a test bed for civilian applications. Specific targets have been set for the use of embedded software in industries such as mobile phone production, automotive industries, defence, shipbuilding and robotics.

In the area of packaged software, there are efforts to support open source software, open innovation and to activate SaaS by leveraging cloud computing. The Government also intends to reinforce its actions to crack down on the use of illegal software.

For IT services, the strategy is to create new businesses through the convergence of software and various other services, such as transportation and public services. For example, there are plans to launch 100 new services conveying information related to public transport, traffic congestion and safe food consumption. Other projects will develop mobile-based services. As discussed in the next section, the Government has also taken steps to facilitate local software industry growth through public procurement.

(b) eGovFrame – a standardized platform for e-government

The Republic of Korea is recognized as a leading provider of e-government (Kang, 2010). To avoid dependency on any single supplier and to avoid the use of multiple frameworks for the development of applications in different parts of the administration, the Ministry of Public Administration and Security in 2007 decided to develop a standardized software framework, called e-Government Standard Framework (eGovFrame). This framework comprises a standardized set of software tools for developing and running e-government applications in order to improve the efficiency of ICT investment and the quality of e-government services. It serves especially to ensure the reusability and interoperability of different applications. Finally, to encourage competition among suppliers, various steps have been taken to build the capabilities and competitiveness of IT SMEs in the country.

(i)   The process of developing the eGovFrame

To standardize the framework, the views of a wide range of stakeholders were solicited. At the outset, many were far from convinced of the merits of the project. Some large companies feared that they would lose market opportunities. Public organizations raised concerns related to future access to stable technical support, while several developers rejected the new tools. Government representatives were afraid that the effectiveness

of e-government services would be negatively affected, and SMEs were worried that the project would mainly serve the interests of large suppliers. The challenge was therefore to ensure that the various stakeholders would eventually support eGovFrame. In response, the Government implemented an open innovation strategy with four dimensions: open sourcing, open process, open output and open ecosystem (figure III.2).

Open sourcing: In order to standardize eGovFrame, the environment and functionality of the frameworks of five major IT companies were analysed. As a result, four environments (table III.5) comprising 13 service layers and 54 service functionalities were identified. Moreover, to prevent repeated development of the same functions across different government systems, 67 e-Government projects from 2004–2007 were reviewed, involving more than 30,000 functionalities. Eventually, 219 common components were defined. Well-known and proven open source software was assessed to allow eGovFrame to be easily adapted as technologies evolve, with 40 kinds of software eventually selected for use.[33]

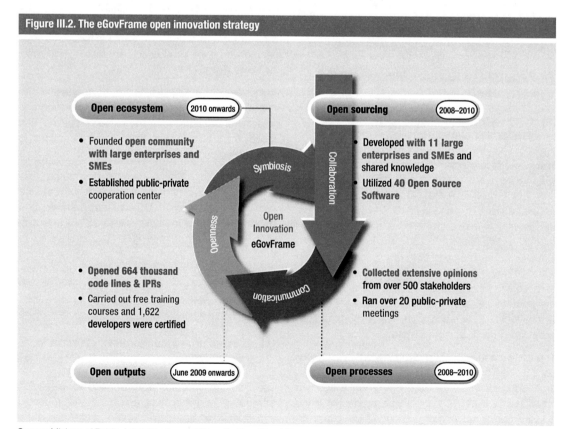

Figure III.2. The eGovFrame open innovation strategy

Source: Ministry of Public Administration and Security, Republic of Korea.

Table III.5. Four eGovFrame environments

Client	Project details
Development environment	Provides a set of tools for the implementation (coding, debugging), testing, deployment and configuration needed to develop applications based on the eGovFrame.
Runtime environment	Provides libraries of common modules that work as a core foundation for running the software application lifecycle.
Management environment	Provides a set of tools for system monitoring and communication for dealing with application faults and communication issues.
Operation environment	Provides a set of tools for technical support and maintenance for responding to customer requests as well as enhancing the eGovFrame.

Source: Ministry of Public Administration and Security, Republic of Korea.

Open processes: Development processes related to eGovFrame are open and reflect comments and inputs from over 500 stakeholders. More than 20 public- or private-sector meetings were organized to foster understanding and consensus among the different stakeholders.

Open outputs: The source code, entity relationship diagrams and other outputs are open and available on the eGovFrame website (http://eng.egovframe.go.kr). This contributes to an open ecosystem with voluntary participation in its implementation by developers and providers as well as government officers. Moreover, between June 2009 and April 2012, the eGovFrame education and training programme was carried out a total of 54 times for IT SME developers and more than 1,600 software developers were certified.[34]

Open ecosystem: The Government formed an open community with enterprises of varying size and set up a public–private sector cooperation centre. This serves as the central point promoting eGovFrame, providing technical support and ensuring continuous

improvement. The development and improvement of eGovFrame is achieved by the open community, quarterly expert meetings and an open forum of partners.

(ii) Effects of eGovFrame

The success of eGovFrame relies on three main components: a standardized framework for developing software applications, reliance on open and neutral software, and efforts to boost the competitiveness of IT SMEs by sharing the tools openly and by providing training.

As of January 2012, eGovFrame had been applied to more than 200 e-government projects, with many more in the pipeline (table III.6).[35] Its main benefits include improved quality of e-government services and higher efficiency of government ICT investment. Developers can avoid duplication of work by making use of eGovFrame's common modules and standard templates. eGovFrame also serves as a platform for developing common functions. By 2013, cost savings of about $294 million[36] are expected from the use of

Table III.6. Ongoing or planned projects for which eGovFrame is applied (number of projects and millions of dollars)

Sections	2009	2010	2011	2012*	2013*	Total
Number of projects	23	69	112	150	200	554
Total budget	85.6	242.0	339.2	400.0	500.0	1 566.8

Source: Information provided by the National Information Society Agency, Republic of Korea, March 2012.
* Forecast.

Table III.7. Cost savings from the use of eGovFrame (millions of dollars)

Sections	2009	2010	2011	2012*	2013*	Total
Common component savings	2.6	7.9	12.8	17.1	22.8	63.2
Framework savings	9.6	28.7	46.6	62.4	83.2	230.4
Total	12.2	36.6	59.4	79.5	106.0	293.6

Source: Information provided by the National Information Society Agency, Republic of Korea, March 2012.
* Forecast.

Table III.8. Selected sectors and projects that have applied eGovFrame

Sector	Projects with eGovFrame	Sector	Projects with eGovFrame
Administration	National Representative portal	Media	Broadcasting telecommunication integration information system
Transportation	Seoul metropolitan rail transit management system	Patent	Patent net system
Medical	Hospital strategy management system	Tax	National tax office ITSMenhanced system
Military	War fighting symbology management system	Port	Incheon U-port system
Customs	Global high-tech port logistics system	Culture	National assembly electronic library system
Land	Land information management system	Education	University information management system

Source: Republic of Korea, Ministry of Public Administration and Security.

eGovFrame for the development of e-government projects (table III.7).[37] Moreover, there is greater scope for reusing components in multiple government systems, and standard interfaces increase interoperability. As a result, the project supports interagency collaboration and information sharing. Finally, the development source code has been standardized.

By providing a standardized interface for e-government services, the level of public satisfaction has increased. Such a one-stop service was unfeasible as long as government agencies used dissimilar interfaces. In addition, e-government implementation providers are now able to improve their core competencies, technological capabilities and productivity by utilizing eGovFrame.

The introduction of eGovFrame has also boosted supplier competition. There is now a better chance for IT SMEs to bid for and win e-government projects. In fact, since its launch, SMEs have won 64 per cent of all projects for which eGovFrame has been applied. Moreover, over 82 per cent of firms responding to a survey stated that they had a plan to introduce the software framework within a year. The eGovFrame has

been applied to a range of systems in both the public and the private sector (table III.8). Ultimately, it should contribute to business opportunities for SMEs as well as large companies, more efficient use of public funds and accelerated national informatization.

With expanded use of advanced mobile devices, such as smartphones and tablets, the demand for mobile-based services is growing in the public as well as private sector. To meet this demand, eGovFrame 2.0 was launched in 2011, incorporating the HTML5, new user interface features and improved quality and efficiency. It is compatible with three mobile browsers (Chrome, Safari and FireFox). Many mobile e-government services in the Republic of Korea have already been developed (figure III.3). To utilize mobile features, such as vibrations, camera control, compass, and the like, eGovFrame 2.0 will also introduce new components that support the creation of mobile applications.

(iii) Opportunities for other countries

There is considerable interest in this standardized framework from other countries that want to address problems of certain supplier companies' monopoly or to rely more on open source software. The eGovFrame has already

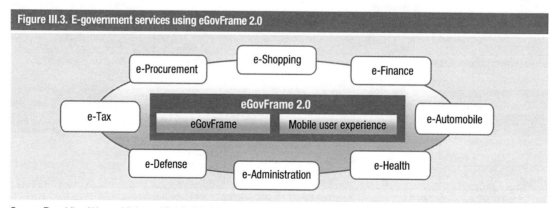

Figure III.3. E-government services using eGovFrame 2.0

Source: Republic of Korea, Ministry of Public Administration and Security.

been applied to an administration system of the University of Sofia in Bulgaria, a single window system of the Ecuador Customs Service, the upgrading and expansion of a water supply system of the National Resources and Environment Ministry in Viet Nam, a state registration system of the General Authority for State Registration in Mongolia, and the e-Procurement System of the National Observatory of Public Procurements in Tunisia.[38]

The Government of the Republic of Korea contributes in various ways to improving e-government services in other countries, including active cooperation with international organizations. To encourage the adoption of eGovFrame, the source code is available to download from the English version of the portal (http://eng.egovframe.go.kr) and online technical support is offered. In addition, eGovFrame training courses are provided through the Korea IT Learning Program and the Information Technologies Cooperation Centre to promote mutual cooperation within the IT sector between the Republic of Korea and partner countries.

2. Brazil – regional software giant

Brazil has by far the largest software market and production in Latin America and the Caribbean, with its sizeable domestic demand absorbing most software produced. Brazil is also among the fastest-growing IT markets in the world (Forrester, 2012c). Software and IT services are considered to be of strategic importance to the Federal Government, and various policies have been adopted to create conditions that can help strengthen the software industry.

(a) Trends in the software and IT services industry

According to the Association for the Promotion of Brazilian Software Excellence (SOFTEX), there were 64,000 enterprises in the software and IT services industry in 2009, a figure expected to climb further to 79,000 by 2014 (Observatorio SOFTEX, 2012). Together, these enterprises employed approximately 450,000 people in 2009, a figure expected to increase to 725,000 by 2014. As in the case of the Republic of Korea, embedded software production plays a major role. In 2009, another 350,000 software and IT services professionals were working in enterprises not belonging to the software and IT industry, mostly in other parts of the ICT sector, banking and finance and various professional and scientific activities.

As in other countries, the software and IT services industry is populated by many SMEs and it is estimated that as many as 96 per cent of companies have less than 20 employees. However, the remaining 4 per cent of companies account for more than three quarters of the industry's total revenue of $25 billion, and for almost 60 per cent of total employment. Considering only the enterprises with at least 20 employees, their main activities in terms of net revenue were customized software development and licensing, followed by IT consulting and computer programming. These three areas in 2009 accounted for 65 per cent of total net revenue and 54 per cent of employees.

Whereas the Brazilian software industry has seen rapid growth in overseas markets in recent years, its focus is clearly domestic. In 2009, exports – mainly to the United States of America – amounted to about $1.6 billion, or just over 6 per cent of the total net revenue that year. Much of the Brazilian software industry is geographically concentrated into a few centres with a historical specialization in electronics and ICT hardware manufacturing, notably in and around Sao Paulo. A number of local enterprises have emerged as international players (ECLAC, 2011), including TOTVS, which in 2011 was among the world's top 100 software enterprises.[39]

(b) Government strategy and policies

A new policy was launched in 2008, stressing the need to promote the software and IT services industry as one of six priority areas. While recognizing the important contribution of the software industry to the domestic private sector, the Government is interested in promoting more exports. The new policy set a target of expanding exports to $3.5 billion by 2010 and creating 100,000 new jobs. It emphasized the importance of investing in technology training and supporting domestic technology-based enterprises (ECLAC, 2011). Technology parks have been established in Sao Paulo, Porto Alegre and Recife.

The Government has been relatively successful in fostering relevant skills. Between 2003 and 2008, the number of students entering higher education courses with a focus on technology rose from 20,000 to 38,000. Meanwhile, the number of technology graduates increased from 7,000 to 13,000 (Observatorio SOFTEX, 2012). There has also been an increase in the number of technology students graduating with a masters or higher degree, from 806 in 2003 to 1,075 in 2009.

Various measures have also been taken to promote the use of FOSS in public administration. For example, when a project called PC Conectado was launched in 2005 with a target of tendering one million low-cost computers, proprietary software was excluded in an attempt to promote local industry development. A significant share of all computers used by Brazilian ministries run on Linux and other open source software (Center for Strategic and International Studies, 2010).

As in India and Sri Lanka, the Brazilian software industry is actively supported by an industry association (SOFTEX). The association manages a programme for the Ministry of Science, Technology and Innovation focused on the development of markets and the sustainable expansion of a more competitive software sector. The actions and projects that have been implemented include the production of relevant information about the industry, export promotion, quality improvements and certification, and funding. A software industry development programme, PROSOFT, is managed by the Brazilian Development Bank and can provide long-term lending that covers up to 85 per cent of the investment up to a certain ceiling. Brazil offers many other financing mechanisms of relevance to software companies. Several seed and venture capital funds have been set up by the State and there are also fully private as well as mixed schemes available. Other programmes offer long-term credit and credit guarantees to innovative enterprises involved in R&D (Zavatta, 2008).

In 2012, the Ministry of Science and Technology in consultation with the academic and private sectors designed a new strategy to boost the country's position in the global IT market. At the time of drafting this report, the national Software and IT Services Policy was launched officially in August 2012.[40] In view of the current strengths and opportunities, the new policy focuses on the development of internal resources and international positioning of the industry. Special attention will be devoted to policy measures that can help accelerate the development of technology-based start-ups, including mentoring, business services, research and investment support, human resources and labour-force development, certification of companies and professionals, R&D incentives and other instruments to strengthen the software and IT ecosystem. The policy also recognizes various needs and opportunities for software development for key sectors, including financial services, extractive industries, aerospace, energy, health care and education. With regard to global linkages, the Government plans to create international hubs located strategically in targeted markets abroad to support the internationalization of Brazilian software and IT services companies.

3. China – a major player domestically and globally

China has traditionally attracted limited attention for its performance in the area of software. This may in part be explained by the country's dominant position as an exporter of ICT goods (UNCTAD, 2011a). However, China has become a major player also in the area of software, and whereas Chinese production of software is overwhelmingly oriented towards the domestic market, exports are also rising rapidly.

Data provided by the Ministry of Industry and Information Technology (MIIT) paint a remarkable picture of the development of the country's software production. In 1999/2000, China's production of software amounted to about $5 billion (table III.9), about as much as India's production of BPO, software services and software products at that time.[41] In China, however, exports accounted for only 5 per cent of software production, as compared with 71 per cent in India. By 2006, production in China had risen to $64 billion – a nearly thirteen-fold increase. Software production in China was thus already considerably higher than that of India, which was about $42 billion (Gregory et al., 2009). But focus was still primarily on serving domestic needs.

According to the MIIT, there were in 2007 more than 18,000 software companies in China with a production in the order of $77 billion and exports of about $10 billion. Production has continued to surge, by 2011 reaching $285 billion, of which $30 billion were related to exports. These exports are to a significant degree the result of joint ventures between Japanese and Chinese companies producing for the Japanese market.

The domestic market still absorbs about 90 per cent of production. As is the case in Brazil and the Republic of Korea, embedded software represents a very important part. Major software players, especially the top three, are equipment makers that are engaged in the production of embedded software (Huawei, ZTE, Haier). In particular, software production in China is closely integrated with the dynamic hardware sector and has a stronger focus on software products than on services (Tschang, 2003; Chaudhuri, 2012).

Table III.9. Production, exports and domestic sales of software, China, 1999–2011 (millions of dollars)

Year	Total	Domestic sales	Exports
1999	5 006	4 754	254
2000	6 772	6 373	399
2001	8 883	8 167	726
2002	13 360	11 860	1 506
2003	18 116	16 304	1 812
2004	29 060	26 260	2 800
2005	48 400	44 810	3 590
2006	64 000	57 940	6 060
2007	77 009	66 769	10 240
2008	109 050	94 850	14 200
2009	145 931	127 431	18 500
2010	197 415	170 715	26 700
2011	285 900	255 500	30 400

Source: UNCTAD based on Gregory et al., 2009 (up to 2006) and MIIT China thereafter.

Note: Data from MIIT was gathered with the help by Professor Liu Xielin, Graduate University of Chinese Academy of Sciences and Professor Zhang Liyan, Tianjin University.

In 2010, the hardware sector comprised 14,836 enterprises with a total production of $820 billion and generating employment for some 7.7 million people.[42] Much of the hardware production in China is exported. In 2010, its ICT-goods exports stood at $459 billion.[43]

Expanded use of ICTs in the Chinese economy and society is also adding to the demand for software. For example, the transaction value of China's e-commerce market in 2011 was about RMB 5.9 trillion ($926 billion), equivalent to 12.5 per cent of GDP.[44] Most of these sales were channelled via Chinese e-commerce platforms, such as Alibaba and Taobao. China has also developed indigenous web platforms for social networking, such as Renren, and local search engines, such as Baidu. The uptake of ICTs and associated software has been supported by government policies and institutions, including publicly financed research into Chinese language software, translation engines and security systems (Tschang, 2003).

The role of government policies in support of the national software system has evolved over time. Whereas China had already launched a programme for software industry development in the 1980s, at end of the 1990s there was still no clear national vision for the industry (Li and Gao, 2003). However, the Government's

supportive policies towards the ICT-manufacturing sector and towards ICT use in the economy have indirectly had a positive effect on the software industry.[45] Moreover, since 2000, a range of government instruments were introduced to support the software industry, ranging from policy documents, the establishment of new software schools in universities, attracting skills, promotion of certification, export promotion and strengthening of intellectual property protection (Yang et al., 2005). In 2010, the Government issued new preferential tax policies and various investments in technology to boost domestic software consumption.[46]

New policies and strategies in this area are the result of close interaction among several government and non-government stakeholders, including the Ministry of Industry and Information Technology, the Tax Office of the Ministry of Finance, the National Development and Reform Commission, the Ministry of Commerce and two trade associations.[47] In addition, various steps have also been taken by municipalities to foster the software industry. Related policies include the setting up of software industry clusters, technology parks and the introduction of incentives (Huang, 2011).

In conclusion, China has developed a vibrant software industry that is primarily geared towards the domestic market. Much of the local production is either embedded in ICT goods and other products manufactured in China (and often subsequently exported to the world market) or developed to meet rapidly growing ICT use in the domestic economy. At the same time, the country's software exports have reached a significant scale. Both national and regional policies have been put in place to support the expansion of the sector.

4. Russian Federation – shifting focus[48]

The Russian software and IT services industry is similarly oriented towards servicing an expanding domestic market and the needs of local firms and public institutions. As noted in chapter II, the software and IT services industry accounts for about one fifth of the total ICT-sector employment in the Russian Federation (figure II.4).

While the software and IT services market is relatively small compared with those in Brazil and China – estimated at about $9 billion in 2011 (EITO, 2011) – it is growing faster. Its expansion is particularly linked to domestic demand from the extractive industry, the public sector and the financial and telecommunications industries. Although domestic sales dominate, exports are rising. Between 2002 and 2010, Russian software and IT services exports surged from $345 million to $3.3 billion, of which products and replicated solutions accounted for 41 per cent(RUSSOFT Association, 2011). The geographical distribution of exports of software and especially IT services has become more diversified over time with less dependency on the United States of America and greater focus on Europe, the Commonwealth of Independent States and various developing countries.

Global links are strengthening in various ways. Russian software producers are expanding internationally. Kaspersky Lab, which started to internationalize in 2001, is now among the world's top 100 software vendors, with software revenues of about $500 million in 2010.[49] It is one of one of the world's four leading antivirus vendors. Another example is Luxoft, which supplies computer services to various international clients.[50]

There is a significant presence of foreign-owned software companies in the Russian market. Beyond marketing and distributing their products and services, global players such as Google, SAP and Oracle have opened innovation centres and are collaborating with Russian universities through course delivery and to some extent on R&D projects. Local companies are also actively involved in the education of specialists. Both domestic and foreign-owned enterprises view the partnering with universities and colleges specializing in engineering as a way to enhance access to skilled engineers and programmers.

The current government strategy for the Russian information society indicates that the software industry will be supported by way of increased demand for local products, investment in education, increased use of ICTs in the public sector, economy and financial sector and the establishment of high-technology parks.[51] A state programme entitled Establishing of Techno Parks in the Field of High-technologies is supporting the establishment of new technology parks and IT clusters.[52] The Skolkovo Innovation Centre is an ambitious project near Moscow in the sphere of innovation clusters and IT. It was established in 2010 under a separate federal law and is considered to be the Silicon Valley of the Russian Federation, supporting innovations in ICTs, space, nuclear and other technologies.[53] In March 2012, the Skolkovo IT cluster had 134 participants and was growing fast.

Local software and IT services producers are supported by two national associations. The Russian Software Developers Association (RUSSOFT), with more than 70 member companies, advocates a more competitive business environment through changes in taxes and customs legislation, improved IT clusters and effective export promotion. In connection with the release of its annual survey of the industry, RUSSOFT also called upon the Government to improve education and customs procedures and reduce red tape to make the environment more enabling.[54] The second body is the Association of Computer and Information Technology Producers, which focuses on support of local companies through influence on macroeconomic and social policy and on combating unfair competition practices.

D. DISCUSSION

The successful development of software capabilities cannot be accomplished solely by market forces – governments have a key role to play. This is reflected in all the cases cited in this chapter. Making available a large pool of skilled personnel at different levels is particularly important to achieve the primary condition for the establishment of a software production base. Brazil, China, India and the Russian Federation have also taken steps to take advantage of agglomeration economies by setting up technology parks within which communication infrastructure and other services facilitate interaction with bureaucracy. Such technology parks can benefit from being in close proximity to the centres of learning such that mutual learning and domestic technological capability are built up over time.

Since the software value chain consists of different activities that call for varying levels of capabilities, many developing countries with skill deficits will make their entry point with software services and IT services, typically targeting the domestic market. A conscious effort towards skill empowerment is required in order to avoid becoming locked up in low technology activity and to facilitate an upward movement along the value chain.

The cases presented in this chapter include countries for which the growth paths of the software industry seem very different. In particular, India and Sri Lanka are highly export-oriented while Brazil, the Republic of Korea, China and the Russian Federation are predominantly driven by the domestic market. In the former countries, there is now growing interest in fostering closer interaction between the software industry and other parts of the domestic economy. In the latter cases, various efforts are being taken by governments as well as industry associations to expand the software exports.

An important distinction between the two categories of economies is the performance of their manufacturing sectors. The relevance of the industry structure of a country matters for the software industry. For example, as noted in one study (Ojo et al., 2008, p. 4):

> countries with large manufacturing bases such as telecommunications, hardware, aerospace, automobile, and aeronautics tend to provide a significant and sophisticated patronage to their local software industries.

In Brazil, China and the Republic of Korea, much of the software production is indeed serving the needs of domestic producers of various manufactured goods for embedded software. And in the Russian Federation, the domestic industry acts as a demanding buyer of software applications. The development of software applications then serves as a strategic tool to improve the competitiveness of enterprises that are operating inside the economy but outside the software sector. This experience illustrates the argument that the social marginal product of a dollar worth of software consumed domestically is higher than that of a dollar worth of export (Kumar and Joseph, 2005).

By contrast, in India and Sri Lanka the main clients for the software products and services sold are located overseas. If the majority of software capabilities are used to supply foreign clients, the chances are smaller that valuable learning opportunities emerge that can support the development of software applications to meet domestic needs (Parthasarathy, 2006). In the case of India, the detachment of individual IT and software firms from other domestic sectors has been noted as a key difference vis-à-vis the Chinese situation (Chaudhuri, 2012, p. 13):

> The roots of Indian firms are purely economic and nothing else, and hence pecuniary returns are both the driving force and the limiting factor of their operations. It is an industry driven not by national needs, but by foreign demand. No Indian company is heavily involved in sectors such has health, education, or even organizational or social knowledge-sharing, commonly known as networking… The vacuum in the sphere of commerce is especially surprising, since the long-run profit potentials are enormous. While e-commerce remains paltry except for niche areas such as airlines ticketing in India, its market size in China was estimated at $681.82 billion in 2010.

In India as well as other countries where the software industry is predominantly export driven, there may be reasons to explore ways of enticing local software enterprises and developers to pay more attention to the domestic market. As noted in the case study, the new Indian ICT policy signals several steps to address this challenge. In less-developed economies, while it is possible to develop software production capabilities for the export market, a policy framework that creates a domestic market base is likely to be desirable for reaping greater development gains from software production.

Various approaches can be explored in this context. Public procurement is one important avenue to consider, and the experience of the Republic of Korea can offer valuable insights. Careful consideration should in this case be given to the role of open standards, open innovation and FOSS (chapter IV). Promoting embedded software in relevant industrial sectors is another option. Useful lessons can be learned from Brazil and China, as well as the Republic of Korea. Moreover, as illustrated in the case of Sri Lanka, growing demand and use of mobile phones and related applications present opportunities to boost domestic demand. Mobile network operators can play a central role as market makers. This domain is particularly relevant in low-income countries in which the current use of computers remains limited while mobile phone use is booming. Stimulating demand in both the public and private sectors for mobile apps, with relevant local content, can help to catalyse the sector and generate more interest in software development among the skilled youth.

Whether the emphasis is on promoting exports or domestic production and development, it is important to establish an ongoing dialogue between the government and other relevant stakeholders. In several of the cases discussed, industry associations – such as NASSCOM (India), SLASSCOM (Sri Lanka), SOFTEX (Brazil) and RUSSOFT (Russian Federation) – play an active role in the system. Various steps should be taken to facilitate interaction among all the actors in the national software system. This can be done by establishing dedicated facilities in conjunction with universities and research centres and by involving stakeholders in the development of national visions, strategies and government policies (chapter V).

NOTES

1   Guatemalan companies, for example, export many of their software solutions to countries like Honduras, Mexico and Nicaragua (SOFEX, 2011). Similarly, in the former Yugoslav Republic of Macedonia, more than half of all software and IT services exports go to neighboring markets in the Balkans, which are less mature and competitive than Western European markets and easier to penetrate (MASIT, 2010).

2   Among the top 10 software exporters, the first three positions are held by Indian firms and only three foreign firms (Cognizant Technology Solutions, IBM and Accenture) are in the top ten list.

3   See http://soft-engineering.blogspot.de/search/label/CMM%20level.

4   See "The Software Products Industry in India", NASSCOM Newsline, October 2009.

5   For instance, Druvaa developed fully automated laptop backup software which protects corporate data for office and remote users. Today the company has over 200 customers spread over 22 countries. See http://blog. nasscom.in/nasscomnewsline/2009/10/the-software-products-industry-in-india/.

6   Including BPO, exports increased from $17 billion to $59 billion during the same period according to NASSCOM. Data from the Electronics and Software Export Promotion Council are similar: from $17 billion to $58 billion.

7   It was also helped by the country's geographical location and strong English-speaking capabilities.

8   As the unique identity database comes into existence, the various identity databases (voter ID, passports, ration cards, licenses, fishing permits, border area ID cards) that already exist in India are planned to be linked to it. See http://uidai.gov.in and NASSCOM, 2011.

9   For the collection of biometric and demographic data 209 agencies have been selected and the services of an additional 91 more will be needed. Telecom companies such as Aircel, Airtel, BSNL, Reliance, Tata Telecom and Railtel have been entrusted with the task of providing connectivity between enrolment agencies and the Central Identities Data Repository.

10 For details, see http://mit.gov.in/sites/upload_files/dit/files/National_Policy_on_Information_Technology_07102011% 281%29.pdf.

11 Including the BPO industry, which is expected to contribute $300 million, the overall IT industry is expected to generate $1 billion in 2015. Statements by SLASSCOM during interviews.

12 See *Overview of the Sri Lankan IT Industry* by Dinesh B. Saparamadu, http://www.hsenid.com/download/EH_ Overview_Of_the_Sri_Lankan_ITDetail.pdf.

13 See http://www.icta.lk/en/e-sri-lanka.html.

14 Sri Lanka Information Technology Report, Q4 2011, Companies and Markets.com, see http://www.compa- niesandmarkets.com/Market/Information-Technology/Market-Research/Sri-Lanka-Information-Technology- Report-Q4-2011/RPT1012855.

15 Source: ITU World Telecommunication/ICT Indicators database.

16 According to data from the ITU World Telecommunication/ICT Indicators database, the number of active mobile broadband subscriptions rose from 294,000 in 2010 to 485,000 in 2011, corresponding to a penetration of 2.3 per 100 inhabitants.

17 The five mobile operators in Sri Lanka are Dialog Axiata, Mobitel, Etisalat, Airtel and Hutch – Dialog Axiata: subsidiary of Axiata Group Berhad of Malaysia; Mobitel: owned by Sri Lanka Telecom, fully state-owned; Etisalat: owned by Etisalat United Arab Emirates; Hutch: owned by Hutchinson Whampoa Limited, Hong Kong (China); Airtel: owned by Bharti Airtel, India.

18 See http://www.lbr.lk/fullstory.php?nid=201103041615077468.

19 Extracted from "Sri Lanka's Internet penetration hits 11.8%", Indi.ca, available at http://indi.ca/2012/02/ sri-lankas-internet-penetration-hits-11-8/.

20 See "Top web sites in Sri Lanka", Alexa.com, 4 March, 2012, available at http://www.alexa.com/topsites/countries/LK.

21 See https://www.odesk.com/oconomy/.

22 Two top 10s for Google Summer of Code, 2008, see http://google-opensource.blogspot.com/2008/04/two-top-10s-for-google-summer-of-code.html.

23 Prices of such handsets declined from LKR 75,000 ($773, HTC Hero) in 2010 to LKR 11,000 ($113, Vodafone 858 Smart) in 2012.

24 Android Market has been converged into Google Play, and that has become the home for Android Apps, see http://googleblog.blogspot.com/2012/03/introducing-google-play-all-your.html.

25 See Dhanka's Thoughts, blog site of Dhanika Perera, http://dhanikauom.blogspot.com/.

26 Started in 2010, Refresh Colombo was inspired and assisted by Refresh Miami in the United States of America. See Refresh Colombo web site, http://www.refreshcolombo.org/.

27 Apple's App Store in Sri Lanka is, nevertheless, open without any restriction to apps produced by locals. Software companies are optimistic that the Android Market will open soon.

28 See http://unctadstat.unctad.org.

29 Based on data from IDC and the Electronics and Telecommunications Research Institute cited in the 2010 Annual Report on the Promotion of IT Industry 2010 (in Korean only) by the Ministry of Knowledge Economy, see http://www.nipa.kr/board/boardView.it?boardNo=79&contentNo=31&menuNo=294&gubn=&page=1.

30 See http://www.softwaretop100.org/global-software-top-100-edition-2011.

31 The highest level of software use is found in telecommunications and broadcasting and the lowest in restaurants/hospitality, food and beverages and agriculture/fishery (Oh, 2011).

32 See http://www.mke.go.kr/news/coverage/bodoView.jsp?seq=58448&pageNo=1&srchType=1&srchWord=&pCtx=1 (in Korean only).

33 The software evaluation process for eGovFrame was defined using an international software evaluation process model (ISO 14598) and a practical software evaluation process (SEI PECA). In the first, logical test, 175 different kinds of open source software were evaluated. In the second, physical test, 85 kinds of open source software remained and were evaluated with regard to their basic functions and non-functional requirements.

34 The eGovFrame Free Education and Training Programme is provided by eGovFrame Center of National Information Society Agency, which reports to the Ministry of Public Administration and Security.

35 Examples include national portal systems, e-authentication, a system for sharing administration information, tracing of imported beef, advanced civil service systems, local administrative information systems, systems for boosting corporate competitiveness, a ubiquitous port system, and integrated management systems for providing firms with policy information.

36 One dollar in tables III.6 and III.7 is calculated as KRW 1,000.

37 Savings from using common components were estimated based on average savings ($114,000) in 11 of 69 projects in 2010. The framework savings were estimated based on the development cost ($416,000) of 9 out of 54 service functionalities when eGovFrame was developed.

38 Based on information provided by the National Information Society Agency, March 2012.

39 See http://www.softwaretop100.org/global-software-top-100-edition-2011.

40 See "Brazil announces $248M investment to boost software, IT services", *RCRWireless.com*, 21 August 2012, available at http://www.rcrwireless.com/americas/20120821/software/brazil-releases-plan-boost-software-it-services-areas-investments-248-m/.

41 See Electronics and Software Export Promotion Council, various years.

42 See China Statistical Yearbook, http://www.stats.gov.cn/english/statisticaldata/yearlydata/.

43 See UNCTAD Stat, http://unctadstat.unctad.org/TableViewer/tableView.aspx.

44 See "China to Become Largest Online Retail Market", *Capital Vue*, 30 May 2012, http://www.capitalvue.com/home/CE-news/inset/@10063/post/10900524.

45 See, for example, UNCTAD, 2011a, 2010.

46 See "New policies to favor software industry", *People's Daily Online*, 4 June 2010.

47 See "Document 4's favorable policies for software and integrated circuit", *China IP Magazine*, 14 July 2011.

48 This section is based mainly on Abramova, 2012.

49 See http://www.softwaretop100.org/global-software-top-100-edition-2011.

50 It was awarded best outsourcing services provider by the European Outsourcing Association in 2011, see http://www.eoasummit.com/awards/.

51 State programme of the Russian Federation – Information Society 2011–2020 – approved in 2010. See http://government.ru/gov/results/12932/.

52 State programme – Establishing Techno Parks in the Field of High-technology – http://www.mininform.ru/ministry/documents/828/2292.shtml, approved in 2006.

53 Established under the Federal Law No. 244-FL, dated 28.09.2010 – Establishment of the Innovation Center Skolkovo.

54 See " Software Makers Seek State Support", *The Moscow Times*, 19 April 2012.

THE ROLE OF FREE AND OPEN SOURCE SOFTWARE

4

One of the features of the evolving ICT landscape highlighted in chapter I is the growing acceptance and use of free and open source software (FOSS). This trend goes hand in hand with the greater openness seen in software development and the reliance on distributed peer-production models. Over the past decade, FOSS applications have continued to gain market share in many areas. Both governments and enterprises recognize the value of using software for which the source code is freely available and which can be adapted and improved upon. This chapter builds on earlier work conducted by UNCTAD on FOSS, documents how the role of FOSS and related policies have evolved during the past decade, and examines opportunities for business development around FOSS. The chapter notes that current trends are likely to reinforce the growing reliance on FOSS, which should therefore be adequately considered in efforts to strengthen national software systems.

A. REVISITING THE ROLE OF FOSS

The development dimension of FOSS was discussed by UNCTAD in its *E-Commerce and Development Report 2003* (UNCTAD, 2003b), which provided an overview at that time when it was still a relatively new phenomenon.[1] The report argued that governments, companies and civil society should seriously consider the potential benefits of taking a positive and pro-active approach to the use of FOSS. It noted that open source software offered possibilities for developing countries to develop their human capital, spur innovation and diffuse software in the domestic economy. It predicted that the increasing adoption of FOSS in the developed world would create business opportunities for software enterprises and developers in developing countries. Today, many of these predictions are being realized.

Since the UNCTAD report was published, the FOSS landscape has evolved and matured in many ways. Open source software is now found in virtually every operating system and professional environment. Networking equipment, cable and satellite television boxes, DVD players and even coffee machines are examples of goods that often include FOSS in their operating systems. An important enabler of FOSS has been the widespread use and adoption of the Internet and increasing bandwidth opportunities, coupled with the transition towards knowledge-based economies. In developing countries, FOSS has gradually made inroads into government policy, business and industry-led R&D and software use. Before reviewing these trends, it will be useful to revisit briefly the basic differences between FOSS and proprietary software.

1. The meaning of FOSS

Software differs in how it is developed, distributed, modified and licensed. The most prominent types are proprietary software and FOSS. Combinations of the two are also common. The main distinction between proprietary software and FOSS is that the source code in the latter case is freely available.

The terms of use for proprietary software are described in end-user licences that include full restrictions set by the copyright owner (an individual or a company) on use, copying and distribution. These licences often come with high costs per device (PC, tablet) or user

and the underlying source code is not distributed. The idea behind such proprietary licences is to ensure that the copyright holder is compensated for the monetary and human resources that have been invested in the development of the code.

Just like proprietary software, FOSS comes with user licences and relies on intellectual property regulation for protection and legal recourse. However, FOSS licences specify certain freedoms to use, copy, study, modify and redistribute the software.[2] These freedoms provide a framework for the usage and sharing of intellectual capital in a way that is applicable to many areas of development. A distinction can be made between free and open source software (box IV.1).[3] While free software encourages intellectual freedom in the philosophical sense (as in free speech rather than free beer), open source software encourages pragmatic freedoms to reuse and adapt software to one's needs. The concept of FOSS is here used without bias towards either approach. Both involve licences that ensure community contributions and engagement on the basis of inclusive, collaborative and open sharing of intellectual capital as a common good.

2. FOSS-related licences

Different FOSS-related licences offer varying levels of protection and therefore serve different needs. Licensing decisions affect which software libraries can be used as well as the size and character of the community that gathers around a project. Licensing decisions therefore need to be made in the context of a project's goals, resources, community and philosophy (Fontana et al., 2008). Some of the more common licences are presented below (Ernst & Young, 2011).[4]

- **GNU is not Unix (GNU) General Public License (GPL):** The central idea of this licence is to prevent cooperatively developed software source code from being turned into proprietary software. The licence relates to the software as a whole and to its individual components. The viral clause of GPL states that users may not add restrictions of their own – all copies, regardless of how much the software is altered, must also use the GPL. It exists in three versions; the most recent one was updated in 2007.[5]

- **GNU Library or Lesser General Public License (LGPL):** In order to avoid forcing the publication of the whole source code, components licensed under

---

Box IV.1.	Defining free and open source software

Free software code is protected under a special form of licensing that provides a safety net for the underlying philosophy and the developers of the software. According to the Free Software Foundation (FSF), a software is free if users have the freedom to:

- Run the programme for any purpose;
- Study how the programme works and adapt it to the needs of the user;
- Redistribute copies in order to help a neighbour;
- Improve the programme and release improvements (and modified versions in general) to the public so that the community as a whole can benefit.

Open source software licences also conform to these four freedoms but may differ in terms of what other forms of software may be added to it. According to the Open Source Initiative definition, software is open if it carries the following features:

- No royalty or other fee is imposed upon redistribution.
- The source code is available.
- Users and developers have the right to create modifications and derivative works.
- Modified versions may be required to be distributed as the original version plus patches.
- There is no discrimination against persons or groups.
- There is no discrimination against fields of endeavour.
- All rights granted must flow through to/with redistributed versions.
- The licence applies to the program as a whole as well as to each of its components.
- The licence must not restrict other software, thus permitting the distribution of open source and closed source software together.

Source: UNCTAD. Based on the Free Software Foundation (www.fsf.org/about) and the Open Source Initiative (www.osi.org). See also http://opensource.org/docs/osd.

---

the LGPL may continue to be used in proprietary software. Any changes made to the LGPL library itself must however be published under a LGPL. In this way, the LGPL offers a weak safeguard of freedoms.

- **GNU Affero General Public License (AGPL):** This licence was also issued by FSF in collaboration with the Affero company.[6] It requires the source code to be disclosed in the case of use via a network connection. This feature may make the AGPL important in the context of the expanding use of cloud computing and SaaS.

- **Massachusetts Institute of Technology (MIT), Berkeley Software Distribution (BSD) and Apache Licenses:** These are considered more permissive licences as they allow the source code to be incorporated into proprietary software under certain conditions. For example, the MIT licence permits reuse within proprietary software provided all copies of the licensed software include a copy of the MIT licence terms. Such proprietary

software retains its proprietary nature even though it incorporates MIT licensed software.

- **Mozilla Public License (MPL):** This licence offers a weak safeguard of freedoms. It is possible to take an MPL-licensed work and build upon it with new components. The resulting work can be distributed with the MPL covering the use of the original work and any licence covering the rest. Thus, closed source components can be added to build a proprietary product.

According to the Open Source Resource Center, as of April 2012 the restrictive GPL versions 2 and 3 together accounted for almost half of the 540,000 known open source projects. However, this share is considerably smaller than the 70 per cent observed in mid-2008. Meanwhile, less restrictive licences, such as MIT, BSD, Apache and Mozilla, have surged and now account for about one quarter of all projects (table IV.1).

Some observers have linked this shift to the growing role of web companies, such as Facebook, Twitter and

Table IV.1. Most commonly used licences in open source projects, April 2012		
Rank	Licence	Share (%)
1	GNU General Public License (GPL) 2.0	42.28
2	MIT License	11.51
3	Artistic License (Perl)	7.97
4	GNU Lesser General Public License (LGPL) 2.1	7.06
5	BSD License 2.0	6.81
6	GNU General Public License (GPL) 3.0	6.40
7	Apache License 2.0	5.51
8	Code Project Open 1.02 License	2.10
9	Microsoft Public License (Ms-PL)	1.90
10	Mozilla Public License (MPL) 1.1	1.02
11	Others	7.44

Source: Open Source Resource Center
(http://osrc.blackducksoftware.com/data/licenses/).

Yahoo, which are not in the business of selling software and may not see a need for the protections offered by a restrictive software licence.[7] They have a strong preference for dual licensing schemes, both open source and proprietary, and tend to use the more permissive collaborative licences (such as Apache) for non-differentiating components. Moreover, cloud computing platforms, such as Hadoop, OpenStack, Cassandra and CloudFoundry, also use Apache. The same applies to Google's Android mobile operating system and the web operating system of Hewlett Packard for its Palm devices. Even larger proprietary software providers, such as IBM and Oracle, have projects using FOSS licences. Thus, for many software vendors, the strategic decision no longer revolves around choosing between either an open source or a proprietary business model, but rather around the proportion of open source used and what licence to choose to best protect the differentiating elements of a business.

3. Pros and cons with FOSS

There are several reasons why software users and producers, especially in developing countries, should consider adopting open source software. As part of their strategies to develop software capabilities, governments may choose to include FOSS policies, not least in connection with software use in the public sector.

Promotion of local learning: FOSS is developed in a process of collaborative production with continuous sharing among peers, a set-up that is conducive to the promotion of learning within and across borders. The way in which FOSS promotes grassroots creativity, innovation, leadership and teamwork is a key value added, especially in developing countries. Various studies of FOSS communities have demonstrated that the process of learning about and adapting software enables users to become creators of knowledge, rather than merely passive consumers of proprietary technologies.[8]

Lower costs and local value creation: Cost reduction is also among the prime arguments for FOSS adoption (Ajila and Wu, 2007; Koh, 2009). In public or private organizations with a large number of users, the total cost of licences for proprietary software can be considerable. By avoiding licence fees, a government may be able to free more resources for software training and capacity-building (UNCTAD, 2003b). Moreover, in developing countries, licence payments are often made to foreign companies. As noted by one Egyptian software executive (Rizk and El-Kassas, 2010: 156): "At least 70 to 80% of expenditures go to licenses and they don't even get injected back in the economy [in the case of proprietary software], thus all of this gets out of the country as royalties." This is not to say that relying on FOSS is costless. Costs may arise, for example, for its development, installation, maintenance and services. However, the main cost involved for using FOSS is the service component, which is related to local labour costs and the availability of ICT skills.

Less dependence on specific technologies and vendors: Software users in the public and private sector may fear that choosing proprietary software will make them dependent on the vendor for future updates, maintenance and adaptation. In e-government project development, for example, software plays a central role. If such projects are developed with proprietary software, for which the source code is not freely accessible, a government may become locked in with the chosen supplier for maintenance and future development. This may also act as a technical barrier for new competitors to enter, giving the original supplier a dominant market position. In effect, the buyer ends up in a weak bargaining position vis-à-vis the supplier and may face high costs for licences and ancillary services. Reliance on FOSS can enable more companies to potentially act as suppliers of the products and related services. With open source code, file formats and protocols are open as well, which makes it easier to migrate to a new application or platform if desirable. Moreover, when the source code is openly accessible, the quality of the software produced is likely to be higher since more developers are able to provide inputs and detect possible bugs or flaws.

Enable adaptation of software to local needs: With a FOSS model, the user is allowed to make changes to an existing source code and adapt it if necessary to the specific context. Any FOSS program can be translated and altered to suit the linguistic, cultural, commercial and regulatory needs and requirements of any location, without having to seek permission from the original authors or exchanging terms and conditions while using legal intermediaries and consultants. This may be important in developing countries, for example when software products and applications are needed in multiple languages. While tailoring is also possible with proprietary software, a buyer becomes tied to the vendor in question and has a weaker bargaining position.

Address concerns related to national security and long-term availability: If the source code is fully known to the government, there is every possibility to review the system and determine whether a particular program contains vulnerabilities that could enable unwanted access to confidential information. The FOSS option may therefore be attractive from a national security perspective.[9] Having access to the source code is essential in the case of critical software use in such domains as military installations, infrastructure management and health-care systems. Contracting software development without receiving the source code adds risk for the procurer. If the developers disband or their company closes, the application may become difficult to service, upgrade or continue developing. Owning the software code gives the option to release it under a FOSS licence, in particular if it is too specialized to have volume sales potential (UNCTAD, 2004).[10]

Despite such advantages, in many countries – including in Governments – there is strong reliance placed on proprietary software, as in the case of Egypt (box IV.2). The predominant reason for proprietary software use in developing countries is the presence of a large number of users familiar with it, sometimes as a result of the widespread use of unlicensed copies of proprietary software. Some buyers may feel more comfortable opting for branded proprietary software produced by a vendor that offers a package of training, maintenance and support. There may also be concerns related to the interoperability between new software and existing systems. Another reason for opting for proprietary software is the notion that ICT-related capacity-building – from basic literacy to higher education and professional development – has mainly focused on proprietary technologies, contributing to building a critical mass of people trained in the particular software, as well as to a resistance to changing to something new and untested. Even in relatively advanced ICT economies, such as Singapore, a perceived lack of FOSS skills has acted as a barrier to greater FOSS adoption (Koh, 2009).

For the foreseeable future, it is therefore likely that users will rely on a mix of proprietary and open source software. The points of interest are the relative importance of the two models and exploring possible complementarities between them. As discussed later in this chapter, the balance between the two is evolving in dissimilar ways for different kinds of software and in various parts of the world. To achieve more use of FOSS in the private and public sectors, it is important to foster the development of relevant skills and capabilities in the ICT sector to ensure that potential users can trust a transition away from proprietary software solutions. As the next section highlights, there are various ways in which local software firms can build a business case around FOSS.

Box IV.2. Factors limiting FOSS uptake in Egypt

Despite potential benefits for most categories of local software companies, FOSS plays only a small role in Egypt. A recent study identified key factors behind this situation. First, many buyers attach importance to the reputation of the brand names of proprietary software vendors. Second, it is not uncommon that public and private sector software users equate price with value, thus avoiding lower cost solutions. Third, aggressive marketing tactics by large vendors vis-à-vis universities and public agencies had established close links between TNCs and the Government. Fourth, and partly a result of the previous factor, educational efforts in Egypt have often emphasized proprietary software systems. Finally, lack of awareness and weak demand have combined to reduce the availability of job opportunities related to FOSS for software developers. Active support for FOSS by the Government was thus deemed necessary to change the status quo.

Source: Rizk and El-Kassas (2010).

B. FOSS AND LOCAL SOFTWARE INDUSTRY DEVELOPMENT

Freely accessible source code does not prevent developers or enterprises from generating revenue for work related to that software. On the contrary, many software enterprises rely on selling ancillary services. Recognizing the possibilities of FOSS as a tool for generating revenue, rather than as a product to be sold, allows companies to share solutions and the improvements reached while performing contracted work for clients. Software made-to-order may be too specific to be commercialized and sold prepackaged in significant volumes. Still, the mainstream proprietary software industry earns a large part of its income from services and after-sales work (UNCTAD, 2004). The

experience of Globant, an Argentine software company, is one example of how enterprises in developing countries can generate revenue from software development and maintenance, sometimes combining FOSS and proprietary software platforms (box IV.3). Excellence Delivered, a Pakistani company, is another example (box IV.4).

Some Governments see FOSS as a means to support domestic software capabilities. Reliance on proprietary software – for example, in the context of public procurement (see also chapter V) – may act as an entry barrier for newcomers and result in vendor lock-in as mentioned above. FOSS offers greater potential for small domestic companies to participate and thereby contribute, making the environment more competitive. However, few studies have empirically examined the impact of FOSS on local software industry development. As a business model able to leverage

---

Box IV.3.   Globant – an Argentine software company

Globant was founded in 2003 by four engineers determined to build a Latin American leader in the creation of innovative software products. Nine years later, Globant has evolved into a global software and IT services player, employing more than 2,400 professionals and servicing clients such as LinkedIn, JWT, Zynga and Google. From its Buenos Aires headquarters, the company has internationalized its operations and delivers services around the globe, supported by offices in other Argentine cities, Colombia, the United Kingdom, the United States of America and Uruguay.

Globant's experience is an example of how to make money in a developing country around new and emerging technologies by rationally combining open source with proprietary software. While it does not charge for licences, the company generates revenue from software solutions to create innovative products. Its turnover surged from $3 million in 2003 to $90 million in 2011. The company attributes its success to strong engineering capabilities combined with creativity and innovation. As part of its commitment to FOSS, Globant has developed a java-based open source software platform called Katari which is used for the development of web applications. Katari is available to the open source community under the Apache Software License 2.0.

Various trends in the software and IT landscape are empowering end users and compelling enterprises to engage and collaborate with users in new and powerful ways. Large-scale adoption of social networking is changing the way users and servers interact. The mobile revolution has resulted in a whole generation of new platforms and devices. Software products have become simpler to use and more entertaining. Finally, the apps business model has led to thousands of freelance developers and small companies attempting to succeed on e-stores and markets.

Source: Information provided by Globant (www.globant.com) and Wegbrait, 2009.

Box IV.4.   Generating revenues on open source in Pakistan: the case of Excellence Delivered

Excellence Delivered (www.exdnow.com) was founded in Pakistan in May 2010 by a native entrepreneur with experience from software TNCs such as SAP and Oracle. From the outset, Excellence Delivered focused on developing FOSS products and technologies. The company has won contracts in competition with leading proprietary software vendors to deploy 1,200 users with OpenOffice and an open source-based operating system for the leading bottler of Pepsi Cola International. The company continues its commitment to open source software and has developed, inter alia, a global human resource management system based on the PostgresSQL database (http://www.postgresql.org/). It competes in the area of feature functions against similar offerings of global vendors and is available online. Excellence Delivered is also developing Android applications for business intelligence and other applications to supplement its technology offering.

Source: UNCTAD.

existing and essentially free-of-cost infrastructure, FOSS is more efficient and appealing than a scenario with a limited number of expensive proprietary software. From the perspective of software suppliers, open source software is interesting particularly for emerging SMEs that may not be able to propose radically new products, but would rather build on existing technology to offer marginally improved solutions. In this sense, FOSS can benefit SMEs through a substantial reduction in the cost of ownership of the non-differentiating software component and avoidance of the locking-in effects associated with proprietary software (Rizk and El-Kassas, 2010).

There are several ways in which software companies in developing countries can build a business case around FOSS and generate revenue (ict@innovation, 2010). In a 2012 survey, open source vendors mainly in developed countries ranked the following business models and the best options for generating revenue around FOSS: annual, repeatable support and service agreements; ad hoc services and support; and value-added subscription.[11] In general, a business-led rather than technology-driven approach to the application of FOSS to projects in the commercial and private sector has been found to be important for project success.[12] If the strategic needs of clients and the needs of user communities are satisfied, FOSS can provide access

to the building blocks of innovation, allowing clients and users to collaborate and operate in a diverse, multivendor business environment.

In Africa, the most common business model is built around providing FOSS training, for example, on how to use FOSS or how to become certified (ict@innovation, 2010). Other common business models include the installation of FOSS systems, maintenance and support as well as various consultancy services. In addition, some software companies in Africa have built their business around helping clients to select the right open source software, integrating FOSS into existing systems, system migration, software localization, technical or legal certification and the development of new FOSS. Some capacity-building tools exist to support companies seeking advice on how to develop FOSS-related businesses (box IV.5).

There are also potential advantages from the open source process for companies or individual developers that write software for sale and engage in outsourcing or freelancing. The release of a working beta version of open source software – and using developer community resources – can reduce the time between the development and marketing of a product. This is followed by a customization phase where a number of iterations of test and code review are performed in close consultation with the client in order to reach

---

Box IV.5. Creating business and learning opportunities with FOSS in Africa: the case of ict@innovation

ict@innovation is a capacity-development programme started in 2008 by the Free Software and Open Source Foundation for Africa (FOSSFA; box IV.9) and GIZ, which is funded by the German Federal Ministry for Economic Cooperation and Development (BMZ). As of May 2012, ict@innovation was active in 15 sub-Saharan African countries. The programme has helped to create a community of more than 1,200 African and international experts who are exchanging knowledge on FOSS as a key technology to drive innovation, add local value and create sustainable and affordable ICT solutions in African economies. More than 200 African ict@innovation trainers have qualified to teach the dynamics of open source software as a business, many of whom are offering regular demand-oriented IT courses on key issues such as African business models in open source or low-cost certification in Linux system administration. As of 2012, ict@innovation trainers had also reached out to more than 600 IT entrepreneurs, students and industry leaders. Two community-built training manuals have been integrated into the curricula of African IT faculties, business schools and training institutes.

ict@innovation supports African ICT industries primarily by spreading FOSS business models for enterprises, fostering FOSS certification and supporting innovative local FOSS applications for development.

FOSS business models training: With the help of more than 80 African IT and business experts, an open-licensed training guide – *Free your IT-Business in Africa!* – was developed on how to generate business with FOSS. It has become a highly demanded learning material in English and French, with at least 5,000 copies in use. The material was designed to allow for further modification, commercial use by African training entrepreneurs and self-study. Five regional training-of-trainer courses in sub-Saharan Africa have produced more than 130 trainers, mainly from African training institutions and universities. The courses, which reach IT entrepreneurs, IT graduates and university students, are complemented by an online knowledge exchange with more than 300 active members.

Box IV.5. Creating business and learning opportunities with FOSS in Africa: the case of ict@innovation (continued)

Certification of Linux system administrators: The programme provides training in low-cost, vendor-neutral certification, using a scheme developed by the Linux Professional Institute. The provision of such courses can in itself be a viable business opportunity. Moreover, by having certified staff, African IT enterprises involved in open source software can improve the quality of their services and win new clients. Open-licensed training material and the regional training-of-trainers courses were implemented jointly by different community stakeholders. Some 30 national trainings have also been offered by ict@innovation trainers. As a result, more than 300 participants can certify to clients that they possess the required Linux system administration skills. Further peer-to-peer learning continues through an online community of about 150 trainers.

Fostering local FOSS innovation: In order to improve the environment for local innovation through FOSS, ict@innovation has worked with universities and entrepreneurs from the African Virtual Open Initiatives and Resources (AVOIR) network. The goal of this collaboration is to give students practical programming skills through a mentored internship programme.

Beyond these areas, a series of regional networking events have assisted members of the African FOSS community to federate, grow and strategize. A search function helps African enterprises or institutions to find specific IT services in a country and contact vendors online. About three to four new members normally join the community every week.

ict@innovation is being evaluated in 2012 to consolidate knowledge on outcomes, impact and further needs. As current funding ends in December 2012, the programme is encouraging local teaching and expanding the various communities described above. In the future, ict@innovation should seek to broaden its regional scope, offer more training-of-trainer courses, further empower the community and catalyse new local course offerings. To this end, GIZ and FOSSFA are seeking partners interested in building capacities in the African ICT sector.

Source: GIZ. See also http://www.ict-innovation.fossfa.net.

---

the desired combination of features and performance. FOSS licences and the absence of non-disclosure agreements make such client–developer interaction easier, potentially of particular value to developers in developing countries (UNCTAD, 2004).

C. TRENDS IN FOSS ADOPTION

During the past decade, FOSS has gained popularity in several segments of the software landscape. While FOSS platforms are responsible for only a fraction of the desktop operating system market, they have emerged as the preferred choice for all server operating system markets – from the entry level to the enterprise level, and across critical Internet infrastructure as well as appliances and mobile devices. Many established Internet business and websites, such as Google, Yahoo and Amazon, use FOSS operating systems or open source web server software. Without the spread of FOSS and open standards, the world would not have witnessed such rapid technological diffusion as it has in the fields of software, Internet, communications, entertainment, health, entertainment, education and e-government.

1. Trends in FOSS usage

A growing number of private and public organizations are using FOSS in various application domains. At the same time, there is little systematic data on the extent to which FOSS is being adopted in the public and private sector in different parts of the world. Available information suggests that the adoption and use of FOSS technologies have so far been the most widespread in developed economies.

In the public sector, Europe reports particularly high average penetration. The most widely used FOSS products are the Linux operating system, the My Structured Query Language (MySQL) database system, the OpenOffice office productivity suite, the Firefox Internet browser and the Thunderbird email clients. Open source mobile operating systems and applications are also gaining in importance. Various Governments are looking at Linux as a viable alternative, such as the city administrations of Munich, Freiburg and Jena in Germany (box IV.6). The Government of France recently signed up to install the open source software suite in 500,000 computers that currently use proprietary applications. Other European Governments have also been examining such schemes.[13]

Box IV.6. Munich's experience with FOSS

When Munich announced Project LiMux in 2004, it was the first major city to shift its internal government system to open source software. The shift to Linux meant that it could retain older hardware and avoid paying licences for proprietary software. In 2012, it was announced that the city's IT department had been able to save about one third of its total budget in 2011 by opting for Linux and OpenOffice. Buying new proprietary software and upgrading systems would have cost an estimated €15 million, with another €2.8 million due in three to four years for licence renewals. The use of Linux also improved the level of user satisfaction, resulting in fewer calls to help desks. By December 2011, some 9,000 desktops had been migrated to the open source system.

Applying open source software to all activities was not possible. For example, the city's educational network was excluded from the outset. In 2011, around 28,000 computers in Munich's educational facilities were upgraded to a more recent version of Microsoft software. It was argued that extensive discounts for software packages used in education reduced the cost of licence fees. Moreover, some 700 proprietary products were being used in the education network, of which only a small proportion worked under Linux. Consequently, it would have been necessary to migrate a large number of specialized tools and methodologies to Linux had there been a switch to open source software. Still, Munich's schools reportedly use open source solutions when it makes sense.

The positive experience of Munich is being followed by other Germany cities, such as Freiburg and Jena. Moreover, the Mayor of Munich has written to the European Commission to encourage wider FOSS adoption among public administrations in Europe.

Source: UNCTAD. Based on Thomson I (29 March 2012). Munich's mayor claims €4m savings from Linux switch", *The Register* (http://www.theregister.co.uk/2012/03/29/munich_linux_savings/), "Munich school network to be migrated to Windows XP", H-Online, 23 February 2011 (http://www.h-online.com/open/news/item/Munich-school-network-to-be-migrated-to-Windows-XP-1195535.html) and "German cities following Munich's open source example", *JoinUp*, 6 January 2012 (https://joinup.ec.europa.eu/news/german-cities-following-munichs-open-source-example).

In New Zealand, the Government has had a policy on FOSS since 2003.[14] There is a community-based Open Source Society (www.nzoss.org.nz) and the State Services Commission (www.scc.govt.nz) supports Government use of FOSS. Half of New Zealand's 20 largest organizations already deploy FOSS operating systems or applications.

Penetration levels are rising fast also in the public sector in Asia and Latin America (Munoz, 2011). Some studies point to even more FOSS use in Governments in selected developing countries, such as Argentina, Brazil and India, than in some developed countries (UNU-MERIT, 2007). In Taiwan Province of China, the Government supports FOSS activities and has developed a database of local FOSS experts that are developing web-based tools for FOSS licence agreements and encouraging the development and use of more open source software in Chinese (Orbicom and IDRC, 2010).[15] The Government of the Republic of Korea has made considerable investments to boost demand for FOSS through large-scale public projects.[16] In 2006, public organizations showed much higher rates of adoption than different parts of the private sector (see also chapter III).

In the Russian Federation, FOSS implementation is also encouraged and expanding. Unofficial estimates from OpenNet.ru suggest that the Russian market for FOSS was worth about $73 million in 2009. At the State level, support to FOSS implementation is provided under the Information Society State Programme. In 2009, the Ministry of Communication and Mass Media prepared the plan for FOSS implementation in public authorities and is working with the Ministry of Economic Development in this area. In 2011, the Ministry of Communication and Mass Media created the National Software Platform, a Linux-based prototype, under State contract with a local producer (Pingwinsoftware). The first steps for its implementation in federal agencies were scheduled to begin in the second half of 2012.

In the private sector, the past decade has also witnessed an increase in the use of FOSS. In a 2012 survey, the main drivers among enterprises for FOSS adoption were found to be freedom from vendor lock-in (60 per cent of respondents), lower acquisition and maintenance cost (51 per cent), better quality (43 per cent) and access to the source code (42 per cent).[17] Some of the leading players in the software and Internet technology industries, such as Google, Facebook

Box IV.7.	Expanding use of Linux among enterprises

A 2012 survey of Linux adoption trends among almost 2,000 enterprise users found that affinity among new and veteran Linux users continued to increase. Eighty-four per cent of organizations currently using Linux reported that they had expanded their usage over the past twelve months, and continued to rely on it as their preferred platform for greenfield deployments, as well as for mission-critical applications. Eight out of ten respondents said that they had added Linux servers in the last 12 months and planned to add more in the next 12 months, with the same number planning to add more Linux servers in the next five years. By comparison, only 22 per cent of respondents stated that they were planning an increase in Windows servers during the next five years. Total cost of ownership, features and overall security top Linux benefits. More than two-thirds of the respondents found Linux to be more secure than other operating systems.

Source: Linux Foundation (2012).

and Twitter, today rely on FOSS-based infrastructure. Major FOSS-focused companies have also evolved, such as Red Hat (the company behind Red Hat Linux, Fedora Linux and CentOS Linux operating systems and communities). As of January 2012, Red Hat had reached $1 billion in revenue. Linux use among enterprises appears set to expand further in the next few years (box IV.7).

Recent evidence on the impact of FOSS use suggests that the trend is likely to continue, in both developed and developing countries. A 2010 study on the impact of software predicted that the share of FOSS in the European software market would exceed five per cent in 2013 and continue to grow up to 2020 (Center for Strategic and International Studies, 2010). Studies in the United Republic of Tanzania and in Norway found that the positive effects of the use of FOSS had encouraged continued reliance on open source products in the public and private sectors (Lungo and Kaasbol, 2007). Despite different development and income levels, organizations achieved satisfactory results from using FOSS products, which were found to be cheaper and helped to avoid vendor lock-in. In another multi-country study, FOSS use in both developed and developing countries was found to have a positive impact on such factors as citizens having platform independent access to government services and the independent exchange of data between public administrations (UNU-MERIT, 2007).

2. Use by type of software/application

Whereas there is a general trend towards greater use of FOSS, the picture varies across areas of application. In the case of desktop operating systems, proprietary solutions retain a strong dominance. In fact, Linux still accounts for a mere 1 per cent of the total market, which is overwhelmingly controlled by Windows (table IV.2). During the past two years, only

small changes have been noticed and mainly in favour of Apple's Mac operating system. To a significant degree, the strong dominance of Windows can be linked to network effects. The software is compatible with a wide range of computer hardware and software, but there have also been incentives for hardware and software producers to ensure that their products are compatible with Windows. Such considerations tend to reinforce a strong market position.

In the server market, Linux has gained market shares in recent years. According to the International Data Corporation (IDC), in the last quarter of 2011, Linux market shares represented 18 per cent of all server revenue, up 1.7 points when compared with the fourth quarter of 2010.[18] Linux server demand has been impacted positively by high performance computing and growing reliance on cloud infrastructure. However, Windows servers still account for almost half of the quarterly factory revenue, up 2.6 points over the prior year's quarterly figure.

In the area of operating systems for mobile phones, the market has seen major shifts in recent years. In May 2010, Symbian (an open source-based system) was the top operating system with a market share of 33 per cent (table IV.3). By May 2012, its share had dropped to 20 per cent, while Android – based on

Table IV.2.	Desktop operating system market shares, March 2010 and February 2012	
	Market share (%)	
Desktop operating system	**March 2010**	**February 2012**
Windows	93.49	91.92
Apple Mac OS	5.44	6.92
Linux	1.05	1.16
Others	0.02	—

Source: Net Applications, March 2012.
Note: Refers to market share of all users.

Table IV.3. Mobile operating system market shares, May 2010 and May 2012		
	Market share (%)	
Mobile operating system	May 2010	May 2012
Android (FOSS)	3.94	23.81
iOS	29.01	22.95
Symbian (FOSS)	32.92	20.25
Series 40 (Nokia)	—	11.84
Samsung	2.86	7.18
Blackberry	14.15	5.65
Others	17.12	8.32

Source: StatCounter Global Stats (http://gs.statcounter.com), June 2012.
Note: These statistics are based on aggregate data collected on a sample exceeding 15 billion page views per month, collected from across a network of more than 3 million websites.

Table IV.4. Web server market, by application, May 2010 and May 2012		
	Market share (%)	
Web server developer	May 2010	May 2012
Apache	65.24	23.81
Microsoft	13.81	22.95
Nginx	10.15	20.25
Google	3.28	11.84

Source: Netcraft (http://news.netcraft.com/archives/2012/03/05/march-2012-web-server-survey.html).
Note: Refers to totals for active sites across all domains.

open source software supported by Google – had surged to the top position, accounting for one quarter of the market.[19] Meanwhile, the share of Apple's proprietary operating system, iOS, had dropped from 29 per cent to 23 per cent.

The Internet software and hardware infrastructure is extensively comprised of FOSS and open standards.[20] Similarly the infrastructure lying on top of the main protocols is also essentially FOSS based. For example, the Berkeley Internet Name Domain (BIND) is the most widely used Internet name system software, containing all the software needed to ask and answer questions on name services.[21] BIND is used across about 80 per cent of the Internet infrastructure for the domain name system.

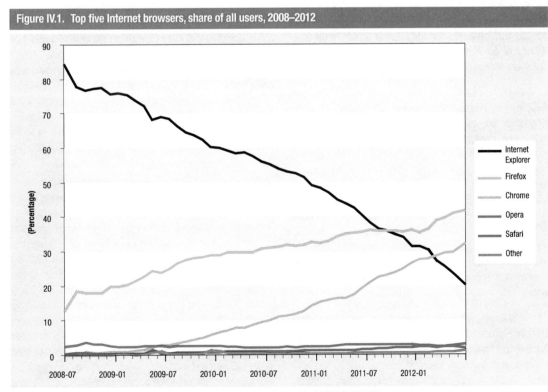

Figure IV.1. Top five Internet browsers, share of all users, 2008–2012

Source: StatCounter. See http://gs.statcounter.com/#browser-af-monthly-200807-201206.

Table IV.5. Examples of FOSS applications	
Area of application	**Example**
Linux distributions	Ubuntu, Fedora, RedHat, CentOS, Software und System Entwicklung (SUSE)
Web markup languages	HTML5
Open source database	MySQL, postgresSQL, NOSQL, SQL Lite
Integrated development environments	Eclipse
Integrated platforms	Linux Apache MySQL Python Perl PHP (LAMP)
Enterprise resource planning systems	OpenBravo, TinyERP
Content management systems	Wordpress, Drupal, Joomla, Alfresco
Education	Moodle, Open Educational Resources, Access to Knowledge A2K
Medical and health	OpenVista, OpenMER
Geographical information systems	Open Street Maps and Data
Disaster management	SAHANA
Electronic commerce	Magento, osCommerce, PrestaShop

Source: UNCTAD.

Web servers are the fundamental software infrastructure for hosting web pages and form another critical part of the Internet's software infrastructure layer. According to a March 2012 survey, there were 646 million websites hosted across the Internet, of which as many as 65 per cent were hosted on Apache, a FOSS-based web server (table IV.4). Apache has been the top web server across one million of the busiest websites since 2008. It is also widely used in the closed source and proprietary software industry.[22]

In the case of web browsers, Microsoft's Internet Explorer dominated the market for a long time, in large part due to the fact that it was delivered on the Windows desktop and server operating systems. However, in the past few years, the picture has changed considerably (figure IV.1). FOSS-based browsers, notably Mozilla Firefox and Google Chrome, have gained in popularity, particularly outside of North America. In Africa, for example, the combined share of Firefox and Chrome exceeded 70 per cent in May 2012. With the rapid diffusion of smartphones and mobile application platforms, more consumers are also expected to connect to the Internet from mobile devices.

Open source software applications have emerged in many areas other than those mentioned above. Table IV.5 provides selected example areas of applications, ranging from e-commerce to education and health applications. For almost all proprietary applications there is now an equivalent FOSS solution.[23]

The future of FOSS appears to be positive in terms of growth in innovative areas such as big data, where it is playing a significant role in managing large volumes of data through a number of platforms. Though currently the market stands at only $311 million in revenue, the industry sees great potential. Some observers predict that big data revenues will surpass $50 billion by 2017.[24] In a 2012 survey of enterprise end users, more than three quarters of respondents expressed a need to address big data, and nearly 72 per cent were choosing Linux to support it. Only 36 per cent were planning to use Windows to meet the demands of this new environment.[25] Similarly, open source software accounts for a growing market share in mobile applications. As of June 2012, there were about 443,000 apps in the Android market, of which three quarters could be downloaded for free.[26]

In summary, FOSS applications have emerged as first, second or third-rung products in terms of market share in several markets, including web servers, server operating systems, desktop operating systems, web browsers, databases, e-mail and other ICT infrastructure systems. FOSS market shares have seen considerable growth in the past few years. In general, FOSS adoption is the most widespread in Europe but there is growing interest in FOSS around the world, including in developing countries. Recent evidence from both developed and developing countries points to considerable benefits from greater reliance on FOSS. This and the fact that recent ICT areas (such as cloud computing and big data) are highly reliant on open source software suggest that the trend towards greater FOSS is likely to be sustained.

D. TRENDS IN FOSS PRODUCTION

Europe is the leading region in FOSS software developers collaborating globally, and leads in terms of global project leaders. Within Europe, FOSS is produced, distributed and supported by both enterprises and thousands of community members.[27] It has been estimated that the European software sector employs more than 2.75 million people and creates an added value of €180 billion.[28] Weighted by regional PC penetration, central Europe and Scandinavia provide disproportionately high numbers of developers (Ghosh, 2006). However, weighted by average income, India was the leading provider of FOSS developers followed by China. Asia and Latin America faced disadvantages at least partly due to language barriers, but may have an increasing share of developers active in local communities. Indeed, the possibility to develop and use software for application in local languages is an important advantage of FOSS.

In India, FOSS has been developed in all 22 Indian languages. This has also facilitated various innovations in hardware. A pioneering innovation addressing illiteracy and affordability was the simputer (simple computer) developed by the Indian Institute of Science in Bangalore. A more recent innovation is the development of Aakash, the world's cheapest tablet computer. With its touch screen, it resembles Apple's iPad but costs only $50. Developed by the Indian Institute of Technology and the Indian Institute of Science in Bangalore, the Aakash uses the Linux operating system and Open Office. One advantage is that it can use either solar panels, batteries or mains electricity as a source of power. It lacks a hard drive but there is access to a USB port, 2GB of memory and a video-conferencing facility as well as Internet browsing. Some 110 million Indian schoolchildren are expected to benefit from the tool.[29]

As stressed in earlier chapters, a wide range of tools and projects is available online. The global FOSS ecosystem has mainly evolved due to the Internet which continues to enable developers and contributors to connect online from across the world, assembling in groups and communities of learning and practice to share their contributions and build software. FOSS development online hubs include Github (github.com), Launchpad.net, Sourceforge.com and Codeplex.com.

An analysis of some freelancing job websites confirms that FOSS skills are in demand (table IV.6). There has been a clear increase in FOSS-related development

Table IV.6. Most requested skills on oDesk.com as of March 2012	
Requested area of skills	Number of jobs posted
PHP (FOSS)	141,086
SEO (search engine optimization)	103,028
HTML	103,028
English (lingual services)	90,847
Wordpress (FOSS)	83,377
CSS (cascading style sheets; open standard)	70,414
Photoshop (proprietary software)	61,814
MySQL (FOSS)	57,850
Javascript (open standard)	45,071
Writing (copywriting, content writing)	16,449

Source: https://www.odesk.com/oconomy and https://www.odesk.com/trends.

work, especially with regard to web and mobile phone applications. PHP and Android appear to be growing with an increasing interest in World Wide Web open standards platforms.[30] Across freelancing websites, there is significant participation of service providers and contractors from developing countries, primarily for work directed towards software and applications for users in developed countries. While FOSS is witnessing more demand, several closed source and proprietary software products appear to be facing declining interest. For example, according to Freelance.com's quarterly Freelancer Fast 50 reports (2012), Windows desktop jobs fell by 37 per cent, and Microsoft jobs were down by 39 per cent. However, the demand for work on proprietary software applications for the iPhone and iPad remains strong.

The open source software community expects their activities to be influenced be recent technology trends. In a 2012 survey of vendors and users of software, cloud computing, mobile applications and mobile enterprises were cited most often as areas where an increased use of open source software was expected.[31] Much of the current cloud infrastructure is based on open source software. At the same time, the cloud can be used for the development of open source software. For example, Canonical has innovated by directly building cloud capabilities into its Ubuntu Server platform.[32] It also offers a developer store platform built on top of its application store, Ubuntu Software Center.[33] The Ubuntu App Developer allows developers anywhere in the world to develop Linux applications for the Ubuntu platform and make them available either for a fee or free of cost. These applications are directly downloadable to the Ubuntu Linux Desktop and Server platforms.

E. TRENDS IN POLICIES SUPPORTING OPEN SOURCE SOFTWARE

Global surveys of FOSS policies have been carried out by the Center for Strategic and International Studies (CSIS) for about a decade.[34] FOSS policies are grouped into four categories, that is R&D, mandates (where the use of FOSS is required), preferences (where the use of FOSS is given preference, but not mandated), and advisory (where the use of FOSS is permitted). The surveys show whether an initiative has been made at the national, regional or local level and whether it has been accepted, is under consideration or has been rejected. In its 2010 edition, the survey tracked a total of 354 governmental policies (based on explicit statements of policy, excluding decisions to use or purchase FOSS) (CSIS, 2010). For the period 2000–2009, 235 national FOSS initiatives and 119 state or local initiatives were identified. Most were associated with giving preference to FOSS.

Of the total 354 open source initiatives identified during the period 2000–2009, 69 per cent had been approved, 9 per cent had failed and the rest remained as proposals (table IV.7). The failure rate was the highest for initiatives aimed at making FOSS use mandatory and the lowest for R&D-related initiatives.

There is considerable regional variation in the intensity of FOSS policy activity, according to the survey. Europe is the most active region, accounting for close to half (46 per cent) of all initiatives and with a high proportion of approved initiatives (table IV.8). Among developing regions, Asia is the front-runner with more than 80 initiatives, followed by Latin America (57) and Africa (9).

During the past decade, both developed and developing countries invested considerable resources in defining and implementing an enabling environment for FOSS. Efforts have been made towards levelling the playing field for FOSS by various Governments. In the United Kingdom, for example, the Government

Table IV.7. Open source policy initiatives, 2000–2009				
	Approved	**Proposed**	**Failed**	**Total**
R&D	81	9	2	92
Advisory	70	19	4	93
Preference	78	27	10	115
Mandatory	16	21	17	54
Total	245	76	33	354

Source: CSIS, 2010.

Table IV.8. Open source policy initiatives, by region, 2000–2009				
	Approved	**Proposed**	**Failed**	**Total**
Europe	126	27	10	163
Asia	59	20	2	81
Latin America and the Caribbean	31	15	11	57
North America	16	11	10	37
Africa	8	1	—	9
Middle East	5	2	—	7

Source: CSIS, 2010.
Note: Regional distribution does not include initiatives from the United Nations or the OECD. Multinational initiatives were counted for each region represented.

has identified the need to reduce costs of public IT systems and to increase supplier diversity in existing procurement contracts. In response, the Cabinet Office is looking at open standards as a means of increasing flexibility and efficiency in Government IT spending.[35] Malaysia has adopted a comprehensive, long-term programme for evolving a parallel open software ecosystem. This effort has helped the Government move significantly towards self-reliance (box IV.8). Such examples may inspire other countries, although the approach chosen would need to be adapted to the specific social, economic and political situation.

A number of regional policy decisions have also been taken to support the use and uptake of FOSS. In Latin America, for example, the Southern Common Market (MERCOSUR) Summit in July 2009 issued a declaration which, among other things, proposed that Governments of its member States adopt policies fostering free and open technologies such as FOSS.[36]

Several initiatives have also been launched, not least in Africa, to support capacity-building, development and usage, educational and business applications, advocacy campaigns, policy implementation and related R&D activities. The following initiatives and others may suggest a gradual but significant trend towards greater reliance on FOSS in Africa and other parts of the developing world:[37]

• The Free Software and Open Source Foundation for Africa (FOSSFA) is a nonprofit pan-African organization with a mission that includes promoting the use and adoption of FOSS in Africa (box IV.9).

• The GIZ programme it@foss has established more than 12 regional expert communities of FOSS

Box IV.8.   The Malaysian Public Sector Open Source Software Programme

The Malaysian Public Sector Open Source Software Master Plan was launched in 2004 to create and enhance value using open source software within the public sector ICT framework. Its main objectives included reducing the total cost of ownership, increasing freedom of choice of software, enhancing interoperability among systems, supporting the growth of the domestic ICT and open source software industry, promoting a knowledge-based society and narrowing the digital divide.

The Master Plan outlined a long-term roadmap comprising three phases to achieve the open source software vision and objectives. Phase I (Laying Foundation and Early Adoption) and Phase II (Accelerated Adoption) were successfully completed in the period 2007–2010. In 2011, the project entered into Phase III (Self Reliance), during which ministries and agencies are expected to champion open source software initiatives to enhance and discover new development projects on application solutions that are unique and aligned to their respective operations and constituency needs.

The Malaysian Administrative Modernization and Management Planning Unit was tasked to establish and operate a new Open Source Competency Centre. This is now the single point of reference to guide, facilitate, coordinate and monitor the implementation of open source software in the public sector. In 2008, the Government of Malaysia claimed it had saved RM40 million ($13 million) from open source software adoption. Savings on licensing fees alone by adopting Open Office.org on 12,760 seats in public agencies had already exceeded RM12 million ($3.9 million). Other open source software projects with substantial savings have been implemented, for example, in the Ministry of Health and the Terengganu State Economic Development Corporation.

As of 2009, more than 70 per cent of Malaysian Government offices were reported to be running open source software. In July 2009, 521 of the country's 724 public sector agencies (72 per cent) had adopted open source software, up from 163 agencies in 2007. As of 2011, other important milestones had been achieved:

- 80 per cent of public sector IT personnel had been trained in open source software (5 per cent were certified and had achieved recognition of certification by an international body).
- 97 per cent of public sector agencies were using open source software.
- 51 per cent of all web servers in public sector agencies were using open source software.
- 42 per cent of web operating systems in public sector agencies were using open source software.
- 30 per cent of agencies were using open source software desktop solutions.
- 30 per cent of institutes of higher learning participated in a certified training provider programme.
- 50 per cent of local IT vendors were providing open source software services.

The continued implementation of the Malaysian Public Sector Open Source Software Master Plan is expected to generate a variety of development gains for the country. For the medium term (2013–2015), a new partnership collaboration platform and ecosystem will be established to promote open source software innovation. The Government also expects to see the production of agency-specific, enhanced application solutions using open source software and the development of new open source software products for both domestic and global use. The longer-term vision (2016–2020) is to make Malaysia a key contributor to global open source software development and an exporter, rather than an importer, of software technology.

Source: UNCTAD, based on information from the Open Source Competency Centre (http://www.oscc.org.my) and the Malaysian Administrative Modernization and Management Planning Unit (http://www.mampu.gov.my/web/bi_mampu/eng_opensource).

multipliers from Cambodia, Indonesia, the Lao People's Democratic Republic, the Philippines and Viet Nam. These communities exchange experiences of their respective IT sectors through peer-to-peer learning activities.[38]

- The Open Society Initiative for Southern Africa seeks to promote and sustain the ideals, values, institutions and practices of an open society.
- The African Virtual Open Initiatives and Resources (AVOIR) is a network of institutions for developing

FOSS and capacity-building in software engineering.

- The African Network for Localization aims to include African people in the digital age by supporting the adaptation of ICT to local languages and culture.
- The Ghana-India Kofi Annan Centre of Excellence in ICT is a capacity-building and training facility that stimulates the growth of the ICT sector, including FOSS, in the Economic Community of West African States.

Box IV.9. The Free Software and Open Source Foundation for Africa

The Free Software and Open Source Foundation for Africa (FOSSFA) was launched in 2003, during a preparatory committee meeting for the World Summit on the Information Society (WSIS). It is a membership organization, consisting of individuals, organizations, government agencies and other partners. Its vision is to promote the use of FOSS and related business models to increase productivity and reduce costs in Africa. To this end, FOSSFA serves as an umbrella organization for FOSS organizations in Africa, creates awareness, sensitizes the public and advocates for FOSS use. The organization helps build capacity in FOSS, facilitates networking and partnering with academia, governments, computer software organizations, the private sector and development partners. In the almost 10 years since its inception, FOSSFA has grown to about 500 members (individuals and organizations) and has many partners.

Largely thanks to the advocacy work of FOSSFA, among its significant contributions are that both the African Union and the Common Market for Eastern and Southern Africa (COMESA) have adopted pro-FOSS policies. In addition, senior government officials now care more about FOSS and the media frequently reports on FOSS-related matters. Through more than 30 sessions, FOSSFA has also trained over 2,000 journalists, students, medical experts, developers, management experts and others on the role of FOSS tools for professional use. Trainings on FOSS business models have graduated 100 trainers who are now rolling out national trainings on wealth creation with FOSS. In addition, FOSSFA has attracted new capacity-building partners, such as the Linux Professional Institute (see chapter V), DiploFoundation (www.diplomacy.edu) and ict@innovation (see box IV.5). In terms of networking, FOSSFA has organized five African FOSS meetings (Idlelos) and it manages a vibrant online FOSS community.

These achievements notwithstanding, FOSSFA also faces challenges, such as inadequate resources and capacity, heavy reliance on volunteers and an uphill battle against the intense lobbying and marketing activities of proprietary software vendors. FOSSFA is advocating several steps to improve this situation. First, African policymakers should ensure that government officials in public procurement, competition and other relevant areas have sufficient knowledge of FOSS to take informed decisions. Secondly, national ICT policies, laws and regulations should be reviewed to ensure that FOSS receives treatment that is equal to that for proprietary software. Finally, policymakers should benchmark their FOSS implementation internationally and participate in South-South cooperation.

FOSSFA sees important roles for development partners, such as adopting transparent FOSS policies, and participating in and supporting FOSS initiatives in Africa. Furthermore, development partners could also participate in knowledge-sharing and be more transparent in the support they provide. The private sector is also an important stakeholder. According to FOSSFA, business users could do more to learn about and benefit from FOSS and private sector ICT providers could offer FOSS training, develop FOSS-based solutions and engage in international FOSS-related cooperation.

Source: FOSSFA (www.fossfa.net).

F. CONCLUSIONS

The spread of FOSS solutions illustrates its growing importance in the global software arena. Data from various private sources and anecdotal evidence confirm that FOSS is coming of age. This trend has various implications, including the reduction of the market power of proprietary software manufacturers and greater reliance on collaborative software development. Furthermore, demand from Europe as well as North America for expertise in FOSS applications is increasing, affecting the market for freelancing.

For software enterprises from developing and transition economies, FOSS offers several opportunities. FOSS can promote domestic software market development and local innovation. Rather than purchasing software licences and services abroad, local FOSS development, sales and services can help keep resources within the

local economy, avoid dependency on specific vendors and provide opportunities for income generation and employment. When based on FOSS, local software companies may be in a better position to develop innovative and cost-effective solutions that are customized to meet specific needs in the domestic market. As noted earlier, such capabilities are essential to seize full development benefits from improved access to ICTs. FOSS also provides the chance to develop innovative software products that are independent of the technical standards of large-scale software manufacturers. FOSS can also enable micro and small local software enterprises in developing countries to establish new niche markets. To capitalize on such opportunities, they need to acquire know-how on FOSS technologies and business models.

FOSS provides new business opportunities in developing countries and can help empower communities to be less technologically dependent. The role of Governments in this regard is important because making correct choices requires taking into account the necessary linkages between all sectors and the overarching ICT policy. Recent technological trends, especially with regard to cloud computing, mobile applications and big data, are set to further accentuate the reliance on FOSS. Governments and their development partners should therefore give adequate attention to this area when designing and implementing strategies aimed at fostering software capabilities and their national software systems (see chapter V).

NOTES

1 The report was followed up with an Expert Meeting on Free and Open Source Software: Policy and Development Implications, held in Geneva, 22–24 September 2004.

2 See http://www.gnu.org/philosophy/free-sw.html.

3 See Open Source Software versus Free Software. http://en.wikipedia.org/wiki/Open_source_software#Open_source_software_versus_free_software.

4 For more information, see http://opensource.org.

5 See http://www.gnu.org/philosophy/free-sw.html.

6 Affero is a privately held company headquartered in San Francisco, California, that hosts personal web pages for authors (http://www.affero.com/ca.html).

7 Metz, C (15 February 2012). Open sources drop software religion for common sense. *Wired* (http://www.wired.com/wiredenterprise/2012/02/cloudera-and-apache/all/1).

8 Examples of FOSS vendors that have implemented these programmes and projects for governments, private sector or academia can be found from Canonical (http://www.canonical.com/about-canonical/resources/case-studies) and RedHat (http://www.redhat.com/resourcelibrary/case-studies).

9 A similar argument can be made with regard to business security considerations.

10 A community may stop supporting an open source software, especially if only a few persons are involved in its development, but it would still be possible to further develop the code. For projects with a large community and hundreds of developers (like Ubuntu), it is unlikely that the project would not ultimately be supported by the community.

11 See Future of open source survey highlights progress, changes, challenges (22 May 2012). *451 CAOS Theory*. It should be noted that such business models can also be built around proprietary software.

12 See Chairperson's summary, Expert Meeting on Free and Open-Source Software: Policy and Development Implications Geneva, 22–24 September 2004, TD/B/COM.3/EM.21/3, 29 October 2004 (http://unctad.org/en/docs/c3em21d3_en.pdf).

13 In Vienna, however, which first chose to start migrating its desktop PCs to Debian-based Wienux, the idea was abandoned because the necessary software was incompatible with Linux (see http://www.freesoftwaremagazine.com/articles/vienna_failed_to_migrate_to_linux_why).

14 See http://www.digital-review.org/uploads/files/pdf/2009-2010/chap-34_new_zealand.pdf.

15 See http://www.digital-review.org/uploads/files/pdf/2009-2010/chap-39_taiwan.pdf.

16 See http://www.digital-review.org/uploads/files/pdf/2009-2010/chap-26_korea_republic.pdf.

17 See "Future of open source survey highlights progress, changes, challenges", *451 CAOS Theory*, 22 May 2012.

18 See http://www.techpowerup.com/161448/IDC-Worldwide-Server-Market-Revenues-Increase-5.8-in-2011.html.

19 In 2011, Android accounted for almost 50 per cent of all smartphones shipped worldwide. See http://mobithinking.com/mobile-marketing-tools/latest-mobile-stats.

20 The Internet Protocol is the set of communications protocols used for the Internet and similar networks. Its most important protocols are the Transmission Control Protocol (TCP) and the Internet Protocol (IP), which were the first networking protocols defined in this standard. This is commonly known as TCP/IP, which stands as an open standard.

21 BIND originated in the early 1980s at the University of California at Berkeley and is an implementation of the Domain Name System (DNS) protocols, which are part of the core standards for the Internet. See http://www.isc.org/software/bind.

22 For example, Oracle Corporation bundles Apache Tomcat web server as part of its relational database offering. Similarly, a multitude of software technology and platforms employ Apache as part of their core service infrastructure.

23 See also the list developed by InWEnt and the International Open Source Network Asean+3of applications for SME: http://fosstoolkit.iosnasean.net.

24 See Big Data Is Big Market & Big Business – $50 Billion Market by 2017. http://www.forbes.com/sites/siliconangle/2012/02/17/big-data-is-big-market-big-business/2/. See also http://wikibon.org/wiki/v/Big_Data_Market_Size_and_Vendor_Revenues.

25 See Linux Foundation and Yeoman Technology Group, 2012. http://go.linuxfoundation.org/l/6342/ux-adoption-trends-report-2012/7l4j7.

26 AppBrain. Distribution of free vs. paid Android apps. http://www.appbrain.com/stats/free-and-paid-android-applications.

27 See Policy Recommendation Paper, 2. OSEPA-Open Source software usage by European Public Administrations. INTERREG IVC, 0918R2. 4.11.2011. CP3 Exchange of experiences. University of Sheffield. http://osepa.eu/pdeliverables/TAL33B_3%207%202_OSEPA_PolicyRecommPaper2.pdf.

28 Economic and Social Impact of Software & Software-Based Services Smart 2009/0041 August 2010. The project "The economic and social impacts of Software and Software based Services" analysed and assessed the development of the European Software Market and Industry and its impact on the economic growth and employment from today to 2020 (http://cordis.europa.eu/fp7/ict/ssai/docs/study-sw-report-final.pdf). All reports are available on the project website: http://cordis.europa.eu/fp7/ict/ssai/study-sw-2009_en.html.

29 See http://www.guardian.co.uk/world/2010/jul/23/india-unveils-cheapest-laptop.

30 According to Elance's Global Online Employment Report for the first quarter of 2012, FOSS technologies and platforms were among the top IT skills in demand, especially Android, PHP and Javascript, which all grew by more than 30 per cent (https://www.elance.com/q/online-employment-report). Job announcements related to open-source applications on Freelancer.com also grew rapidly in 2011.

31 See Future of open source survey highlights progress, changes, challenges, *451 CAOS Theory*, 22 May 2012.

32 Ubuntu Linux Cloud (http://www.ubuntu.com/download/cloud).

33 Ubuntu Software Center (https://wiki.ubuntu.com/SoftwareCenter).

34 For more information, see http://csis.org/files/publication/100416_Open_Source_Policies.pdf.

35 See Open Standards: Open Opportunities – Flexibility and efficiency in Government IT, Cabinet Office, United Kingdom. 2012. Formal consultation on the definition and mandating of open standards for software interoperability, data and document formats in Government IT.http://www.cabinetoffice.gov.uk/resource-library/open-standards-open-opportunities-flexibility-and-efficiency-government-it.

36 See http://www.solar.org.ar/spip.php?article617.

37 See http://unu.edu/articles/science-technology-society/free-and-open-source-software-in-sub-saharan-africa.

38 See http://www.it-foss.net/e3076/index_eng.html.

POLICIES TO ENABLE NATIONAL SOFTWARE SYSTEMS

5

Making effective use of opportunities created by the evolving ICT landscape is a priority task for most developing countries. ICTs are increasingly recognized as a vehicle to improve the provision of government services, health care, education and essential information, including in low-income economies. At the same time, in order to seize the full potential of ICTs, developing countries need to go beyond simply relying on imports of technologies developed abroad. Building relevant domestic capabilities in the ICT producing sector is essential for ICT services and applications to be appropriately adapted to the prevailing realities in each context. As software constitutes the brain of ICT devices, nurturing capabilities in this area is particularly relevant.

This chapter discusses policy options that Governments should consider to accelerate the development of domestic software capabilities and a stronger national software system with a view to making ICTs a more effective enabler of development. While not every country may become a successful exporter of software, all countries need certain domestic software capabilities to achieve an inclusive information society. Compared with only a few years ago, there is greater scope for policymakers to catalyse progress in this area through a clear vision and supportive policies, laws and regulations. Other stakeholders – donors, the private sector and civil society – should also contribute to this process.

A. MAKING SOFTWARE A POLICY PRIORITY

It is necessary for countries to build domestic capabilities that allow individual, firms and organizations to engage in learning processes in order to facilitate structural transformation and be technologically up to date (Nelson, 2008; Cimoli et al., 2009). Governments should seek to adopt policies that can help expand such learning especially in new industries that offer wide learning opportunities (Cimoli et al., 2009). The software industry represents a good example. As a general purpose technology, software has applications throughout the economy and society. It also has relatively low entry barriers and is likely to remain highly relevant in the future.

The national software system introduced in chapter I can serve as a useful framework for governments to identify areas to address that foster relevant capabilities at the individual, firm and organizational levels. As depicted in figure I.3, the national vision, strategies and government policies influence the development of the system. In fact, in most countries that have successfully managed to nurture domestic software capabilities and a competitive software industry, active government involvement was instrumental, especially at the early stages of development (chapter I). Similarly, in most of the cases reviewed in chapter III as well as in countries found in the top right quadrant in figure II.9 – such as Argentina (box V.1) and Malaysia (box IV.8) – Governments have taken a proactive stance to strengthening the national software system.

A prime role of Government is to catalyse an effective policy process (Rodrik, 2004) and constructive dialogue with other stakeholders in the national software system. As part of a process to develop a national strategy, Governments should play the role of a proactive coordinator rather than seeking to impose a top-down vision (Nicholson and Sahay, 2009). The strategy may include guidelines and a road map for effective cooperation and development. Information from other stakeholders about both opportunities and bottlenecks is crucial in order to allow policymakers to make the right policy choices. This is especially true in the area of ICT and software which is rapidly evolving. There is a need for continuous adaptation to changing market conditions and emerging technology trends (for example, related to FOSS, mobile applications, cloud computing and Web 2.0 technologies).

Policy areas to consider include the quality and availability of key supporting factors – such as infrastructure, human resources, an enabling business environment and an adequate legal framework – as well as those that can facilitate greater interaction between software producers and users, and between domestic and international networks. Given the cross-cutting and multipurpose nature of software, with consequences for both public service delivery and business competitiveness, it is important to integrate the strategy effectively into the overall development plan. A detailed implementation plan should also be crafted for the execution, monitoring and evaluation of the strategy.[1]

The appropriate approach to developing software capabilities has to be carefully adapted to the specific context, based on the prevailing realities of each country. When designing the strategy, a natural starting point is to identify the development objectives towards which it should contribute. At this stage, a series of questions can be raised. What are the current status, strengths and weaknesses of the national software system? Who are the main potential users of the software developed or distributed locally? How much emphasis should be given to export promotion as opposed to servicing domestic market needs? What weight should be given to different types of software? What are the main barriers facing enterprises and other stakeholders involved in the national software system?

Surveying the local software industry can generate valuable inputs to some of the questions posed above. The UNCTAD–WITSA Survey of IT/Software Associations (box V.2) conducted for this report found that most such associations actively contribute to the process of national policymaking (figure V.1). All responding associations support national policy formulation and engage in policy advocacy and lobbying. The country studies in chapter III confirmed that such associations play an active role in the national software system.

Inputs from industry associations can also help to identify priority areas for policy interventions. In the UNCTAD–WITSA Survey, associations were asked to identify the main barriers for the growth and development of the software and IT services industry in their respective countries. The factor mentioned by the largest number of respondents was limited access to venture capital, followed by shortages of qualified people and a lack of government procurement (table V.1).

Box V.1.   Software promotion in Argentina

Argentina is among the developing countries that have relatively high domestic spending on computer software and services as well as significant software exports (chapter II). The Government of Argentina regards the software sector as a value added service export as well as of strategic importance to the country.It is working on promoting the industry in close partnership with the private sector to provide a more enabling environment.

Before the economic crisis (1999–2002), Argentina's software sector focused primarily on providing services to domestic institutions and companies. After a significant devaluation of the peso in 2002, exports surged from 17 per cent to 26 per cent of total software sales, with exports valued at $775 million in 2011. During the same period, the number of people working in the sector rose from 20,000 to 56,000 people. This strong performance has been facilitated by the more competitive cost situation, time zone compatibility with the United States of America, the high quality of human resources and Government policies. In addition, new software start-ups have taken advantage of growing use of the Internet and opportunities created around online and cloud-based services.

Soon after the devaluation, the Government, local companies, chambers of commerce and others came together to develop a strategic plan for the development of the software and IT sector in Argentina. This resulted in a 10-year plan (2004–2014) aimed at making the national software system more competitive internationally. The software law of 2004 (Law 25.922) provides tax incentives and other benefits to legal entities established or operating in Argentina, as long as they export software services, pursue quality certifications and dedicate efforts to R&D. In 2011, Law 26.692 modified some of the measures and extended certain tax benefits targeting the software industry until the end of 2019. Entities that meet the conditions under the software industry promotion regime are exempt from withholding tax and value added tax. In addition, they are allowed a 60 per cent income tax reduction for certain software-related activities.

In the area of human resources, the Government is promoting higher level education and offers incentives to young students who pursue IT-related careers. Incentives are promoted by the Ministry of Labour jointly with the national Software Chamber of Commerce and selected universities. Some companies also actively support the initiative. University students pursuing engineering or other scientific careers, including software and networking certification studies, can apply for special scholarships. Various training programmes are organized and financed by the Ministry of Education with private sector support. According to the Government, some 80,000 students are enrolled in IT courses offered by 77 different educational centres across the country.

In order to boost ICT usage, a national plan, Argentina conectada, intends to build a nationwide fibre-optic network for national backbone Internet access, including in rural and semirural areas. Meanwhile, another state policy, Conectar Igualdad, set out to distribute three million netbooks in the 2010–2012 period to each student and teacher at public high schools, special education schools and teacher training institutes.[a]

In regards to innovation, the Ministry for Science and Technology funds basic and applied science, including software-related research. A dedicated Trust Fund for the Promotion of the Software Industry (FONSOFT) has been established. Managed by the National Agency of Scientific and Technological Promotion, it supports R&D projects, professional training, quality improvement and start-ups. It targets individuals as well as new firms. Financial support includes a subsidy of $45,000 to be executed over a two-year period. Activities eligible for funding include hiring professional services, obtaining technical assistance and a certain proportion of the entrepreneurs' salaries. Since its inception, more than 330 proposals have been approved, totalling $7.8 million in funding.[b]

FONSOFT also has non-reimbursable grants for innovative firms in the software industry. These grants finance quality certification processes, product and process development and pre-competitive R&D. The grants have a maximum amount of $150,000 and should not exceed 50 per cent of the total value of the project. The remaining share must be invested by the beneficiary. More than 540 projects have received funding, at a total of $12 million, through this programme.[c]

Source: UNCTAD, based on data and information provided by the Government of Argentina, (Argentina, Ministry of Economy and Production, 2004) and Proposals for an Action Plan 2008–2011, CESSI, Cámara de Empresas de Software y Servicios Informáticos, September 2009 (http://www.cessi.org.ar).

[a]   See http://www.conectarigualdad.gob.ar/ingles/about-the-program-2/what-is-conectar-igualdad/.

[b]   See http://sites.kauffman.org/irpr/resources/Kantis,%20Hugo%20-%20Entrepreneurial%20Ecosystems%20in%20 Latin%20America.pdf.

[c]   Ibid.

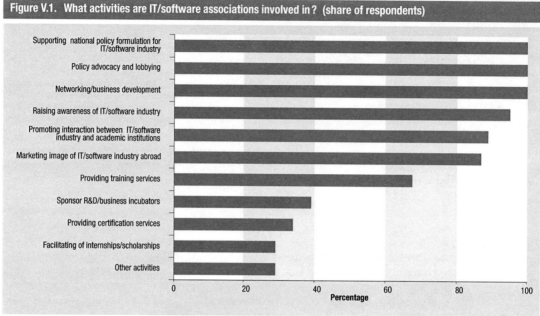

Figure V.1. What activities are IT/software associations involved in? (share of respondents)

Source: UNCTAD–WITSA Survey of IT/Software Associations, 2012.
Note: Based on responses from 38 associations.

Regional differences exist. For example, whereas none of the associations in developed economies identified software piracy as a barrier, this factor was highlighted by almost half of those in Latin America and the Caribbean. Venture capital was the top rated barrier in all regions except in Asia and the Pacific, where access to skills was the most often mentioned barrier. In the Middle East and Africa, more than 70 per cent of respondents found that the lack of public procurement constituted a barrier – reflecting the role of Government as a potential creator of demand in these economies.

A common challenge, especially in low-income countries, is the lack of reliable data that can be used as a basis for informed policymaking. This is another area in which collaboration with the private sector can help. As noted in chapter II, few countries compile official data on the size and composition of the software sector. However, the UNCTAD–WITSA Survey found that two-

thirds of the associations survey their members regularly and almost half of them do so at least annually. A relatively large share (31 per cent) of the associations does not yet survey their members. With a view to enhancing wider availability of internationally comparable data, the IT Industry Barometer may serve as a useful platform (box V.3).

In the remainder of this chapter, attention is given to selected policy areas relevant to developing domestic capabilities needed in the national software system. Although the framework can be applied to countries at all levels of development, the emphasis on different parts of the software system and policy choices must be adapted to the circumstances and priorities of each country. Section B discusses policies to support the local software industry. Section C explores the role of public procurement. Skills development is considered in section D, while selected aspects of the legal and regulatory framework are addressed in section E.

Box V.2. The UNCTAD–WITSA Survey of IT/software associations

The survey was conducted in March–April 2012. Out of 80 associations invited to participate, 38 respondents completed the online questionnaire. The countries represented through these associations account for more than half of global spending on software and IT services and more than half of all ICT spending. Eight of the respondents were based in a developed country, 26 in a developing country and the remaining four in a transition economy. Three LDCs were included (Bangladesh, the Gambia and Haiti).

Source: UNCTAD.

Table V.1.   Main barriers to the growth and development of the software and IT services industry (share in percentage of respondents mentioning factor)

Barrier	Developed economies	Asia-Pacific*	LAC**	Middle East and Africa	Transition economies	All regions
Limited capabilities in domestic software/ IT services companies	13	38	45	43	50	34
Lack of qualified human resources	63	63	55	43	75	56
Limited access to venture capital	63	50	73	86	75	66
Weak demand among private enterprises for software and IT services	25	25	18	57	50	29
Lack of government procurement of software and IT services	13	50	45	71	50	44
Limited demand from export markets	13	25	18	29	25	22
Inadequate protection of intellectual property rights	25	25	27	14	—	22
High rates of software piracy	—	13	45	29	25	24
Unfavourable general business climate	13	13	27	14	50	20

Source: UNCTAD–WITSA Survey of IT/Software Associations, 2012.
Note: * Excluding West Asia; ** Latin America and the Caribbean. Based on 38 responses.

Box V.3.   The IT Industry Barometer – a tool to improve data availability

As noted in chapter II, detailed information on the software sector in developing countries, and especially in low-income countries, is generally unavailable. Moreover, to the extent that private market research companies collect such information, the analysis and data sets published are often too expensive for many developing country institutions. Information collected by industry associations can thus be a valuable input into the policy formulation related to the development of national software systems. Some associations are already gathering various data from their members, while others have yet to start.

From a policy perspective, access to internationally harmonized time series data is desirable to allow for benchmarking against other countries and to monitor developments over time. Information on the composition, capabilities and size of the software and IT services production sector is of value. Such information can serve as a basis for assessing the economic impact of the sector and when considering new public procurement of software and IT services.

In this context, the IT Industry Barometer developed by GIZ could be considered by software associations (Germany, Federal Ministry for Economic Cooperation and Development, 2011b). This web-based tool is designed to gather and analyse both quantitative and qualitative information on the IT industry and to identify relevant market and industry trends. It covers topics such as general company information (products/services, certification, etc.), statistics (for example, turnover, exports), human resources (for example, employment, salary structures), forecasts and current subjects and concerns (feedback function for companies). The IT Industry Barometer can help to monitor and evaluate the sector as well as provide statistical information for research and economic planning purposes. The IT Industry Barometer has already been applied by software associations in some developing and transition economies, such as El Salvador, Guatemala, Honduras and the former Yugoslav Republic of Macedonia.

A possible solution to the overall problem of missing and inconsistent statistics on software industries in developing and transition economies could be to further develop the IT Industry Barometer with a view to promoting its use on a global level as a step towards an internationally harmonized and standardized approach. As the agency responsible for ICT sector measurement within the Partnership on Measuring ICT for Development, UNCTAD intends to explore this possibility with relevant stakeholders in the coming year.

Source: UNCTAD.

B. STRENGTHENING THE CAPABILITIES OF THE LOCAL SOFTWARE INDUSTRY AND DEVELOPER COMMUNITY

The structure and capabilities of the local software industry are central to the ability of a country to supply the software services and products required in different areas. In order to facilitate new start-up firms in this industry as well as the upgrading and growth of software SMEs, Governments can seek to ensure a competitive general business environment, promote upgrading through quality certification, improve access to finance and establish software or technology parks.

1. Creating an enabling business environment

The general business environment is a key factor influencing the ability of the software industry to develop. Moreover, about a fifth of the software associations surveyed for this report stressed that the general business environment in their countries constituted a barrier to growth. Given the variety of issues that can be considered under such a broad area, a discussion of relevant policy options needs to remain fairly general.

The status of the ICT infrastructure was noted in chapter II to be of high relevance. Access to adequate and affordable ICT infrastructure (notably national and international broadband connectivity) is essential for the development of the software industry. This involves consideration of the role of network operators, Internet exchange points, data centres and related regulation. While it is beyond the scope of this report to discuss related policies for broadband development in detail, several publications from international organizations address this topic in detail.[2]

Technology parks, innovation hubs and incubators are sometimes set up with the aim of making it easier for software enterprises to get started, innovate and expand (see also chapter III). Such facilities are of particular value when weak basic infrastructure (electricity, broadband connectivity) represents an obstacle to business development. In these instances, the establishment of specialized parks, centres or labs tailored to software development and ICT can

become a short cut to creating a more enabling business environment in which small companies and individual developers may interact and learn from each other. Co-location of software skills and enterprises can spur innovation and cross-fertilization between enterprises and the developer community. Facilitating the creation of informal networks can also facilitate transfers of tacit knowledge among software producers and users.

Government initiatives in this area have been used in several countries that have successfully developed software capabilities (see also chapter III).[3] They have helped to overcome basic infrastructure shortages, reduced red tape, offered incentives and facilitated exports. When designing a national software strategy, Governments should take into account the tendency among software enterprises and developers to cluster into certain locations. In India, Bangalore was the location of the first software centre, followed by others such as New Delhi, Chennai, Hyderabad, Pune, Mumbai and Kolkata.[4] Similar agglomeration trends have also been observed, for example, in Argentina, Brazil, China, Costa Rica and Kenya. At the same time, Governments may want to avoid enclave-type situations, with limited interaction between enterprises operating inside and stakeholders on the outside of the dedicated premises. The setting up of parks, hubs or labs to provide adequate facilities should ideally be located close to, and have interaction with, relevant centres of learning to build up mutual interaction and domestic technological capability in the long term. Such agglomeration economies may become less important as more software development work gets distributed over online platforms.

It should be kept in mind that the most successful business clusters have emerged spontaneously (Tessler et al., 2002). By far, most government- or donor-funded incubators or technology parks do not become success cases. Conversely, not all labs have been set up by Governments. In Guatemala, for example, Campus Tecnológico – a single building with workspaces and programming classes – was established by an Internet entrepreneur who returned from Silicon Valley and now hosts a number of entrepreneurial start-up software firms.[5] Such market-driven initiatives may stand a better chance of long-term success, although governments may have an important role in acting as a catalyst. Meanwhile, there is a need for more systematic impact assessments of factors determining the rate of success of incubators, technology parks and software labs.

Box V.4.	**Android for Developing initiative in Africa**

In Africa, mobile apps development is supported by an initiative led by Fraunhofer Portugal Research Center for Assistive In-formation and Communication Solutions (Fraunhofer Portugal AICOS) – a non-profit applied research centre – in collaboration with local academic, industrial and civil society partners. Android for Developing, a pilot project, was launched in Mozambique in 2010 and is expected to be replicated and further developed in other contexts. The pilot project is part of the first phase of cooperation between Fraunhofer Portugal AICOS and its African partners aimed at fostering the joint development of high technology products that can respond to local demand and thereby have a potential to become commercially viable.

For Android for Developing, strengthening the capacity of local developers and entrepreneurs is essential to ensure that innovative software solutions take into account relevant legislative, cultural, social and physical environments. The open source Android platform was chosen as it enables powerful applications for smartphones. Moreover, Android applications are programmed in Java, a widely used, standard programming language. Finally, low-cost Android devices are appearing in the African market, with prices under $80 and expected to decline further.

The first part of the initiative was implemented in Maputo from March to November 2010. Together with the Centro de Informática da Universidade Eduardo Mondlane, PT Inovação and SAP Research South Africa, Fraunhofer Portugal AICOS invited university students to submit ideas for mobile applications. Some 25 proposals were received, many of which related to software applications for microenterprises and for the management of personal finances. The four most promising ones in terms of marketing were given financial, technical and project management support over a period of six months to help in the implementation of software prototypes. The winners were presented at the AFRICOMM conference in South Africa. Some students were also offered company internships.

This part of the initiative concentrated on technical capacity-building. However, in line with the market-oriented, applied research approach promoted by Fraunhofer Portugal AICOS, several industrial partners were engaged. In the future, Android for Developing will be further strengthened by adding a business incubation component and involving experts evaluating the socioeconomic dimension of the solutions developed. Both extensions are seen as crucial for the success-ful implementation of local solutions that can enhance the lives of people.

Throughout 2013, the project is being replicated in Zambia together with MachaWorks, a local NGO targeting mobile health solutions and working with rural communities as part of a Global Research Alliance project. The approach will involve the close participatory integration of end users (community health workers) in the design and implementation phases.

Source: UNCTAD, based on information from Fraunhofer Portugal AICOS.

In view of the increased demand for mobile apps, various initiatives have been undertaken in developing countries to create spaces for strengthening informal networks of developers and software SMEs and for incubation of mobile businesses (World Bank, 2012). Grameen Foundation has established AppLabs in Indonesia and Uganda, while infoDev – a World Bank programme – has partnered with Nokia and the Minis-try of Foreign Affairs in Finland to establish a network of mLabs in Armenia, Kenya, Pakistan, South Africa and Viet Nam. In addition to offering state-of-the-art equipment, they provide training and workshops as well as opportunities for developers, entrepreneurs, investors, experts and policymakers to interact. Mobile apps development is also supported by a re-cent initiative called Android for Developing (box V.4).

2. Encouraging quality certification

The building of new capabilities among individuals and firms tends to take place through learning

opportunities in the production process (Rodrik, 2004). Attention to quality is crucial to encourage and enable enterprises to upgrade their capabilities and move towards higher-level value added activities. In the current globalization process, the standardization of production processes is a way to ensure that the production of each unit follows the same process.

Software enterprises can improve their overall efficiency and quality by implementing internationally recognized quality standards and models. This involves optimizing processes and reducing defects to achieve better management and more efficient use of time and resources. This in turn can lead to greater customer satisfaction and an enlarged client base – domestically (for example, in public procurement) or internationally. For firms and developers in developing and transition economies, quality standards are relevant to building trust among potential foreign clients – a key param-eter to win offshoring contracts. International quality standards send a message to potential clients that software providers and developers work according to clearly defined norms and procedures and subject themselves to global standards (Heeks and Nicholson, 2004). At the national level, quality standards and certification schemes can contribute to the increased international competitiveness of the entire industry, facilitate international cooperation by applying a common language and quality culture, and create local capacity and know-how in quality management and software process improvement.

There is a broad range of IT-related quality models, certification schemes, standards and methodologies for companies to consider, depending on their activities, capabilities and market orientation. Which schemes are more appropriate in a country depends on the existing availability of skills and capabilities, financial resources and target markets. A short overview follows that presents selected quality models, standards and methodologies of varying relevance for software industries in developing and transition economies.

(a) Different quality standards and certification schemes

One of the most well-known quality standards is the International Organization for Standardization (ISO) 9000. ISO consists of a family of standards and guidelines for quality management systems and related supporting standards. ISO 9001, a widely used quality management system,[6] provides a set of standardized requirements related to customers, focus, leadership, the involvement of people, a systematic approach to management and more. Unlike other standards discussed below, it is not IT-specific and can be applied regardless of the enterprise size and industry. There are several other relevant ISO standards. ISO 20000 – developed on the basis of the Information Technology Infrastructure Library (ITIL) standard (see below) – focuses on IT services management (for example, technical support, global delivery centres and call centres). ISO 12207 provides guidelines for software life cycle processes, while ISO 15504 is for the assessment of software development processes and their improvement. Moreover, ISO/International Electrotechnical Commission (IEC) 15288 is applied to system engineering, while ISO 27000 contains information security standards that often need to be met to qualify for public procurement and e-government tenders.

The Capability Maturity Model Integration (CMMI) is a process improvement approach and de facto standard for the software and IT industry. It describes the principles and practices underlying software process maturity and is intended to support software organizations in improving their software processes. CMMI was developed by the Software Engineering Institute at the Carnegie Mellon University. A characteristic of this model is the five maturity levels for process areas ranging from level one (initial) to level five (optimizing). CMMI allows for effective usage and combination with other approaches, standards and tools in the area of software and IT.[7] At the same time, the approach is comparatively complex and demanding, which may challenge the resources and capabilities of smaller enterprises, especially in low-income countries. The scheme is most commonly used among companies that service the North American market.

ITMark is a certification scheme, specifically for software SMEs, developed by the European Software Institute (ESI).[8] It combines a quick assessment in the areas of business maturity, information security and internal process development. ITMark can be used as a coaching scheme for SMEs as well as a facilitator to bypass some typical entry barriers and obstacles to quality certification, such as a lack of resources and the complexity of existing certification schemes (for example, CMMI).[9] The implementation of ITMark includes a one-day, in-company training, followed by coaching to initiate the internal process improvement programme, a short three-day appraisal by ITMark and a report on the major gaps identified. If the required compliance level is not achieved, a three-month improvement plan is recommended and a remedial assessment is performed. It can be seen as a more affordable entry-level step for SMEs towards increased competitiveness through process and quality improvement. To date, it has been implemented by software SMEs in Eastern Europe and Colombia.

The Brazilian Software Process Improvement Programme (MPS.br) was established in 2003 as a result of a joint initiative between SOFTEX, universities, the Ministry of Science and Technology, the Brazilian innovation agency Financiadora de Estudos e Projetos (FINEP) and the Inter-American Development Bank.[10] Its two main goals are to establish and improve the MPS.br model and to disseminate the model in the market, targeting both SMEs and large public and private organizations.[11] It was designed to provide cost-effective quality certification for Brazilian software SMEs and there are plans to export the model to other Latin American countries.

The Information Technology Infrastructure Library (ITIL) is a widely adopted approach for IT service management. It provides a practical framework for identifying, planning, delivering and supporting IT services to organizations. In its current version (ITILv3 and ITIL 2011), best practices are structured within five core publications, each of them covering an IT service management life cycle.[12]

Software testing is performed to detect defects in software by contrasting an application's expected results with its actual results for a given set of inputs. Software quality assurance implies the implementation of policies, procedures and processes within an organization to prevent defects from occurring. Relevant certifications in this area include the Certified Software Tester and the Certified Manager of Software Quality, both offered by the Quality Assurance Institute;[13] the Certified Software Test Professional offered by the International Institute for Software Testing; and the International Software Testing[14] Qualifications Board Certified Tester, by the International Software Testing Qualification Board (ISTQB).[15]

The degree to which software enterprises in different countries are certified according to different standards and systems varies considerably. For example, the export-oriented software industry in India – for which the United States of America is by far the most important target market – has made large investments into software process improvement and quality certification (chapter III). As of December 2010, 58 Indian companies were certified at the highest level (five) of CMMI, the most complex and challenging quality certification in the software industry. India is also very close to hosting the highest number of ISO companies in the world (Vijayabaskar and Suresh Babu, 2009). By contrast, in many developing and transition economies comparatively few software companies have obtained relevant certification. For example, in Guatemala and Honduras only 20 per cent and less than 10 per cent, respectively, of software companies have any kind of certification (SOFEX, 2011; AHTI, 2011). In the Russian Federation, the majority (69 per cent) of software companies in 2011 did not have such certifications, though almost 30 per cent were certified according to some ISO standard (Russoft Association, 2011). In Kenya, there were only four ISO certified software enterprises in 2010 (UNCTAD and BMZ, forthcoming).

(b) Pros and cons of different schemes

External driving forces, such as increased competition, tend to promote the successful adoption of

quality standards and associated changes within software companies in developing and transition economies (Macias-Garza and Heeks, 2006). In view of the diversity of schemes available, it is important to consider their possible strengths and weaknesses.

While the benefits of applying quality models and standards were highlighted above, there are also potential pitfalls. The implementation of quality standards involves costs to train and hire staff, and pay for auditors and appraisers. There are also costs in staff time and resources used in the planning, learning and managing of new methods and processes. New processes introduced in the framework of quality certification may not be compatible with the process models of customers. This can lead to friction in relations with clients and along supply chains. In addition, applying quality standards by necessity adds bureaucracy and paperwork. It is also sometimes argued that quality models and standards constrain the creativity of software engineers and developers by establishing processes and structures that are too rigid. Finally, quality standards can effectively act as an entry barrier for companies from developing countries, especially when they require substantial financial resources. Some schemes are simply unaffordable for microenterprises and small enterprises in developing countries.

Although relevant quality models and standards share most of these benefits and drawbacks, each has specific pros and cons (table V.2). Thus, government and software companies have to choose on the basis of their strategic goals, area of expertise, business model and available capabilities and resources.

For many software enterprises in low-income countries, ISO 9001 as well as specialized quality standards such as ITMark and MPS.br offer attractive features. They are less complex than CMMI and less demanding to implement. They also provide a foundation for the implementation of other, more complex IT standards at a later stage, when companies have improved their software process maturity and established a culture of continuous improvement. In addition, they are more accessible for SMEs in terms of complexity, time and financial investment (ESI Eastern Europe, 2007).

(c) Measures to encourage certification

In view of the potential benefits from greater adoption of international standards and certifications, governments in developing and transition economies

Table V.2.	Pros and cons of selected schemes for quality assurance and certification	
System	**Pros**	**Cons**
ISO	• This family of standards is internationally well known and addresses systemic management. • ISO 9001 is one of the most widely used quality standards • ISO 9001 certification often required in private and public procurement • Applicable to companies from different industries and regardless of their size • Additional IT-specific standards are available (for example, ISO 15504, ISO 27000)	• ISO 9001 standard is not software specific • ISO certification involves substantial investments of resources • Can create additional overhead and slow down processes
CMMI	• Probably the most renowned standard for the IT industry • Widely used by IT and software companies around the world • Designed specifically for the IT and software industry • Provides guidance for efficient improvement across multiple process disciplines in an organization. • Compatible with other methods such as ISO standards, ITIL and Agile • Continuous improvement of the CMMI model	• Comparatively complex and demanding quality model which might overstretch the resources and capabilities of SMEs • Requires highly trained employees to manage the system • Implementation incurs substantial costs
ITMark	• Less complex than other standards and therefore easier to implement • Specifically designed for IT and software SMEs • Relatively cost-effective standard • Combination of CMMI, ISO 27000 and 10-squared method • Provides effective quality management coaching system for SMEs	• Still relatively unknown at the international level • Lack of awareness and market penetration • Only a small number of companies certified • Benefits not sufficiently communicated within the IT industry
MPS.br	• Specifically developed for IT SMEs in Brazil • Based on the standards ISO/EIC 12207, ISO/EIC15504 and CMMI • Continuous improvement of the standard • Allows for gradual implementation making it particularly suitable for SMEs • Provides cost-effective quality certification • Based on an integrated approach, including marketing of the standard as well as special financial support schemes and training programmes for SMEs	• Currently confined to the Brazilian market • Lack of international awareness and reputation • Lack of market penetration
ITIL	• Well-established and internationally recognized standard for IT service management • Maps the entire IT service life cycle, • Underpins the ISO/IEC 20000 standard	• No organizational certification possible • Only focused on IT services

Source: UNCTAD

may address this area in their national software strategies. Options to consider include quality strategy development, awareness-raising, capacity-building, training and quality certification and education. What schemes to focus on would need to be determined in consultations between the government and the software industry.

Quality strategy: In order to promote a culture of quality and continuous improvement, governments may develop specific strategies or integrate quality management into IT and software sector development strategies. For example, in the Export Promotion Strategy for the Software and IT Services Industry in the former Yugoslav Republic of Macedonia, a range of measures are dedicated exclusively to fostering quality management and certification (MASIT, 2010).

Awareness-raising and capacity-building: Lack of awareness of quality standards and their benefits is a common problem.[17] In addition, SMEs often find it difficult to determine which is the most appropriate model or standard for their organization. Special information events can provide local companies with detailed and up-to-date information on different standards. It is also important to build local capabilities and expertise in terms of quality certification, consulting and training. This may involve the establishment of institutions for training and certifications, such as the Software Engineering Competence Center (SECC) in Egypt which is training and testing individual specialists and is a member of ISTQB (UNCTAD, 2011b).[18]

Support to training and quality certification: Once local capacities and a quality infrastructure are in place, software companies need to be trained in quality models. Companies may require support for the implementation of the required quality procedures and processes to prepare for audits, appraisals and certification. In El Salvador, the software cluster Asociación de Empresas de Tecnologías de Información (ASETI) has developed and implemented a special training programme on quality management for its member companies.[19] In Egypt, SECC delivers courses and advisory services to domestic companies to assess their maturity level (UNCTAD, 2011b). Over thirty companies have attended these courses and achieved certification for CMMI maturity levels two to five. So far, SECC has been focusing especially on lower-level certifications, with only a handful of companies having achieved certification levels four or five.

Education: To increase efficiency and sustainability of initiatives for quality improvement in the software industry, quality models, standards and certification should also be included into the curricula of university programmes (for example, computer science, business informatics and business administration).

In order to avoid overstretching the resources and organizational capabilities of SMEs, an incremental approach is recommended, with early initiatives focusing on less complex and more easily implemented standards (for example, ISO 9001, ITMark, MPS.br). Once companies have improved their process maturity and quality management capabilities, more complex and advanced standards can be introduced. As proposed in a recent review of science, technology and innovation policies in El Salvador, it may also be advisable for the education sector and the private sector to work together in order to help prioritize among the various certification programmes available in the market (UNCTAD, 2011c).

3. Facilitating access to finance

Limited access to investment funding, especially venture capital, is the barrier to growth of the software industry most mentioned by software associations. This was particularly accentuated in the Middle East and Africa, where 86 per cent of the respondents cited this factor. When financing software-related SMEs, various forms of equity financing are often preferred over debt financing. The latter option is structurally less suitable due to the need for regular repayments and often stringent collateral requirements. When there is an intellectual property element in business activities, as is often the case in software development, it may be possible to attract venture capital. The investor takes a certain equity share in the company and may also offer access to technical or managerial advice and networks. For less sophisticated activities, such as web design and software customization, other forms of risk capital, such as shareholder loans and unincorporated joint ventures, may be more appropriate (Zavatta, 2008).

The market for private equity (including venture capital) is generally more mature in developed economies (figure V.2). Moreover, most software-related projects are concentrated in a few locations, notably the BRIC countries (chapter II). In developing countries, the financing situation may be aggravated by the absence of well-functioning banking sectors and a lack of public financing schemes for technology start-ups.

In developed countries, various initiatives have been launched to improve the financing of software enterprises. For example, Enterprise Ireland introduced a venture capital programme for supporting software

Figure V.2. Private equity investment relative to GDP, selected countries and regions, 2011 (percentage)

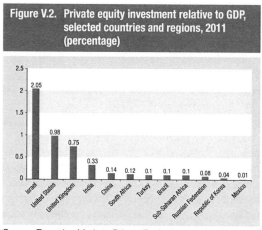

Source: Emerging Markets Private Equity Association (EMPEA) (2012).

entrepreneurship (Tessler et al., 2002). In Israel, the Government played an important role in fostering the country's venture capital and making use of the diaspora to support the software industry (Kenney et al., 2002). In Bulgaria, the software association BASSCOM and the Bulgarian ICT cluster conduct match-making events with foreign business angels as well as venture capitalists.[20]

There is generally little data on the size and composition of the venture capital sector in developing and transition economies. A review of selected countries in 2008 found wide differences in the availability of venture capital (Zavatta, 2008). Not surprisingly, India was found to have the most developed market for such financial instruments, with a range of different schemes. By contrast, in sub-Saharan Africa and parts of Latin America there were virtually no such services. The review distinguished between generalist

funds, development-oriented funds, high-tech funds and business angels (box V.5).

There are indications that developing countries (especially in Asia) are becoming a more attractive target for investments by venture capital firms based in developed countries (Bruton and Ahlstrom, 2003; Dauterive and Fok, 2004). The stronger presence of such firms in the software industry would contribute not only financial capital, but also much needed management expertise, advice and networks.

Some developing countries have launched special initiatives targeting the ICT sector, including software. These involve the provision of credit lines of refinancing facilities with an interest subsidy or mechanisms to reduce risk (for example, through credit guarantees). Many such initiatives were noted especially in Brazil and India (Zavatta, 2008).

Several developing countries have also established dedicated funds to support innovation and production in the software industry. In Mexico, three instruments have been put in place to support greater access to financial resources. The Prosoft Fund focuses on financing infrastructure and training; the Guarantee Fund secures up to 80 per cent of the credit of businesses in the IT industry; and the third instrument involves the promotion of risk capital.[21] The Government of Argentina has set up a dedicated Trust Fund for the Promotion of the Software Industry to finance R&D projects, professional training, quality improvement and start-ups in the software industry (box V.1) and Chile offers direct incentives to training, technology infrastructure co-financing and long-term leases (ECLAC, 2011). Nigeria's new software strategy includes the establishment of an IT Innovation Fund (box I.2).

Box V.5.   Different forms of equity financing in developing countries

Generalist funds: These funds seldom invest in early stage deals and typically target relatively large investments (more than $1.5 million).

Development-oriented funds: These are normally funded by international financial institutions (IFIs) or bilateral donors. While they have a clear focus on SMEs, the ICT sector is not a main target.

High-tech funds: There are three types of high-tech funds: private initiatives, public financed funds and hybrids. The first type tends to focus on later stage and larger deals, whereas the latter two more frequently support early stage investments. Some are supported by IFIs or donors. High-tech funds are common in Brazil and India and some examples were also noted in Morocco, the Philippines, Ukraine and Viet Nam.

Business angels: This form can be an attractive option for SMEs as they can offer financing on the order of $50,000–$250,000. In addition, business angels often have experience in the industries in which they invest. In the review, mature networks of business angels were found only in India and, to a lesser extent, Argentina, Brazil and the Philippines.

Source: Zavatta (2008).

While there are promising initiatives, the most relevant financing mechanisms for nurturing national software capabilities are mostly poorly developed in low-income developing countries. Further empirical assessment of the situation in this area is needed to identify and develop appropriate policy responses.

C. SECURING ACCESS TO RELEVANT SKILLS

The importance of human resources has been emphasized throughout this and other studies of the software sector. More than half of the software associations surveyed by UNCTAD and WITSA identified the lack of relevant skills as a key barrier to the sector's expansion (table V.1). There are several avenues to generate adequate human resources. This section briefly highlights the areas of skills development through the regular education system (from secondary to higher education), specialized training institutions and in-house training.[22]

1. Skills development through the education system

The main way of fostering skills is through the regular education system, particularly secondary and tertiary schools. A key challenge is to produce human resources that the market is actually requires. While this applies to all areas of education, it is particularly demanding in the case of ICTs and software as these technologies change rapidly, affecting the kind of education and training to be included in the curricula. In addition, practical experience is as important as theoretical skills. In general, a sound foundation in mathematics and other science subjects is important, complemented by courses aimed at developing the specifics of coding.

The skills needed also evolve as the software system matures. One study identified the following capability requirements for a software industry to transform over time from being a low-wage based producer of data entry and software services to becoming a producer of a range of software products and services (Vijayabaskar and Suresh Babu, 2009):

- Basic programming skills;
- Communication skills;
- High-end programming and low-end domain knowledge for turnkey projects;
- High-end domain knowledge for embedded software and domain-specific software development;

- Intra-firm coordination capabilities for turnkey projects;
- Firm-level process capabilities to trap and consolidate project-specific learnings for building up dynamic sectoral capabilities;
- Simultaneous need for large pools of basic programming skills in diverse languages and packages.

Technical skills in the software development cycle are typically analysis, design, development/coding, implementation and maintenance. Detailed recommendations on the specific technologies and programming languages to be covered are difficult, but they should try to reflect the requirements of the current market and customers targeted. Regular surveys of the software industry can help governments in the design of curricula.

For example, in a recent survey of skills needs in South Africa, application development and software as a service emerged at the top, with mobile computing skills among those rising the fastest in importance (Schofiled, 2011). Several open source platforms are also gaining in importance (chapter IV). A study of Costa Rica found that in software and support services, the skills pyramid was too heavy in the middle, with the Bachelor of Arts the most frequent final degree and the number of graduates from community colleges and technical high schools insufficient (Mata et al., 2009). The sector needed a greater quantity of graduates qualified as mid-level technicians.

Furthermore, hybrid skills that combine sound technical skills with entrepreneurial skills and vertical and business process management expertise play a role, particularly for companies trying to move up the software value chain towards specialized services such as IT consulting. Management skills such as marketing and sales, project management, business process and human resources management are relevant for software companies to improve their efficiency and competitiveness.

Many developing and transition economies seeking to expand their software industries face common structural challenges in university education (Germany, Federal Ministry for Economic Cooperation and Development, 2011a; UNCTAD, 2011b):

- The output of IT education in terms of quality and quantity of IT graduates is insufficient due to limited financial resources and capacities.
- Existing curricula for computer science/informatics are outdated and/or not in line with software industry requirements.

- There is insufficient coordination and cooperation between universities and the software industry.
- Academic staff teaching at the universities lack the necessary technical qualifications and/or do not meet international standards.
- Study programmes do not meet international quality standards and lack accreditation.

Various initiatives have been adopted to address such structural problems. For example, India's NASS-COM created its special assessment and certification programme. NASSCOM Assessment of Competence-Technology, for the recruitment of entry-level talent. The idea was to identify the level of talent available and provide feedback to universities on the areas in which more work is needed to improve the employ-ability of their graduates.[23] In the Russian Federation, domestic and foreign-owned software enterprises actively engage in university training courses (chapter IV). The Government of Argentina offers special incentives to young students who pursue IT-related careers (box V.1).

The growing importance of mobile technologies and related programming languages should also be taken into account. In response to the rapid surge in demand for new mobile apps, the IT faculty at Strathmore University in Kenya launched two courses on mobile applications, and interactive mobile and web. The first is designed to train students to develop commercially viable, easy-to-use, interactive mobile applications. It covers relevant concepts, essentials tools and methods. The second course teaches students in web development, interface design and interactivity in addition to functionality, with an emphasis on access from mobile devices. The two courses use current industry standards and tools and involve training that enables students to acquire the practical knowledge required.[24]

2. Specialized institutions and in-house training

Professional qualifications and training of people in the software industry are crucial complements to regular education systems.[25] Specialized training institutions generally do not offer university degrees but rather various kinds of certificate and diploma courses. Some provide quite sophisticated training. In India, for example, one of the largest training institutions with around 10,000 students, NIIT, offers a three-and-a-half-year programme that includes

one year of professional practice (internship) with a software development firm. Professionals trained with this degree are usually offered employment with the firm on completing the internship. Another major player is Aptech, which concentrates on training for graduates specializing in software development (Vijayabaskar and Suresh Babu, 2009).

In Egypt, SECC has been delivering courses and offering advisory services to Egyptian software companies since 2003. SECC also undertakes the training and testing of individual specialists as a member of ISTQB. SECC has trained around 11,000 people from over 500 companies (UNCTAD, 2011b).

In Ghana, the Meltwater Foundation offers a three-phase entrepreneurial programme designed to foster software companies in Africa. It begins with a two-year training programme at the Meltwater Entrepreneurial School of Technology campus in Accra. IT entrepreneurs with business ideas deemed viable can move to the Meltwater Entrepreneurial School of Technology Incubator for assistance in getting their businesses off the ground.[26]

In some countries, national IT/software associations provide training services. In the UNCTAD–WITSA Survey, almost 70 per cent of respondents stated that they were engaged in such activities.[27] The Guatemalan software cluster, SOFEX, introduced a special working group on education and training that developed suggestions on how to improve the conditions for capacity-building and training in the software industry. The proposals included the introduction of a revolving fund for qualification, five days of annual training holidays as well as compulsory training activities for cluster members.[28] In order to provide specialized technical and management training at affordable prices, software clusters in Albania, El Salvador, Honduras and the former Yugoslav Republic of Macedonia have established cluster training academies. Their main objective is to identify the concrete training needs of IT cluster member companies and coordinate corresponding training activities. As a one-stop shop for its members, the academies organize training events and conduct quality control, while the training sessions are mostly implemented by external training providers. Elements covered by the programme of the Salvadoran software and IT cluster, ASETI, are depicted in table V.3.[29]

The leading training and certification activities in FOSS focus on Linux and related applications. Several internationally recognized schemes offer training

Table V.3.   Training programme for the ASETI IT Cluster Academy

Technical training	Management training
• Software engineering	• Human resources management in the IT industry
• Software process improvement and quality management	• IT project management
• Agile methods	• Marketing and sales for export
• OSS/LAMP technologies	• Business development and trade fair management
• Enterprise resource planning/SAP	• IT tender management
• Requirements engineering and management	• Business process analysis and optimization
• Technical documentation	• IT controlling
• Software testing	• Key account management
• Mobile technologies	• IT product management
• ISO	
• ITIL	

Source: ASETI (http://aseti.org/).

in this area, such as the Linux Professional Institute (box V.6), Red Hat Linux Certifications, Novell SUSE Certifications and FOSS Capacity-Building for the Developing World.

Several related initiatives are supported by donors and civil society to boost the availability of relevant skills for the software industry and developer community. Coders4Africa is one project that seeks to support the development of a community of software programmers in Africa and the diaspora and to facilitate the sharing and transfer of knowledge (box V.7). There are also training-of-trainer networks and skills upgrading

for core personnel at IT educational institutions that target representatives of different institutions (such as universities, technical schools and training providers), IT SMEs with outreach potential and other change agents. These courses are entirely needs driven. The pan-African IT-learning and trainer network, ict@innovation (box IV.5), is an example of such a regional capacity development network.

Still, many countries face obstacles that impede efficient training and qualification for the software industry.[30] Specialized professional training services for further qualification of local IT experts are frequently

Box V.6.   Linux training and certification in Arab countries

ITU and the Linux Professional Institute (LPI) launched an initiative in 2011 to support the roll-out of a Linux certification and training programme.a For both organizations, the objective of the programme is to unlock the potential of ICTs to deliver employment opportunities and to empower ICT trainees in their careers. Training and certifications on Linux and other open source software had already been jointly delivered by the two institutions in Afghanistan, the Lao People's Democratic Republic, Occupied Palestinian Territory, Pakistan, Syrian Arab Republic and Yemen.

Building on this initial experience, the two organizations joined efforts in March 2012 and put together a comprehensive three-year project to be implemented in the 22 members of the League of Arab States. The project responds to the growing interest in open source software from the region's Governments and corporations and proposes establishing more than 130 Linux train-the-trainer centres to develop and strengthen local ICT capacity in human resources. The project has an initial budget of $5.8 million and is expected to reach some 13,200 direct beneficiaries.

The LPI network of IT industry representatives, enterprise customers and Linux professionals recognize an economic interest in this training programme as it connects to a community which speaks the local language. LPI's mandate is to promote professional standards and global adoption of Linux and other open source software through training. It is expected that open source software will quickly become attractive for the majority of the region's young ICT trainees as it has deep roots in community and collaborative work groups.

Source: UNCTAD, based on information provided by ITU and LPI.

a   See http://www.lpi.org/news/lpi-announces-linux-training-program-international-telecommunication-union-league-arab-states .

Box V.7.   Coders4Africa

Coders4Africa is a recent initiative that seeks to support the development of a community of programmers in Africa and the diaspora to facilitate the sharing and transfer of knowledge. The initiative contributes practically and effectively by connecting communities and providing services to its members.

The overall goal of Coders4Africa is to help ensure that the pan-African community can act as a catalyst and play an active role in providing technology-based tools to address development challenges. Coders4Africa aims to nurture a community of internationally certified IT professionals and software developers to create free open source solutions that respond to local African problems and demands and reduce dependence on imported software. By leveraging software solutions more effectively, African countries would be better equipped to streamline various processes in the public and private sectors. Locally trained people are best positioned to understand local cultural dynamics and produce solutions tailored to local needs and capabilities. There is a particular need for user interfaces and back-end mobile and web development skills.

A first step for Coders4Africa was to galvanize software developers and IT professionals by organizing technology conferences in Ghana, Kenya, Mali and Senegal. In 2011, such conferences brought together some 800 professional developers, computer science students and small software start-ups, all with a focus on the role of breakthrough technologies in alleviating the problems facing their communities. The conferences featured workshops, training, hack-athons, demonstrations and discussions on a vision for a pan-African community of software developers. These events were supported by private companies, including Microsoft, Oracle, Strathmore University, the Advanced Information Technology Institute, Safaricom, IBM and EcoBand. As of March 2012, the Coders4Africa online community had reached more than 1,000 members in 23 countries. To sustain itself, the initiative created local chapters that organize Coders4Africa in Action events – monthly gatherings where workshops and boot camps are held.

Coders4Africa plans to introduce development hubs to train young people with a view to helping them find jobs in the software industry or become entrepreneurs. These hubs would provide an open space to innovate and create solutions aimed at solving development problems. Coders4Africa is currently in the process of securing support from donors and the private sector.

Source: Coders4Africa (www.coders4africa.org).

---

insufficient or not available (Germany, Federal Ministry for Economic Cooperation and Development, 2011a: 72). In view of the need for tailored skills to perform various kinds of software development, it is often necessary for enterprises to invest in training their staff. The emphasis in recruitment on the ability to learn and the importance of tacit knowledge for some of the skills required further underline the need for firms develop in-house and on-the-job training. In addition, short innovation cycles in the IT industry add pressure on software enterprises to upgrade their capabilities.

In the Indian software industry, formal training programmes exist in all large enterprises, especially those catering to the export market (Vijayabaskar and Suresh Babu, 2009). Such programmes typically aim at equipping new employees with programming and problem-solving skills, as well as exposing them to organizational procedures and routines.

In some countries, special incentive programmes have been introduced to boost in-house investment in training. In Mexico, for example, several instruments were developed to address weaknesses in the availability of

trained/certified IT professionals and to attract foreign IT firms. The MexicoFirst initiative financially supports the certification of IT specialists and others working in the IT and ICT-enabled service industries, covering up to 70 per cent of the cost. The programme is administered through the national competitive fund, Prosoft, and expects to support the certification of 12,000 professionals annually.[31] The IT talent programme also certifies graduates in specific competencies required by the industry. By April 2011, five different profiles had been identified and 48 people had been certified as software architects.[32]

Nonetheless, in many developing countries most software companies are small and may lack the necessary resources to invest in training and developing the capacity of their employees. An idea arising out of a study of Costa Rica is the introduction of a dual training system for vocational training on a broad scale (Paus, 2010). This would aim at keeping curricula current and training students in line with the state of skills and knowledge in the industry. Making apprenticeships in firms an integral part of vocational training could institutionalize an ongoing discussion and feedback process between the private sector and the training institution about the skills requirements in the sector.

D. FOSTERING SOFTWARE DEMAND

A key barrier to the development of the domestic software industry in developing countries is weak domestic demand. As the domestic market represents the natural starting point for local software firms to provide services, local demand is particularly important in the early stages of the industry's development. Moreover, once software companies have developed a certain level of capabilities, demanding clients in the domestic market can spur local software developers and firms to innovate and improve their process and outputs. Governments can support domestic demand creation primarily through IT-related public procurement and measures to increase ICT uptake in the private sector. In addition, governments and other stakeholders can seek to expand demand by promoting exports.

1. Public procurement as a tool to boost domestic demand

The public sector represents a major potential client for software companies in developing countries. This is particularly true in countries where ICT use in the private sector is nascent. Public tenders for e-government are a crucial growth driver for domestic software market development as well as local innovation. Accordingly, Governments in developing and transition economies should seek to use public IT projects as a way to foster active participation and development of local software companies. The relevance of public procurement was confirmed in the UNCTAD–WITSA Survey of IT/Software Associations, where the lack of such procurement of software and IT services was mentioned as a barrier by more than half of all responding associations based in developing and transition economies, and especially in Africa and the Middle East (table V.1).

In chapter III, examples were given of how Governments in India, the Republic of Korea and Sri Lanka are now using projects in e-government as a tool to spur local software growth. This strategic mechanism can be further developed to create domestic demand.

Governments and their various agencies should recognize their role as buyers within the national software system. Various factors need to be addressed for public procurement to have the intended effect on local enterprises regarding demand (UNCTAD and BMZ, forthcoming).

An important first step is to recognize the link between public procurement and local industry development. As noted in the Industrial Policy Action Plan of South Africa: "Much public procurement is currently conducted on an ad hoc rather than strategic basis and does not deliver adequately on either value-for-money or key industrial policy objectives" (South Africa, Department of Trade and Industry, 2010: 33).

The government body dealing with procurement may not feel accountable for the promotion of the domestic industry. The main focus is typically obtaining the best possible value for money when procuring goods and services. For the economy as a whole, however, encouraging the development of local software suppliers in the short term may increase the number of potential bidders competing for government tenders in the long term, thereby also enhancing the value for money in future procurements. Thus, the successful use of public procurement as a strategic tool to promote local software industry development requires all relevant parts of government to agree on a strategy that is in line with broader development plans.

A second step may be to map existing opportunities and barriers to leveraging public procurement for ICT sector development. This may involve the identification of public service delivery projects suited to involving local software suppliers. The characteristics of such projects will depend on the capabilities of the local software industry. Thus, mapping the skills, competencies and expertise available domestically is important. In many instances, government agencies responsible for public procurement are today unaware of the size and structure of the domestic IT sector (UNCTAD and BMZ, forthcoming).

Conversely, there may also be limited knowledge among domestic software firms about public procurement opportunities. This may call for dedicated training of enterprises – by the government or the industry association – on tender procedures and how to complete tender documents. In Sri Lanka, for example, active steps were taken to address this challenge. When the ICT agency, ICTA, noticed that many non-compliant bids were being received, its procurement advisers organized workshops to train local bidders on tender guidelines. This initiative helped to reduce the number of non-compliant bids and led to greater involvement of the local private sector in winning bids (UNCTAD and BMZ, forthcoming).

Governments should also try to ensure that their procurement practices are conducive to greater involvement of domestic suppliers, especially SMEs. This involves attention to transparency, openness and clarity of specifications. Making use of e-procurement is useful in this context, as has been noted in countries such as Canada and Chile (UNCTAD, 2011b). In addition, the structure of the procurement process can be adapted in many ways to fit the skills and capabilities of software SMEs, for example (UNCTAD and BMZ, forthcoming):

- Adopt, where possible, a modular design of the software systems procured. If systems are procured in a larger package, fewer bidders are likely to have the required qualifications, experience or financial resources.

- Adopt, where possible, an e-government architecture that is reusable, modular and open. A good example of this approach is the Republic of Korea's eGovFrame (chapter III). Such an approach creates opportunities for multiple small

procurements and reduces the risk of duplication of work in developing new software solutions.

- Set interoperability standards to allow different e-government systems to work together effectively. Such standards are particularly important in situations when modularity is given priority. A further step is to apply open standards and open document formats.

- Give preference to FOSS in public procurement. As highlighted in chapter IV, there are strong arguments for relying on FOSS when developing public software systems. If e-government architectures are highly modular, it is more likely that FOSS applications can be found or developed for each small component. This may also give local firms a better chance to compete with foreign suppliers.

- When running international competitive tenders, explore possible approaches to give local software enterprises a fair chance to compete, without jeopardizing the quality of software products and services delivered. This may involve encouraging joint ventures, a local presence to ensure post-implementation support or local language capabilities when appropriate.

But even when a government applies all of the above to the design of the public procurement strategy, local

---

Box V.8. Coded in Country: Linking local software skills to development projects

Coded in Country was launched in 2010 as a not-for-profit initiative to promote greater involvement of local software firms in the design, implementation and ongoing support of software solutions to be used in international development projects. With a team based in the United States of America, and globally active participants, its goal is to facilitate greater engagement between international development organizations (for example, United Nations and bilateral development agencies) and local software firms.

Coded in Country's activities concentrate on making the capabilities of their local in-country partners better known. Coded in Country identifies and establishes relationships with local firms, then helps them to develop corporate profiles and case studies to highlight their skills. Profiles are published on the Coded in Country website (codedincountry.org) and communicated through the initiative's network of international development partners and professionals. These same channels are used to notify local partners of upcoming business opportunities. As of April 2012, Coded in Country had built relationships with and developed company profiles for 20 software firms in 14 countries, with significant representation in sub-Saharan Africa.

With growing emphasis on international development through locally driven solutions, Coded in Country can help development agencies identify and connect with local software partners. Using the website, organizations can learn about local software firms, read about their successes, determine their competencies and ultimately connect with a local partner. Coded in Country is also currently developing a new service called Coded in Country-Connect. It aims at helping the international development community to identify appropriate local software partners based on their project's needs. This service is scheduled to be rolled out in the third quarter of 2012.

While still at an early stage, Coded in Country hopes that its approach will become the norm in international development to bring down long-term projects costs, make solutions more locally-appropriate and strengthen local software capacity.

Source: UNCTAD, based on information from Coded in Country.

software firms will only be able to compete effectively if they have the necessary skills and capabilities. Thus, it is important to connect strategies with efforts aimed at strengthening the capabilities of the local software industry and developer community (section V.B). Close collaboration with a local IT/software association may again be useful.

Procurement by the international development community can also contribute to generating more demand for software development in developing countries. Mobile phones, the Internet and social media are assuming a growing role as tools to address development challenges, such as coping with natural disasters, promoting democratization and enhancing social economic development. Much of the software for such development projects is today designed and implemented by firms located in developed countries. For example, in the case of mHealth for development projects in sub-Saharan Africa, most software used was developed by firms in the United States of America and Europe (Vital Wave Consulting, 2009). Although such software may meet the needs of the project objectives, relying on firms in developed countries may make projects unnecessarily expensive. In addition, the potential to strengthen the local software development sector in developing countries is lost. The Coded in Country initiative was recently launched to promote greater usage of local software capabilities in such contexts (box V.8).

2. Promoting greater ICT use in the private sector

The extent to which the domestic market offers opportunities for the software industry also depends on the nature of ICT use in the economy and society. In general, the more sophisticated ICT usage is in the public and private sectors, the greater the demand for various kinds of software products and services. But even in low-income countries, there is now rapidly expanding use of some ICTs, especially mobile phones and related applications.

Governments can take different measures to boost ICT uptake and use within traditional industries and particularly among SMEs, including computers and the Internet as well as mobile phones and smartphones. The growing use of mobile devices has in itself created new domestic demand for software (chapter II). A more enabling environment for ICT uptake can be created by fostering competitive markets for the provision of ICT services, providing a supportive legal and regulatory environment for electronic transactions (see below) and enhancing technological diffusion. Governments can also seek to overcome market failures through demand aggregation (for example, by developing e-government services and encouraging firms to use them) and by supporting the development of ICT skills (Qiang et al., 2006; UNCTAD, 2011a). Governments can contribute to enhanced access to different ICTs by opening up ICT markets and improving competition. Where connectivity is lacking due to market failures, such as in the case of mobile networks in rural areas of LDCs, governments and their development partners may need to explore approaches to extending network access (UNCTAD, 2010).

A prerequisite for more widespread uptake of ICTs for commercial purposes is that enterprises and consumers trust systems. Many governments need to adopt and enforce adequate legal frameworks to unleash the full potential of electronic transactions, in particular by improving consumer and business confidence. This is becoming more relevant also in low-income countries where mobile platforms are emerging as enablers of electronic transactions for businesses, governments and consumers. As recently highlighted in a study on the use of mobile money services in the East African Community, the existing legal framework for e-commerce does not suffice to address relevant concerns (box V.9) (UNCTAD, 2012).

Such broad efforts at creating an environment conducive to ICT use can be complemented with more targeted measures. For example, to take advantage of opportunities in the domestic market, the national software association in Brazil, SOFTEX, has developed initiatives to stimulate the use of ICT in microenterprises and small businesses. In addition, it provides support for IT specification, purchase, implementation and management. SOFTEX also stimulates domestic development of software and solutions suitable for the specific needs of Brazilian clients. Many of these initiatives were developed in partnership with IT sector bodies and supported by the Brazilian Service of Support for Micro and Small Enterprises (SEBRAE).[33] In Mexico, one of the Prosoft objectives for promoting the software sector is similarly to promote greater business use of IT. Among other things, Prosoft offers financial support (of up to 50 per cent of the cost) to firms looking to buy custom-made software. Only software businesses with quality certification qualify to participate in this initiative.[34]

Box V.9.	Mobile money regulations in the East African Community

A recent UNCTAD study analysed mobile money developments in the East African Community in order to address the legal and regulatory challenges (UNCTAD, 2012). As of April 2012, the East African Community accounted for one quarter of all mobile money systems in Africa. Each month, more than half a billion dollars are transferred in the region using mobile phones.

The use of mobile money raises specific issues for consumers and regulators. Mobile money transactions involve electronic transfers of funds and electronic payments. As such, they are affected by applicable legal frameworks for electronic commerce. While the East African Community Task Force on Cyberlaws has made considerable progress in preparing regional guidelines on electronic transactions, electronic signatures and authentication, data protection and privacy, consumer protection and computer crime, increased regulatory collaboration and harmonization are needed in the area of mobile money services. To ensure that mobile money services bring about the desired broad benefits, especially for the poor, various regulatory issues in telecommunication, financial services and competition overlap and need to be addressed. Mobile money providers have to operate according to the regulatory requirements of all three regulators and comply with all applicable laws and regulations.

Convergence between the ICT and the financial sector generates several regulatory issues, such as consumer protection, privacy and data protection, registration and transaction limits, competition, interoperability between telecommunication and mobile money networks, and cross-border transfers. For example, currently no comprehensive multi-sectoral consumer protection legislation and no mandated authority exist in East African Community countries to protect mobile money consumers. The study recommends regulators to start paying more attention to consumer-related issues and to define standards for mobile network operators and partner banks to protect consumer interests. East African Community countries are also advised to continue their work towards adopting harmonized legislation on electronic and mobile payments.

Source: UNCTAD.

3. Promoting software exports

In countries with nascent domestic software markets, exploring export opportunities may be necessary to generate significant demand for the local industry and developer community. Different export strategy options may be considered depending on domestic capabilities and resources. Software companies have to decide whether to enter export markets with software products or services and where to position themselves within the software export value chain, which ranges from simple coding activities to complex software development projects, IT consulting and software products.

Exporting can be highly challenging and complex, especially for SMEs. Challenges include the lack of export know-how and market intelligence, insufficient financial and human resources as well as the absence of suitable support institutions. A broad range of measures have been explored to overcome such obstacles and promote software exports. For example:

- Export information services as well as business-to-business export promotion services were developed and implemented by the Guatemalan software cluster Sofex (SOFEX, 2011).

- The Lebanese software industry used the Lebanese diaspora in France for export-oriented software development.[35]

- In Brazil, SOFTEX collaborates with the Brazilian Trade and Investment Promotion Agency to develop marketing campaigns. Activities include participation in business events and trade shows overseas, mapping and selection of potential buyers of Brazilian software and IT services and the development of market studies, in addition to technical and commercial consulting services.[36]

- In India, export promotion is handled by the Electronics and Software Export Promotion Council, an autonomous body under the Government of India and the Ministry of Information Technology.

Neighbouring and regional markets often represent important destinations. Software companies in Guatemala export software solutions to Honduras, Mexico (SOFEX, 2011) and Nicaragua. In Nigeria, some companies have emerged as a provider of software applications for other African markets (box I.2). In the former Yugoslav Republic of Macedonia, more than half of all software and IT service exports go to regional markets in the Balkans, which are less mature and competitive than Western European markets and easier to penetrate (MASIT, 2010).

E. TOWARDS A MODERN LEGAL FRAMEWORK FOR BOOSTING SOFTWARE DEVELOPMENT AND USE

The legal and regulatory environment needs to be conducive to software production and development. This is important from the perspective of facilitating greater use of electronic services, such as e-commerce and e-government, and thereby enhancing the demand for software applications. The regulatory framework also influences the ability of the local software industry and developer community to engage in domestic and international software development projects. While there are many legal issues that potentially impact on the software system, this section pays particular attention to intellectual property protection, laws related to electronic transactions and the legal environment for electronic payments.[37]

1. Intellectual property regulation and enforcement

Intellectual property protection is a regulatory domain to consider in the context of software. Stakeholders within the system are affected differently by intellectual property regulation and there is no consensus on what constitutes an optimal approach. In the UNCTAD–WITSA survey, relatively few IT/software associations identified inadequate intellectual property protection as a barrier to growth (table V.1), although several associations in Latin America and transition economies found software piracy to be a key challenge. When designing an intellectual property framework, governments should take into account the level of software capabilities as well as the development path along which they would prefer to see the national software system evolve.

The main purpose of protecting intellectual property is to provide an incentive to invest resources in bringing new products to market. Encouraging local firms to develop new solutions has the advantage of promoting indigenous innovation and its commercialization, as well as of promoting more sustainable employment (Fu et al., 2011).

Questions on who produces software and provides software services in an economy and what kind of software is produced are crucial for the choice of intellectual property strategy. The relevance of intel-

lectual property policies and their enforcement grows as the capabilities of local software developers and enterprises improve (UNCTAD, 2002). In the early stages of development, when most indigenous software firms are engaged in relatively simple software services for the local market, the protection of intellectual property may be of limited concern. By contrast, the ease with which programmes are copied represents a disincentive for producers of packaged software to develop new and innovative products. However, such producers are unlikely to be found in most LDCs and indeed in many other developing countries (chapter I). In addition, while proprietary software may generate very large monopoly profits, it can also stifle competition by discouraging domestic SMEs from entering the software market, especially if a certain software becomes the de facto standard. In particular, stringent protection may restrict the extent to which SMEs can do research on the underlying principles of existing software to achieve interoperability.

As stressed in chapter IV, FOSS is fully intellectual property compliant. Indeed, it needs and uses copyright to maintain and promote its openness. While its spirit is anti-restrictive, it does not challenge current intellectual property from a formal, technical or legal perspective. Countries, institutions, businesses and individuals that switch from using unlicensed software to FOSS work to fulfil their obligations as designated by the World Intellectual Property Organization and the WTO Agreement on Trade-related Aspects of Intellectual Property Rights. Moreover, while FOSS licences oblige users to respect the terms and conditions of free access, copying and distribution as defined by a software's author(s), proprietary licensing allows only the owner to commercialize the intellectual property. Some experts have warned that for ICT the proprietary model can lead to excessive copyrighting and patent hoarding, with the final outcome being less R&D investment and innovation (Bessen, 2002; Bessen and Hunt, 2003).

The intellectual property system can be used as a tool to protect and reward creative software development, whether based on FOSS or proprietary models. Free software licences use the current copyright system in order to overcome conventional limitations on the creation, distribution and use of software.[38] Nevertheless, the widespread reliance on unlicensed copies of proprietary software offers little cost incentive for users to switch to FOSS-based programs. Efforts to decrease the use of unlicensed software may therefore improve the fundamental conditions for increased adoption of open source software.[39]

With the advent of cloud computing, an increasing number of organizations are embracing the concept of SaaS to manage their ICT resources. Cloud-based software does not necessarily require software distribution, which therefore enhances the control of the software developer and reduces the need for intellectual property protection and enforcement regimes. However, cloud computing is built on the same intellectual property rights that drive the general economy. Although cloud-computing contracts relate to the provision of services rather than the supply of software to customers, appropriate software licences may still need to be granted to customers to enable them to use software legally and correctly, without the risk of committing copyright infringement.

In India, stricter enforcement of intellectual property protection had an impact on software piracy and helped the country to attract more offshore software product development. Changes to the Indian Copy Right Law in 1994 made it illegal to make or distribute copies of copyrighted software and therefore punishable. In addition, the Government, in cooperation with NASSCOM, conducted regular anti-piracy raids to discourage software piracy.[40] In Brazil, increased enforcement of intellectual property protections also made the market more attractive for software product development (UNCTAD, 2002).

In deciding its policy on intellectual property in the software sector, each country must reflect upon its level of development, status of domestic software sector capabilities and current system for intellectual property protection, including its capacity to enforce intellectual property law and provide legal recourse. In principle, stronger intellectual property protection creates stronger incentives to develop new products – open source as well as proprietary software. However, for the local industry to benefit from such protection, it needs the capabilities to produce what the market demands. Thus, what initially seems to be a policy choice of favouring more or less FOSS or open standards becomes a nuanced decision dependent on local conditions.

Three common policy propositions require consideration. First, software purchased as-is for use by government or public offices should, as a minimum, conform to open data standards and file formats. Software product and service providers can be left to choose the intellectual property protection and restrictiveness of their products and thus the nature of their business model. Most standards-making bodies permit the use of proprietary works, but only if licences are on reasonable and non-discriminatory terms. Intellectual property protection and interoperability can also be addressed by reducing such protection to those parts of the software (that is, application program interfaces) that enable interoperability.

Second, software that is made to specification for use in government and public service should be delivered with the full source code. This gives the procurer the choice to release it – or not – under the optimal public or proprietary licence that will have a maximum positive economic impact, while giving due consideration to public data security issues. This is particularly important in the case of critical software related to, for example, national health data, national security and infrastructure management.

Finally, in cases where policymakers expect the domestic software sector to become a global player in the outsourcing business, heightened requirements need to be met not only in the strength of intellectual property regulations, but also in the capacity to enforce them and deal with legal misconduct in a decisive and swift manner. This is a prioritization issue and implies deciding to commit money and human capacity which may otherwise be used for other development activities. For low-income countries, and LDCs in particular, finding the resources for intellectual property enforcement represents a significant challenge.

Against this backdrop, intellectual property policies should not be discussed in isolation but rather as part of a broader range of policies. It may be appropriate for countries at various levels of development to consider a combination of (a) increased emphasis on FOSS in public procurement, (b) dedicated efforts to promote capacity-building in the local software sector and developer community, (c) gradually making software intellectual property protection and enforcement more stringent as an incentive for the local industry to develop software applications that can effectively serve local needs and (d) implementing regulations to safeguard fair competition among software developers and protect consumers.

2. Electronic transactions

In view of Government's role as a buyer of locally developed software products and services (section V. D) especially in relation to various e-government projects, it is important to consider the legal framework for electronic transactions. E-transactions also facilitate e-commerce and mobile commerce. E-transactions are carried out remotely, that is, without the simultaneous physical presence of the supplier and the consumer, and the substance of the transaction itself is intangible – in the form of digital information products and services such as software.

Electronic contracting raises questions and issues that do not arise with traditional paper-based contracting, particularly with regard to the validity and enforceability of the transactions. Hence, policymakers should seek to adopt a modern regulatory framework that addresses certain basic issues. In particular, the framework needs to establish that:

- E-transactions shall not be discriminated against solely because of their nature;
- Under certain conditions, the legal value of electronic transactions shall be equivalent to that of written or other forms of communication, without the need to review all existing legislation that establishes formal requirements;
- The law is flexible enough to address all relevant technologies.

These needs are embodied, respectively, in the principles of non-discrimination, functional equivalence and technological neutrality.

The United Nations Convention on the Use of Electronic Communications in International Contracts, prepared in 2005 by the United Nations Commission on International Trade Law (UNCITRAL),[41] aims at enhancing legal certainty and commercial predictability when electronic communications are used in international contracts. It addresses the determination of a party's location in an electronic environment; the time and place of dispatch and receipt of electronic communications; the use of automated message systems for contract formation; and the criteria to be used for establishing functional equivalence between electronic communications and paper documents – including original paper documents – as well as between electronic authentication methods and handwritten signatures. The Convention also contains a provision on input errors made by natural persons in electronic communications.

No global monitoring exists concerning the progress of developing countries in adapting their legislation to e-commerce. However, regional studies have been conducted by UNCTAD to take stock of legal advances in Latin America (UNCTAD, 2009a, 2009b) and in the Association of Southeast Asian Nations (ASEAN) (UNCTAD, 2008). Studies for other regions are under way.

3. Electronic and mobile payments

The issue of electronic payment systems has been touched upon in this report, particularly in connection with the new opportunities created by freelancing for software development work in developing countries. Without the ability to receive payments online, developers are at a disadvantage. Moreover, with the market demand for mobile applications also rising in developing countries, the possibility of paying electronically is important.

In Bangladesh, more than 10,000 freelancers offer their services online according to the Bangladeshi Software and Information Services Association. Until recently, the Central Bank of Bangladesh considered payments related to freelancing assignments and channelled through Western Union and similar services as remittances and taxed them accordingly. However, a directive issued in May 2011 by the Central Bank of Bangladesh recognized that these funds should be treated as export-related commercial income, which is tax exempt. This is significant for freelancers, who are now asking that PayPal be formally allowed as a means of electronic payment (UNCTAD, 2011a)

E-payments – and increasingly mobile payments – raise challenging issues for developing countries where payment facilities such as credit cards are scarce even in a physical environment, and where online payments are not backed by adequate legal frameworks. Since there is no face-to-face interaction in the majority of e-transactions, payment systems must be secure to build the confidence of users. Towards this end, most e-payment systems used for e-commerce rely on a trusted third party scheme. Such a scheme provides trust, security, identification and authentication. Its specific role varies from one system to another. Some schemes enable financial transactions over the Internet, such as PayPal where both buyers and sellers have to open an account in the trusted third party to transfer money into their trusted third party account.

Information regarding e-payment systems, which include the payment infrastructure and the legal framework, is only available for a few developing countries.[42] To facilitate e-payment systems, developing countries need to play a proactive role in encouraging the rapid adoption of market-friendly laws and regulations. Institutional cooperation among government agencies, regulatory bodies, central banks, financial institutions, telecommunications operators and industry associations is key to the success of adapting payment systems to online means (UNCTAD, 2012).

F. CONCLUDING REMARKS

This chapter has reviewed selected policy areas for developing countries to build software capabilities and strengthen their national software systems. While these policy domains are relevant for countries at all levels of development, each country has to adapt any strategy to its specific realities. Building local capabilities is important in order for developing countries to make effective use of imported software, adapt imported technology to their needs and eventually start to produce home-grown software services and products.

Given the rapid changes in technologies and markets of the software industry, governments face a challenge in ensuring that the policy approach they opt for will deliver the desired outcomes. This makes it particularly important for governments to establish an effective policy process which involves all relevant stakeholders. The fact that official data on the software industry are often missing, especially in low-income countries, makes regular dialogue with the software industry, the developer community and relevant universities and research institutes very important.

Significant knowledge gaps remain about how best to tailor national strategies aimed at fostering the software sector. In most developing countries, such strategies remain nascent. Moreover, the relevance of national strategies in helping to ensure that ICT-related services are well adapted to the needs of the country may not yet be well recognized. Indeed, developing countries that have launched national strategies for the sector have tended to focus more on its potential as a generator of export revenue than as a provider of domestic solutions.

As noted in this chapter, there are many policy measures and tools available to governments to promote the development of relevant capabilities. Together, these policy measures and tools can contribute to building skills and technological upgrading, create demand for local software developers and enterprises, promote interaction and learning among relevant stakeholders and over time strengthen the entire software system with a view to enhancing the development impact of ICT use. Developing countries about to make the development of software capabilities a development priority may draw lessons from countries that have already gained experience in this area and adapt them to fit their specific contexts.

NOTES

1 A useful tool for Governments to consider is the IT Sector Manual and Toolbox developed by BMZ in Germany (Germany, Federal Ministry for Economic Cooperation and Development, 2011a).

2 See, for example, http://broadbandtoolkit.org/en/home and http://www.broadbandcommission.org/work/documents.aspx.

3 See http://ec.europa.eu/research/regions/pdf/sc_park.pdf.

4 In Argentina, 60 per cent of all software enterprises are located in Buenos Aires and in Brazil most software firms are found in and around Sao Paulo. A similar situation prevails in Mexico, where software development centres are mainly located in Guadalajara and Monterrey (ECLAC, 2011).

5 See "A Silicon Valley Dream Grows in Guatemala, Despite the Risks", New York Times, 16 November 2011.

6 See ISO (http://www.iso.org/iso/home.html).

7 For example, with Agile, Scrum, ITIL, Control Objectives for Information and related Technology (COBIT), ISO 9000 and Rational Unified Process (RUP). For more information, see http://www.sei.cmu.edu/cmmi.

8 ESI Center Eastern Europe (http://www.esicenter.bg).

9 See http://it-mark.eu.

10 See SOFTEX (http://softex.br/mpsbr).

11 The MPS.br model for software process improvement is based on the standards ISO/EIC 12207, ISO/EIC15504 and CMMI version 1.2.

12 ITIL underpins the foundations of ISO/IEC 20000, the international service management standard for IT service management. See http://www.itil-officialsite.com/AboutITIL/WhatisITIL.aspx.

13 See www.qaiglobalinstitute.com/.

14 See www.iist.org/.

15 See www.istqb.org/.

16 See http://soft-engineering.blogspot.de/search/label/CMM%20level.

17 In South Africa, for example, this challenge was identified in the Industrial Policy Action Plan for 2012/13-2014/15 (South Africa, Department of Trade and Industry, 2010).

18 Another example is the ESI Center Eastern Europe in Sofia, Bulgaria (www.esicenter.bg/). It was established in the framework of a project involving BASSCOM, the Bulgarian Ministry of Transport and GIZ. It has become a leading provider of training and certification in quality standards such as CMMI, ITMark and ISO 15504.

19 See http://aseti.org/.

20 See http://ictcluster.bg/en.

21 The Prosoft Fund disbursed $45 million in 2010, which were matched by the private sector ($68 million), state entities ($17 million) and to a lesser degree higher education institutions ($450,000), for a total of $132 million. By November 2010, more than 6,600 firms had been supported. (Based on information provided by the Vice Ministry of Industry and Trade, Ministry of Economy (Mexico City, March 2011)).

22 In addition to these two areas, countries may address skills shortages through migration of relevant expertise.

23 See http://www.nac.nasscom.in/nactech.

24 See http://www.strathmore.edu/fit/component/content/article/320.

25 On industry-based education and training for the Egyptian ICT industry (UNCTAD, 2011b: 27).

26 See http://www.meltwater.org/about/.

27 See http://unctad.org/en/PublicationsLibrary/dtlstictmisc2012d4_en.pdf.

28 See http://www.sofex.org.gt.

29 See http://aseti.org/.

30 See, for example, UNCTAD, 2011c and UNCTAD, 2011d.

31 Certifications are offered in areas such as multimedia, IT and BPO, English and project management. See www.mexico-first.org.

32 Based on information provided by the Vice Ministry of Industry and Trade, Ministry of Economy (Mexico City, March 2011).

33 See http://www.softex.br/softexEn/_projects/business.asp. Private sector partners include the Association of Brazilian Information Technology Companies (ASSESPRO) and the National Federation of Information Technology Companies (FENAINFO).

34 See http://www.mexico-it.net/index.php?Itemid=12&id=11&layout=blog&option=com_content&view=category.

35 See http://alsionline.org.

36 See http://www.softex.br/softexEn/_projects/business.asp.

37 In general, to favour ICT uptake, special attention should be paid to the following legal issues: electronic transactions, electronic signatures and authentication, data protection and privacy, consumer protection, computer crime, intellectual property, competition, taxation and information security at large.

38 Some FOSS advocates question the use of software idea patents (UNCTAD, 2004).

39 Other FOSS advocates have argued in favour of relaxing intellectual property protection, using the infant industry argument in reverse (Rizk and El-Kassas, 2010: 140): "Effectively, open source software remains the infant domestic industry that needs protection. In this case, protection does not refer to blocking imports by imposing tariff barriers, but rather to shielding open source software firms by freeing them from the threat of market dominance by larger business structures, which is partly due to proprietary intellectual property rights protection."

40 For a detailed account of the NASSCOM activities in promoting IT, see "Power Lobbying", Business India, 19 February to 4 March 2001.

41 Information on UNCITRAL texts on e-commerce is available in English athttp://www.uncitral.org/uncitral/en/uncitral_texts/electronic_commerce.html (the same content is also available in Arabic, Chinese, French, Russian and Spanish).

42 See for instance http://www.bis.org/publ/cpss97.htm.

CONCLUSIONS AND POLICY RECOMMENDATIONS

6

Governments have a key role to play in fostering software capabilities. In countries that have succeeded in strengthening their software industries, the development of a national strategy, based on consultations with all relevant stakeholders, has been a useful starting point. But such strategies need to be adapted to the specific context of each country.

Drawing on the analysis in preceding parts of the report, this final chapter presents overall conclusions related to the role of software in developing countries and identifies a set of policy recommendations.

The ability of a country to adopt, adapt and develop appropriate technological solutions and applications depends on the strength of its domestic capabilities. This applies in particular to software as a general-purpose technology relevant to a wide range of economic and social development fields. As ICTs permeate societies in countries at all levels of development, developing the technological capabilities to adopt and adapt existing software solutions, and eventually to innovate, becomes increasingly important. Access to such capabilities can make ICTs a more powerful enabler of government, health care, education, business and other services. To maximize the development value of software applications, they should be geared to the precise needs of different countries and contexts.

Locally trained expertise can be better positioned to understand cultural and linguistic dynamics and to produce adequately tailored solutions. The important role of locally developed applications was illustrated in earlier chapters, for example, in making poverty reduction initiatives more effective in Lao People's Democratic Republic, improving market access services for farmers in Bangladesh, producing mobile apps in local languages in Sri Lanka and reducing the dependency in Nigeria on imports of foreign software.

Once a basic level of capabilities is in place, countries may seek to develop their national software system along different paths towards higher-level value added activities targeted at the domestic and/or export market. Such technological upgrading has been witnessed especially in India and the other BRIC countries, but also in several other developing countries. In some cases it has been associated primarily with exports of software services (for example, Costa Rica, India, Sri Lanka). In other cases, improved software capabilities have been applied domestically, often as critical inputs to other export-oriented industries or to the public sector (for example, Brazil, China, the Republic of Korea).

Current changes in the global software landscape are also widening the scope for countries at lower levels of development to participate in production, learning and innovation networks for software development and production. Improved mobile connectivity, rapid diffusion of smartphones and greater reliance on open systems of innovation and open source software all contribute to this wider scope. At the same time, available data indicate significant potential for more investment in software in developing countries.

Governments should take an active part in fostering their national software systems. Intentionally or unintentionally, they are influencing the evolution of these systems. Governments are important buyers of software. They determine the curricula for the education of new software engineers as well as the availability of affordable ICT infrastructure. They also shape the legal and regulatory frameworks that influence the extent to which ICTs are taken up and productively used in the economy and society.

Inadequate attention to the national software system can imply several missed opportunities. When this is the case, the costs for software users in the private and public sectors are higher as there are fewer domestic software enterprises competing in the market. Moreover, a larger proportion of money invested in software ends up abroad. Fewer software jobs emerge in the local economy – jobs that might otherwise be attractive for skilled young people. Imported software is likely to be less than optimally adapted to the specific needs of the country. Finally, and as a result of the previous observations, the level of informatization is lower, thereby reducing the development benefits from ICTs and slowing down the transition to an inclusive information society. Several policy recommendations can be made in this context.

Strategies must be tailored to each context: The experience of countries that have successfully managed to strengthen their national software systems suggests that the development of a national strategy, based on consultations with relevant stakeholders, is a useful starting point. Although a national software system framework is relevant to all countries, not every country will be able to repeat the export success of India. For the large majority of developing countries, the main focus should be on nurturing the capabilities needed to supply relevant solutions to users in the domestic market. Needs specific to the domestic market are less likely to be addressed by foreign providers. The expanding demand for locally developed mobile apps (as witnessed, for example, in Sri Lanka) and growing reliance on FOSS create opportunities for entrepreneurs to build a business and for individual developers to generate income. Over time, it may be possible to upgrade and diversify software-related activities by expanding the range of services offered, venturing into software product development or seeking clients abroad.

In order for a software strategy to have the desired effects, it needs to be rooted in a thorough understanding of economic realities, industrial capabilities, the availability of skills and current and expected future needs for software in the private and public sectors. A careful diagnosis is therefore needed to assess how the software sector can be promoted and what approach will realistically deliver good results. Such an assessment should consider the producers and the users of software as well as the various enabling factors highlighted in chapter I. The outcome of an analysis of existing strengths, weaknesses, opportunities and threats can help to identify critical underlying challenges and enable Governments to set priorities for the short- and long-term development of a system.

Software strategies should be integrated into broader development plans: A national software strategy should be consistent with the overall policy framework governing the development and use of ICTs across sectors to help meet development objectives. This is important in order to ensure that outputs from the software system contribute effectively to a government's development goals and that policies in relevant areas support rather than undermine strengthening the software system. To this end, effective coordination between all relevant government bodies is of essence. The case of public procurement is illustrative. The government body dealing with procurement may not feel accountable for promoting the domestic industry. Its main focus is typically on obtaining the best possible value for money when procuring goods and services. For the economy as a whole, however, encouraging the development of local software suppliers in the short term may increase the number of potential bidders competing for government tenders in the long term, thereby also enhancing the value for money in future procurements. Coordination is particularly important in view of the range of factors that can influence the performance of the software system, including the regulatory environment, education policies, e-government plans and enterprise development.

Partner with other stakeholders in designing the strategy: A key role of Government is to catalyse and steer a strategy development process and the implementation of the key elements of a national software system. In this process, other actors – the software industry, the software developer community, universities and research centres – should be engaged and consulted. Such collaboration is especially important in view of the rapid speed at which the software sector is evolving. The software industry can provide vital information on market and technology trends, skill needs, barriers to growth and policy changes that could help strengthen the system as a whole. National IT/software associations are strategically positioned to contribute in these areas. Universities and research centres can provide information on the education of engineers and possibilities for joint software development activities.

Strike a balance between domestic and export market promotion: Exports of software and IT services can be an attractive option to generate foreign exchange, reduce trade deficits, induce job creation and transfer technology. Moreover, software exports can accelerate the integration into global value chains and contribute to economic diversification. To harness the value of software in local economic development, however, it is important to ensure that software services and capabilities are available to support the local needs of the public and private sectors. Domestic use of software can be instrumental in enhancing the competitiveness of enterprises and the welfare of society. The domestic market also provides a potentially important foundation for developing relevant skills and innovative products. Countries may therefore seek to strike a balance between export sales and software development for domestic consumption. Where domestic demand is constrained by weak purchasing power, active government policies are particularly important to create demand for domestic software producers.

Adapt education and training schemes to the new ICT landscape: The strategy should include efforts to make available a pool of skilled personnel. The availability of an educated workforce and students enrolled in computer-related education fundamentally affects the potential of a national software system. The regular education system and training facilities for professionals should adapt their curricula to match the evolving needs of the software system. This necessitates close dialogue with private sector stakeholders, universities and software users. Particular focus should be given to skills development around new models of networking, community building and international knowledge-sharing. At the same time, education should be generic, flexible and adaptable, rather than target certain programming languages or tools. Software enterprises value in particular employees with the ability to learn new things on the job as projects evolve. Governments may also consider the use of incentives to encourage software enterprises to invest in in-house training and to introduce apprenticeships as part of vocational training programmes.

Encourage technological upgrading: Attention to quality is crucial to encourage and enable enterprises to upgrade their capabilities and move towards higher-level value added activities. In this context, governments may seek to encourage and facilitate greater adoption of relevant international standards and certifications. Options to be considered include quality strategy development, awareness-raising, capacity-building, training and quality certification and education. In countries with nascent software capabilities, an incremental approach is recommended in which early initiatives focus on less complex and easier to implement standards. This is important to avoid overstretching the resources and organizational capabilities of microenterprises and small enterprises.

Facilitate the strengthening of developer communities: The innovation process in the global software industry is transforming towards greater reliance on networked, peer-to-peer and co-creation models. This offers new opportunities that governments, donors and private sector actors can leverage by organizing events to which the local developer community can contribute as well as from which to learn. Relevant initiatives include developer meetings devoted to specific software platforms or certain development concerns (clean water, disaster risk reduction, open government), Google Summer of Code and various technology conferences. Governments can also facilitate the participation of local software freelancers by ensuring that the legal framework permits electronic payment. Without the ability to receive payments online, local developers are at a disadvantage. Ensuring that there is a marketplace for local developers to sell their apps is central to making apps development sustainable. Governments may help catalyse such developments by incentivizing mobile operators to develop mobile apps marketplaces and by identifying their own needs for new mobile applications, thereby creating demand.

Give adequate attention to FOSS, especially in public procurement: While the adoption of FOSS is currently most widely promoted in Europe, there are strong reasons for developing and transition economies to rely more on FOSS. For software

enterprises and developers, FOSS can promote domestic market development and local innovation. Rather than purchasing software licences and services abroad, local FOSS development, sales and services can help keep resources within the local economy, avoid dependency on specific vendors and provide opportunities for income generation and employment. FOSS can also enable local software SMEs to establish new niche markets. Governments should seize the various advantages of relying on FOSS when this offers a competitive solution to their software needs. Technological trends, especially with regard to cloud computing, mobile applications and big data, are further accentuating the reliance on FOSS.

Development partners should offer support: In the spirit of WSIS, and to make ICTs a more powerful enabler of development, development partners should expand their assistance to developing countries in the software sector. Examples cited in this report offer a basis on which to build, including with regard to training, application development, support to strengthening legal and regulatory frameworks, supporting IT/software associations and clusters, meetings of developers and software SME development. Development partners can also make a contribution by using local software industries when procuring software services and applications for use in development assistance projects.

Leverage South-South cooperation: The level of software capabilities and the market orientation of software industries in developing countries vary considerably. At the same time, some of the leading producers of software products and services are based in the South, and there is considerable experience in developing countries with public procurement and the use of software, skills development and the promotion of new business models. This combination of diversity and excellence makes software an attractive area for South-South cooperation. Several examples of such collaboration already exist (Ojo et al., 2008) but can be further enhanced through research backed by theory and empirical evidence. Through its three pillars, UNCTAD could offer a platform for developing countries to discuss using South-South cooperation to bridge the digital divide, develop software capabilities and harness the software and ICT sector for development. In particular, the platform could facilitate integrated development of the ICT sector wherein both production and use are promoted to avoid a one-sided approach with which many developing countries become mere passive adopters of technology.

REFERENCES

Abramova A (2012). Russian software industry profile. Background unpublished paper prepared for UNCTAD.

Asociación Hondureña de Tecnologías de Información (AHTI) (2011). *Honduran IT Industry Barometer 2011*.

Ajila SA and Wu D (2007). Empirical study of the effects of open source adoption on software development economics. *Journal of Systems and Software*. 80(9):1517–1529.

Argentina, Ministry of Economy and Production (2004). *Software and IT Services Blue and White Book. Strategic Plan 2004-2014 and Action Plan 2004–2007*. Ministry of Economy and Production. Buenos Aires.

Arora A, Arunachalam VS, Asundi J and Ronald F (2001). The Indian software services industry. *Research Policy*. 30(8):1267–87.

AT Kearney (2011). The app frenzy: Just a short-lived fad? AT Kearney Inc. Chicago.

Balakrishnan P (2006). Benign neglect or strategic intent? Contested lineage of Indian software industry. *Economic and Political Weekly*. 41(36).Bamiro OA (2007). *The Vision and Challenges of ICT Production in Africa: Software Production and Services*. ICT project Working Papers. Paper No. ICTWP_05.

BASSCOM (2011). *Bulgarian IT Industry Barometer 2011*.

Berkman Center for Internet & Society (2005). *Roadmap for Open ICT Ecosystems*. Available at http://cyber.law.harvard.edu/epolicy.

Bessen J (2002). What good is free software? In: Hahn RW, ed., *Government Policy toward Open Source Software*. AEI-Brookings Joint Center for Regulatory Studies. Washington D.C. 12–33.

Bessen J and Hunt RM (2003). *An Empirical Look at Software Patents*. Federal Reserve Bank of Philadelphia.

Broadband Commission for Digital Development (2011). *Broadband: A Platform for Progress*. ITU and UNESCO. Geneva and Paris.

Bruegge C (2011). *Measuring Digital Local Content*. No. 188. OECD Publishing. Paris.

Bruell N (2003). Exporting software from Indonesia. *The Electronic Journal on Information Systems in Developing Countries*. 13(7):1–9.

Bruton G and Ahlstrom D (2003). An institutional view of China's venture capital industry: Explaining the differences between China and the West. *Journal of Business Venturing*. 18:233–259.

Business Software Association and IDC (2011). *2010 Piracy Study*. Business Software Association. Washington D.C.

Capgemini (2011). *World Quality Report 2011–2012*.

Carmel E (2003). The new software exporting nations: Success factors. *The Electronic Journal on Information Systems in Developing Countries*. 13(4):1–12.

Center for Strategic and International Studies (CSIS) (2010). Government Open Source Policies. Available at http://csis.org/files/publication/100416_Open_Source_Policies.pdf.

Chaudhuri A (2012). *Creeping Tiger, Soaring Dragon: India, China and Competition in Information Technologies*. National Institute of Science, Technology and Development Studies. New Delhi.

Chesbrough HW (2003). The era of open innovation. *MIT Sloan Management Review*. 44(3):35–41.

Chesbrough HW (2005). *Open Innovation: The New Imperative for Creating And Profiting from Technology*. Harvard Business Review Press.

Cimoli M, Dosi G and Stiglitz JE, eds. (2009). *Industrial Policy and Development: The Political Economy of Capabilities Accumulation*. Oxford University Press. Oxford.

Cohen W and Levinthal D (1989). Innovation and learning: Two faces of R&D. *Economic Journal*. 99:569–96.

D'Costa AP (2003). Uneven and combined development: Understanding India's software exports. *World Development*. 31(1):211–26.

Dauterive J and Fok W (2004). Venture capital for China: Opportunities and challenges. *Managerial Finance*. 30(2):3–15.

ECLAC (2011). *Foreign Direct Investment in Latin America and the Caribbean 2010*. United Nations. Santiago, Chile.

Edquist C, ed. (1997). *Systems of Innovation: Technologies, Institutions and Organizations*. Routledge.

EITO (2011). *European Information Technology Observatory 2011*. Available at http://www.eito.com/EITO-2011.

Electronics and Computer Software Export Promotion Council (various years). *Statistical Yearbook*. Electronics and Computer Software Export Promotion Council. New Dehli.

Emerging Markets Private Equity Association (EMPEA) (2012). *EMPEA Industry Statistics*. Available at http://www.empea.net/Main-Menu-Category/Resources/EMPEA-Research/Industry-Statistics.aspx.

Ernst & Young (2011). Open source software in business-critical environments. Available at http://www.ey.com/Publication/vwLUAssets/Open_Source_Software_in_business_critical_environments/$FILE/Open_Source_Software_EN.pdf.

European Software Institute (ESI) Eastern Europe (2007). Final report on the mapping of IT industry related international standards project implementation. Sofia, Bulgaria.

Fontana R, Kuhn BM, Moglen E, Norwood M, Ravicher DB, Sandler K, Vasile J and Williamson A (2008). *A Legal Issues Primer for Open Source and Free Software Projects*. Available at http://www.softwarefreedom.org/resources/2008/foss-primer.pdf.

Forrester (2012a). Africa's ICT forecast looks increasingly cloudy. Forrester. Cambridge, Massachusetts.

Forrester (2012b). Emerging markets and technologies drive tech industry growth. Forrester, Cambridge, Massachusetts.

Forrester (2012c). Global tech market outlook for 2012 and 2013. Forrester, Cambridge, Massachusetts.

Fransman M (2010). *The New ICT Ecosystem: Implications for Policy and Regulation*. Cambridge University Press.

Fu X, Pietrobelli C and Soete L (2011). The role of foreign technology and indigenous innovation in the emerging economies: Technological change and catching-up. *World Development*. 39(7):1204–1212.

Galpaya H (2011). *Internet Case Studies: Broadband in Sri Lanka: Glass Half Full or Half Empty?* infoDev/World Bank.

Gantz JF (2006). *The Contribution of Software and IT Services Industries to the Chinese Economy*. IDC.

Gengler EB (2003). Ukraine and success criteria for the software exports industry. *The Electronic Journal on Information Systems in Developing Countries*. 13(8):1–18.

Germany, Federal Ministry for Economic Cooperation and Development (2011a). *IT Sector Promotion in Developing and Emerging Countries: Manual*. Deutsche Gesellschaft für Internationale Zusammenarbeit (GIZ) GmbH. Bonn and Eschborn.

Germany, Federal Ministry for Economic Cooperation and Development (2011b). *IT Sector Promotion in Developing and Emerging Countries: Toolbox*. Deutsche Gesellschaft für Internationale Zusammenarbeit (GIZ) GmbH. Bonn and Eschborn.

Ghosh RA (2006). Economic impact of open source software on innovation and the competitiveness of the Information and Communication Technologies (ICT) sector in the EU. UNU-MERIT.

Gregory N, Nollen S and Tenev S (2009). *New Industries from New Places: The Emergence of the Hardware and Software Industries in China and India*. Stanford Economics and Finance.

Heeks RB (1999). Software strategies in developing countries. *Communications of the ACM*. 42(6):15–20.

Heeks RB and Nicholson B (2004). Software export success factors and strategies in "follower" nations. *Competition & Change*. 8(3):267–303.

Huang Y (2011). Understanding the software industry in China: export performance and regional development. *Journal of Emerging Knowledge on Emerging Markets*. 3:289–307.

ict@innovation (2010). *ict@innovation: Free your IT-Business in Africa!* InWent and FOSSFA. Bonn.

IDC (2009). Aid to recovery: The economic impact of IT, software, and the Microsoft Ecosystem on the global economy. Available at www.idc.com.

Ilavarasan PV (2011). "Center for global" or "local for global"? R&D centers of ICT multinationals in India. In: Howlett RJ, Howlett RJ, and Jain LC, eds., *Innovation Through Knowledge Transfer 2010*. Smart Innovation, Systems and Technologies. Springer Berlin Heidelberg: 275–282.

India, Ministry of Communications and Information Technology (various years). *Annual Report*. Ministry of Communications and Information Technology. New Delhi.

India, Ministry of Finance (2012). *Economic Survey 2012–13*. Ministry of Finance. New Delhi.

IMAP (2010). *Computing & Internet Software Global Report 2010*. IMAP. Delaware.

ITEdgenews.com (2012). Nigeria software industry: An industry in search of a present and a future. 9 January.

Joseph KJ (2006). *Information Technology, Innovation System and Trade Regime in Developing Countries: India and the ASEAN*. Palgrave Macmillan.

Joseph KJ (2010). Sectoral innovation systems in developing countries: the case of India's ICT in India. In: Lundvall B-A, Joseph KJ, Chaminade C and Vang J, eds., *Handbook on Innovation Systems and Developing Countries: Building Domestic Capabilities in a Global Setting*. Edward Elgar. Cheltenham.

Joseph KJ and Harilal KN (2001). Structure and growth of India's IT exports: Implications of an export-oriented growth strategy. *Economic and Political Weekly*. 36(34):3263–70.

Kang J-H (2010). E-Government in Korea. *Journal of E-Governance*. 33(3):130–138.

Kattuman P and Iyer K (2001). Human capital development in the move up the value chain: The case of the Indian software and services industry. In: Kagami M and Tsuji M, eds., *The "IT" Revolution and Developing Countries: Late-comer Advantage?* Institute of Developing Economies and Japan External Trade Organization. Tokyo: 208–227.

Kenney M, Han K and Tanaka S (2002). *Scattering Geese: The Venture Capital Industries of East Asia: A Report to the World Bank*. Berkeley Roundtable on the International Economy. University of California, Berkeley. Berkeley.

Koh EKY (2009). *The Adoption of Open Source Software by Singaporean Companies*. Quensland University of Technology.

Kumar N (2001). Indian software industry development: international and national perspective. *Economic and Political Weekly*. 36(45):4278–4290.

Kumar N and Joseph K (2005). Export of software and business process outsourcing from developing countries: Lessons from India. *Asia Pacific Trade and Investment Review*. 1(1):91–108.

Kumar N and Joseph KJ (2006). National innovation systems and India's IT capability: Are there any lessons for ASEAN new comers? In: Lundvall B-A, Intarakumnerd P and Vang J, eds., *Asia's Innovation System in Transition*. Edward Elgar Publishers. Northampton, Massachusetts: 227–256.

Lall S (2001). *Competitiveness, Technology and Skills*. Edward Elgar Publishers. Northampton, Massachussets.

Lall S (2005). Rethinking industrial strategy: The role of the State in the face of globalization. In: Gallagher K, ed., *Putting Development First: The Importance of Policy Space in the WTO and IFIs*. Zed Books. London and New York.

Li M and Gao M (2003). Strategies for developing China's software industry. *Information Technologies and International Development*. 1(1):61–73.

Linux Foundation (2012). *Linux adoption trends 2012: A survey of enterprise end users*. Linux Foundation Report.

Lundvall B-A, ed. (1992). *National Systems of Innovation: Towards a Theory of Innovation and Interactive Learning*. Pinter Pub Ltd.

Lungo JH and Kaasbol JJ (2007). Experiences of open source software in institutions: Cases from Tanzania and Norway. In: *Proceedings of the 9th International Conference on Social Implications of Computers in Developing Countries*, São Paulo, Brazil, May 2007.

Macias-Garza M and Heeks RB (2006). *Analysing the Organisational Risk and Change of CMM Software Process Improvement in a Nearshoring Firm*. Development Informatics Working Paper No. 28. Institute for Development Policy and Management University of Manchester.

Malerba F (2005). Sectoral systems of innovation: a framework for linking innovation to the knowledge base, structure and dynamics of sectors. *Economics of Innovation and New Technology*. 14(1–2):63–82.

Mandel M (2012). Where the jobs are: The app economy. TechNet.

MASIT (Macedonian Information and Communication Technology Chamber of Commerce) (2010). *Export Promotion Strategy for the Macedonian Software and IT Services Industry*. Macedonian Information and Communication Technology Chamber of Commerce. Skopje.

MASIT (2011). *Macedonian Information Technology Industry Barometer 2011*. Macedonian Information and Communication Technology Chamber of Commerce. Skopje.

Mata FJ, Matarrita R and Pinto C (2009). Situación de la oferta de recurso humano para el sector de tecnología y comunicación en Costa Rica: Análisis para el decenio 1997–2006 y recomendaciones de política. Observatorio de Tecnología de Información y Comunicación, Universidad Nacional. San Jose, (unpublished).

Metcalfe JS (1995). Technology systems and technology policy in an evolutionary framework. *Cambridge Journal of Economics*. 19(1):25–46.

Mickoleit A, Reimsbach-Kounatze C, Serra-Vallejo C, Vickery G and Wunsch-Vincent S (2009). *The Impact of the Crisis on ICTs and their Role in the Recovery*. No. 163. OECD Publishing. Paris.

Munoz C (2011). Free/open source software in Latin America: An annotated bibliography. Available at http://takhteyev.org/papers/Munoz-2011.pdf.

NASSCOM (various years). *The IT-BPO sector in India; Strategic Review*. NASSCOM. New Delhi.

NASSCOM (2011). *Nasscom Strategic Review 2011*. NASSCOM. New Delhi.

NASSCOM (2012). *The IT-BPO sector in India; Strategic Review*. NASSCOM. New Delhi.

Nelson RR (2008). Economic development from the perspective of evolutionary economic theory. *Oxford Development Studies*. 36(1):9–23.

Nelson RR, ed. (1993). *National Innovation Systems: A Comparative Analysis*. Oxford University Press. Oxford.

Nicholson B and Sahay S (2003). Building Iran's software industry: An assessment of plans and prospects. *The Electronic Journal on Information Systems in Developing Countries*. 13(6):1–19.

Nicholson B and Sahay S (2009). Software exports development in Costa Rica: Potential for policy reforms. *Information Technology for Development*. 15(1):4–16.

North DC (1990). *Institutions, Institutional Change and Economic Performance*. Cambridge University Press. Cambridge.

Observatorio SOFTEX (2012). *Software and IT Services: The Brazilian Industry in Perspective (Short Version)*. Association for the Promotion of Brazilian Software Excellence. Sao Paulo.

OECD (2008). *Open Innovation in Global Networks*. OECD Publishing. Paris.

Oh D-H (2011). Ways to strengthen Korea's software industry. *Korea Economic Trends*. 9–13. Samsung Economic Research Institute. 14 March.

Ojo A, Janowski T, Basanya R and Reed M (2008). *Developing and Harnessing Software Technology in the South – The Roles of China, India, Brazil, and South Africa*. No. 2008/89. Center for Electronic Governance, United Nations University, IIST.

Orbicom and IDRC (2010). *Digital Review of Asia Pacific 2009-2010*. Sage Publications.

Parthasarathy B (2006). The Political Economy of the Indian Software Industry. In: Parayil G, ed., *Political Economy & Information Capitalism in India: Digital Divide, Development Divide & Equity*. Palgrave Macmillan: 153–173.

Paus E (2010). *The Uneven Development of Local Technological Capabilities in Costa Rica*. No. mimeo. ILO. Geneva.

Porter ME (1998). *Competitive Advantage of Nations*. Free Press.

Qiang CZ-W, Clarke GR and Halewood N (2006). The role of ICT in doing business. *2006 Information and Communications for Development: Global Trends and Policies*. World Bank. Washington, D.C.

Rizk N and El-Kassas S (2010). The software industry in Egypt: What role for open source? In: Rizk N and Shaver L, eds., *Access to Knowledge in Egypt, New Research on Intellectual Property, Innovation, and Development*. Bloomsbury United States of America: 134–173.

Rodrik D (2004). Industrial policy for the twenty-first century. United Nations publication. Cambridge, Massachusetts. Available at http://www.hks.harvard.edu/fs/drodrik/Research%20papers/UNIDOSep.pdf. .

Roeding CR, Purkert G, Kindner SK and Ralph M (1999). *Secrets of Software Success: Management Insights from 100 Software Firms Around the World*. Harvard Business Press.

Russoft Association (2011). *Russian Software Developing Industry and Software Exports: 8th Annual Survey*. Russoft. St. Petersburg.

Schofiled A (2011). 2011 JCSE-ITWeb Skills Survey: Summary of Main Findings. Joburg Centre for Software Engineering. Johannesburg.

Schware R (1992). Software entry strategies for developing countries. *World Development*. 20(2):143–64.

Seibold B (2010). *Unleashing Open Innovation Systems. Strengthening Innovation Systems in the Context of Development Cooperation.* Deutsche Gesellschaft für Technische Zusammenarbeit GmbH. Eschborn: 87–92.

Smith M and Elder L (2010). Open ICT Ecosystems Transforming the Developing World. *Journal of International Technology and International Development.* 6(1):65–71.

SOFEX (Commission de Software de Exportación) (Guatemala) (2011). *Guatemalan IT Industry Barometer 2011.* SOFEX. Guatemala City.

Soriyan HA and Heeks RB (2004). A Profile of Nigeria's Software Industry. Working Paper 21, Institute for Development Policy and Management, University of Manchester.

South Africa, Department of Communications (2012). Defining a new era in ICTs for all South Africans: The path to creating a National Integrated ICT Policy for South Africa. Government Gazette No. 35255. Department of Pretoria.

South Africa, Department of Trade and Industry (2010). *Industrial Policy Action Plan 2012/13–2014/15.* Department of Trade and Industry. Pretoria.

Sri Lanka, Export Development Board (2007). *Export Value Survey 2007.* Export Development Board. Colombo.

Sri Lanka, Export Development Board (2008). *Sri Lanka IT/ITES Industry, 2008.* Export Development Board. Colombo.

Sri Lanka, Export Development Board (2010). *ICT Export Value Survey, 2010.* Sri Lanka Export Development Board. Colombo.

Sri Lanka, Department of Census and Statistics (2009). *Computer Literacy Survey.* Department of Census and Statistics. Colombo.

Sri Lanka, Department of Census and Statistics (2011). *Household Income and Expenditure Survey Final Report.* Ministry of Finance and Planning. Colombo.

Sri Lanka, Ministry of Finance and Planning (2010). *Sri Lanka, The Emerging Wonder of Asia. Mahinda Chintana – Vision for the Future. 2010.* Department of National Planning, Ministry of Finance and Planning.

Stryszowski P (2009). *Innovation in the Software Sector.* OECD Publishing. Paris.

Sudan R, Ayers S, Dongier P, Muente-Kunigami A and Qiang CZ-W (2010). *The Global Opportunity in IT Based Services: Assessing and Enhancing Country Competitiveness.* World Bank Publications.

Sung K-J (2011). Comparison of ICT Development Strategies in Asia. *International Telecommunications Policy Review.* 18(4):1–25.

Tessler S, Barr A and Hanna N (2002). National software industry development: Considerations for government planners. *The Electronic Journal of Information Systems in Developing Countries.* 13(10):1–17.

Tschang T (2003). *China's Software Industry and Its Implications for India.* Working Paper No. 205. OECD Development Centre. Paris.

UNCTAD (2002). *Changing Dynamics of Global Computer Software and Services Industry: Implications for Developing Countries: Technology for Development.* United Nations publications. New York and Geneva.

UNCTAD (2003a). Free and open source software: Implications for ICT policy and development. *E-Commerce and Development Report 2003.* United Nations publications. New York and Geneva: 95–134.

UNCTAD (2003b). *E-Commerce and Development Report 2003.* United Nations publications. New York and Geneva.

UNCTAD (2004). Free and open sources software: Policy and development implications. Expert Meeting on Free and Open Source Software: Policy and Development Implications Geneva, 22–24 September 2004, No. TD/B/COM.3/EM.21/2. Commission on Enterprise, Business Facilitation and Development. Geneva.

UNCTAD (2008). *Information Economy Report 2007–2008: Science and technology for development: The new paradigm of ICT.* United Nations publications. New York and Geneva.

UNCTAD (2009a). *Estudio Sobre las Perspectivas de la Armonización de la Ciberlegislación en Centroamérica y el Caribe.* United Nations publications. New York and Geneva.

UNCTAD (2009b). *Study on Prospects for Harmonizing Cyberlegislation in Latin America.* UNCTAD/DTL/STICT/2009/1. United Nations publications. New York and Geneva.

UNCTAD (2010). *Information Economy Report 2010: ICTs, Enterprises and Poverty Alleviation*. United Nations publications. Geneva and New York.

UNCTAD (2011a). *Information Economy Report 2011: ICTs as an enabler to private sector development*. United Nations publications. New York and Geneva.

UNCTAD (2011b). *ICT Policy Review Egypt*. United Nations publications. New York and Geneva.

UNCTAD (2011c). *Science, Technology & Innovation Policy Review : El Salvador*. UNCTAD/DTL/STICT/2011/4. United Nations publications. New York and Geneva.

UNCTAD (2011d). *Science, Technology & Innovation Policy Review: Peru*. UNCTAD/DTL/STICT/2010/2. United Nations publications. New York and Geneva.

UNCTAD (2012). *Mobile Money for Business Development in the East African Community: A Comparative Study of Existing Platforms and Regulations*. United Nations. New York and Geneva.

UNCTAD and BMZ (forthcoming). *Promoting Local IT Sector Development Through Public Procurement*. United Nations publications. New York and Geneva.

UNESCO (2010). *UNESCO Science Report, 2010*. UNESCO.

UNU-MERIT (2007). *Free/Libre and Open Source Software: Worldwide Impact Study*. United Nations University. Maastricht.

Vijayabaskar M and Suresh Babu M (2009). The Development of Technological Capabilities in India: Information and Communication Technology in selected sectors. Background paper prepared for the International Labour Organisation (unpublished).

Vital Wave Consulting (2009). *mHealth for Development: The Opportunity of Mobile Technology for Healthcare in the Developing World*. UN Foundation-Vodafone Foundation Partnership. Washington, D.C. and Berkshire.

Walker M (2009). The Economic Impact of IT, Software and Microsoft in South Africa. IDC (Powerpoint presentation).

WITSA (2010). *Digital Planet 2010*. World Information Technology and Services Alliance. Washington D.C.

World Bank (2010). *Implementation status and results report: E-Lanka development*. World Bank publications. Washington D.C.

World Bank (2012). *Information and Communications for Development 2012: Maximizing Mobile*. World Bank publications. Washington D.C.

Yang D, Ghauri P and Sonmez M (2005). Competitive analysis of the software industry in China. *International Journal of Technology Management*. 29(1/2):64–91.

Zavatta R (2008). *Financing Technology Entrepreneurs & SMEs in Developing Countries: Challenges and Opportunities*. World Bank. Washington, D.C.

STATISTICAL ANNEX

Annex table II.1.	Regions used by WITSA/IHS Global Insight					
North America	**Latin America and the Caribbean**	**Europe (EU/EFTA)**	**Europe (Non-EU/ European Free Trade Association)**	**Asia-Pacific**	**Middle East**	**Africa**
Canada	Argentina	Austria	Russian Federation	Australia	Egypt	Algeria
Mexico	Bolivia, Plurinational State of	Belgium	Turkey	Bangladesh	Iran, Islamic Republic of	Cameroon
United States	Brazil	Bulgaria	Ukraine	China	Israel	Kenya
	Chile	Czech Republic		China, Hong Kong SAR	Jordan	Morocco
	Colombia	Denmark		China, Taiwan Province of	Kuwait	Nigeria
	Costa Rica	Finland		India	Saudi Arabia	Senegal
	Ecuador	France		Indonesia	United Arab Emirates	South Africa
	Honduras	Germany		Japan		Tunisia
	Jamaica	Greece		Malaysia		Zimbabwe
	Panama	Hungary		New Zealand		
	Peru	Ireland		Pakistan		
	Uruguay	Italy		Philippines		
	Venezuela, Bolivarian Republic of	Netherlands		Republic of Korea		
		Norway		Singapore		
		Poland		Sri Lanka		
		Portugal		Thailand		
		Romania		Viet Nam		
		Slovakia				
		Slovenia				
		Spain				
		Sweden				
		Switzerland				
		United Kingdom				

Annex table II.2.   Computer software and services indicators, selected economies

Economy	ICT spending $ millions, 2011				Computer software and services spending		PC software, 2010			Computer software & services employees			Computer software and information services exports			
	Total ICT	Software	Services	Computer software & services	As percentage of total ICT	As percentage of GDP	Estimated licensed spending, $ millions	Estimated unlicensed value, $ millions	Estimated licensed spending as percentage of computer software spending	Employees	Year	As percentage of total employment	Total $ millions	Year	Ratio to total computer software & services spending	As percentage of GDP
Algeria	4 586	144	228	372	8.1%	0.2%	14	69	0.1				17	2009	0.1	0.0%
Argentina	16 986	481	1 327	1 808	10.6%	0.6%	292	681	0.7				1 184	2010	0.7	0.4%
Australia	57 876	4 269	9 906	14 174	24.5%	1.2%	2 084	658	0.5	162 000	2010	1.5%	1 496	2010	0.1	0.1%
Austria	24 545	3 357	4 261	7 619	31.0%	1.8%	662	209	0.2	55 700	2010	1.4%	2 021	2010	0.3	0.5%
Bangladesh	10 903	73	248	321	2.9%	0.3%	15	137	0.2	30 000	2010	0.1%	38	2010	0.1	0.0%
Belgium	28 613	4 131	5 859	9 991	34.9%	1.9%	699	233	0.2	47 500	2010	1.2%	4 080	2010	0.4	0.8%
Bolivia, Plurinational State of	1 072	15	38	53	5.0%	0.3%	14	54	1.0				1	2009	0.0	0.0%
Brazil	104 466	3 069	9 310	12 379	11.9%	0.7%	2 231	2 619	0.8	442 535	2006	0.5%	210	2010	0.0	0.0%
Bulgaria	3 873	134	139	273	7.1%	0.5%	61	113	0.5	32 670	2009	1.0%	380	2010	1.5	0.8%
Cameroon	1 804	20	29	49	2.7%	0.2%	2	7	0.1				1	2010	0.0	0.0%
Canada	106 565	10 609	23 366	33 975	31.9%	2.2%	2 741	1 066	0.3	286 356	2008	1.7%	4 893	2010	0.2	0.3%
Chile	9 806	361	1 007	1 368	14.0%	0.7%	214	349	0.7				91	2010	0.1	0.1%
China	427 285	18 668	31 624	50 293	11.8%	0.8%	2 194	7 779	0.1	1 290 000	2006	0.2%	9 256	2010	0.2	0.2%
China, Hong Kong SAR	20 340	540	1 130	1 670	8.2%	0.7%	277	227	0.6	..	..	..	683	2009	0.4	0.3%
China, Taiwan Province of	26 330	1 521	2 650	4 170	15.8%	0.9%	429	252	0.3	..	..	..	218	2010	0.1	0.1%
Colombia	14 797	285	699	984	6.7%	0.4%	232	272	0.9				46	2010	0.1	0.0%

Economy	ICT spending $ millions, 2011				Computer software and services spending		PC software, 2010			Computer software & services employees			Computer software and information services exports			
	Total ICT	Software	Services	Computer software & services	As percentage of total ICT spending	As percentage of GDP	Estimated licensed spending, $ millions	Estimated unlicensed value, $ millions	Estimated licensed spending as percentage of computer software spending	Employees	Year	As percentage of total employment	Total $ millions	Year	Ratio to total computer software & services spending	As percentage of GDP
Costa Rica	2 164	44	80	125	5.8%	0.4%	40	55	1.0	14 760	2010	0.8%	1 214	2010	10.5	3.6%
Czech Republic	19 867	2 943	1 827	4 770	24.0%	2.1%	347	195	0.1	75 200	2010	1.5%	1 213	2010	0.3	0.6%
Denmark	18 138	2 866	4 805	7 671	42.3%	2.2%	592	208	0.2	54 000	2010	2.0%	1 760	2010	0.3	0.5%
Ecuador	3 755	58	127	184	4.9%	0.3%	39	79	0.8	..	..	..	..	2009	0.3	0.5%
Egypt	14 082	262	487	749	5.3%	0.3%	131	196	0.6	..	..	..	171	2009	0.3	0.1%
Finland	19 561	2 353	3 010	5 363	27.4%	2.0%	579	193	0.3	49 800	2010	2.0%	5 696	2010	1.1	2.2%
France	159 107	17 432	47 292	64 724	40.7%	2.2%	4 034	2 579	0.3	407 700	2009	1.6%	1 397	2010	0.0	0.1%
Germany	216 338	24 215	49 953	74 168	34.3%	2.0%	5 667	2 096	0.3	657 000	2009	1.7%	16 017	2010	0.2	0.5%
Greece	20 312	1 090	1 266	2 356	11.6%	0.7%	209	301	0.2	20 100	2010	0.5%	473	2010	0.2	0.1%
Honduras	1 619	27	46	73	4.5%	0.5%	8	22	0.3	..	..	..	0	2009	0.0	0.0%
Hungary	13 969	1 421	950	2 371	17.0%	1.6%	189	131	0.1	40 200	2010	1.1%	1 221	2010	0.5	0.9%
India	96 431	2 271	6 162	8 432	8.7%	0.5%	1 541	2 739	0.8	2 500 000	2010-11	0.6%	33 807	2009	4.3	2.4%
Indonesia	27 360	1 186	1 004	2 190	8.0%	0.3%	198	1 322	0.2	..	..	..	114	2010	0.1	0.0%
Iran, Islamic Republic of	17 721	520	1 705	2 225	12.6%	0.5%	..	..	..	..	..	..	82	2009	0.0	0.0%
Ireland	13 436	2 163	2 126	4 289	31.9%	1.7%	254	137	0.1	41 400	2010	2.1%	37 251	2010	9.3	15.5%
Israel	11 816	931	1 965	2 896	24.5%	1.4%	378	170	0.5	112 112	2010	4.0%	7 700	2010	2.9	4.0%
Italy	114 382	11 356	25 492	36 848	32.2%	1.6%	1 956	1 879	0.2	398 800	2010	1.7%	2 067	2010	0.1	0.1%
Jamaica	446	17	27	44	9.9%	0.5%	..	..	..	..	..	..	37	2009	0.9	0.4%
Japan	363 851	14 766	71 332	86 098	23.7%	1.6%	6 496	1 624	0.5	959 193	2009	1.6%	1 052	2010	0.0	0.0%
Jordan	2 177	38	96	134	6.2%	0.5%	21	28	0.6	8 327	2008	0.4%	..	2009	..	..

Economy	ICT spending $ millions, 2011				Computer software and services spending		PC software, 2010			Computer software & services employees			Computer software and information services exports			
	Total ICT	Software	Services	Computer software & services	As percentage of total ICT spending	As percentage of GDP	Estimated licensed spending, $ millions	Estimated unlicensed value, $ millions	Estimated licensed spending as percentage of computer software spending	Employees	Year	As percentage of total employment	Total $ millions	Year	Ratio to total computer software & services spending	As percentage of GDP
Kenya	3 178	111	184	295	9.3%	0.8%	23	85	0.2	..	..	..	0	2009	0.0	0.0%
Kuwait	5 770	202	508	710	12.3%	0.5%	45	68	0.3	..	..	..	..	2009	..	..
Malaysia	25 996	755	1 261	2 017	7.8%	0.8%	476	606	0.7	47 357	2007	0.4%	1 454	2009	0.8	0.7%
Mexico	52 061	1 513	3 584	5 098	9.8%	0.5%	868	1 199	0.6	57 764	2008	0.1%	..	2009	..	..
Morocco	13 254	159	295	454	3.4%	0.4%	40	75	0.3	..	..	..	297	2010	0.7	0.3%
Netherlands	57 720	9 676	12 390	22 066	38.2%	2.5%	1 520	591	0.2	159 900	2010	2.2%	6 141	2010	0.3	0.7%
New Zealand	7 828	379	1 300	1 678	21.4%	1.3%	301	85	0.8	15 506	2010	0.7%	256	2010	0.2	0.2%
Nigeria	18 990	68	87	155	0.8%	0.1%	49	225	1.0	..	..	..	..	2009	..	..
Norway	18 195	2 801	4 445	7 246	39.8%	1.6%	639	261	0.3	37 000	2009	1.5%	2 192	2010	0.3	0.5%
Pakistan	7 099	272	636	908	12.8%	0.5%	41	217	0.2	..	..	..	193	2010	0.2	0.1%
Panama	1 682	14	96	110	6.5%	0.4%	26	68	2.1	..	..	..	25	2010	0.3	0.1%
Peru	6 620	179	463	642	9.7%	0.4%	83	176	0.5	..	..	..	20	2009	0.0	0.0%
Philippines	13 505	125	999	1 124	8.3%	0.6%	125	278	1.1	67 198	2008	0.2%	2 151	2010	2.1	1.2%
Poland	32 132	2 198	3 065	5 263	16.4%	1.0%	471	553	0.2	129 614	2009	1.0%	1 545	2010	0.3	0.3%
Portugal	16 299	1 387	1 408	2 795	17.2%	1.1%	342	228	0.3	36 300	2009	0.7%	350	2010	0.1	0.2%
Korea, Republic of	88 109	2 864	8 844	11 708	13.3%	1.0%	1 083	722	0.4	..	..	..	235	2010	0.0	0.0%
Romania	13 368	412	509	921	6.9%	0.5%	110	195	0.3	35 000	2009	0.4%	890	2010	1.1	0.5%
Russian Federation	61 422	4 238	6 435	10 673	17.4%	0.7%	1 530	2 842	0.4	296 227	2008	0.4%	1 359	2010	0.1	0.1%
Saudi Arabia	36 409	1 107	3 068	4 175	11.5%	0.9%	382	414	0.4	..	..	..	..	2009	..	..
Senegal	2 570	28	50	78	3.1%	0.6%	2	7	0.1	..	..	..	6	2009	0.1	0.0%

Economy	ICT spending $ millions, 2011				Computer software and services spending		PC software, 2010			Computer software & services employees			Computer software and information services exports			
	Total ICT	Software	Services	Computer software & services	As percentage of total ICT	As percentage of GDP	Estimated licensed spending, $ millions	Estimated unlicensed value, $ millions	Estimated licensed spending as percentage of computer software spending	Employees	Year	As percentage of total employment	Total $ millions	Year	Ratio to total computer software & services spending	As percentage of GDP
Singapore	13 887	1 200	2 351	3 551	25.6%	1.7%	452	233	0.4	..	..	..	1 788	2010	0.5	0.9%
Slovakia	8 330	418	611	1 029	12.4%	1.0%	87	63	0.2	26 100	2010	1.1%	307	2010	0.3	0.3%
Slovenia	2 726	265	260	525	19.3%	0.9%	53	47	0.2	12 300	2010	1.4%	157	2010	0.3	0.3%
South Africa	37 523	2 844	5 574	8 417	22.4%	2.2%	953	513	0.4	83 800	2009	0.7%	290	2010	0.0	0.1%
Spain	79 009	10 492	12 126	22 618	28.6%	1.5%	1 465	1 105	0.2	234 400	2010	1.3%	6 358	2010	0.3	0.4%
Sri Lanka	3 127	3	53	56	1.8%	0.1%	14	83	4.8	..	..	..	265	2010	5.1	0.6%
Sweden	29 591	4 803	10 376	15 179	51.3%	3.2%	1 233	411	0.3	92 000	2009	2.1%	6 651	2010	0.5	1.5%
Switzerland	38 339	8 022	7 247	15 269	39.8%	2.9%	1 207	424	0.2	81 900	2010	2.1%	..	2009	..	..
Thailand	20 176	1 963	1 546	3 510	17.4%	1.1%	287	777	0.2	58 000	2009	0.2%	..	2009	..	..
Tunisia	2 711	96	188	285	10.5%	0.6%	20	52	0.2	..	..	..	41	2009	0.2	0.1%
Turkey	28 405	1 157	2 118	3 275	11.5%	0.5%	316	516	0.3	..	..	..	16	2010	0.0	0.0%
Ukraine	10 039	445	670	1 115	11.1%	0.8%	93	571	0.2	..	..	..	429	2010	0.4	0.3%
United Arab Emirates	13 749	374	1 316	1 690	12.3%	0.7%	308	173	1.0	..	..	..	..	2009	..	..
United Kingdom	186 646	24 034	60 719	84 753	45.4%	3.2%	4 991	1 846	0.2	478 220	2010	1.7%	10 856	2010	0.1	0.5%
United States of America	1 133 256	138 491	375 899	514 390	45.4%	3.3%	38 060	9 515	0.3	867 100	2008	0.6%	13 830	2010	0.0	0.1%
Uruguay	1 521	33	88	121	8.0%	0.3%	35	78	1.2	2 280	2007	0.1%	180	2010	1.6	0.5%
Venezuela, Bolivarian Republic of	10 037	343	1 059	1 402	14.0%	0.3%	90	662	0.3	..	..	..	9	2010	0.0	0.0%
Zimbabwe	1 242	0	2	2	0.2%	0.0%	1	6	1.8	..	..	..	..	2009	..	..

.. – Data not available.

LIST OF SELECTED PUBLICATIONS IN THE AREA OF SCIENCE, TECHNOLOGY AND ICT FOR DEVELOPMENT

A. Flagship reports

Information Economy Report 2012: The Software Industry and Developing Countries. United Nations publication. Sales no. (forthcoming). New York and Geneva.

Information Economy Report 2011: ICTs as an Enabler for Private Sector Development. United Nations publication. Sales no. E.11.II.D.6. New York and Geneva.

Technology and Innovation Report 2011: Powering Development with Renewable Energy Technologies. United Nations publication. UNCTAD/TIR/2011. New York and Geneva.

Technology and Innovation Report 2010: Enhancing Food Security in Africa through Science, Technology and Innovation. United Nations publication. UNCTAD/TIR/2009. New York and Geneva.

Information Economy Report 2010: ICTs, Enterprises and Poverty Alleviation. United Nations publication. Sales no. E.10.II.D.17. New York and Geneva.

Information Economy Report 2009: Trends and Outlook in Turbulent Times. United Nations publication. Sales no. E.09.II.D.18. New York and Geneva.

Information Economy Report 2007–2008: Science and Technology for Development – The New Paradigm of ICT. United Nations publication. Sales no. E.07.II.D.13. New York and Geneva.

Information Economy Report 2006: The Development Perspective. United Nations publication. Sales no. E.06 II.D.8. New York and Geneva.

Information Economy Report 2005: E-commerce and Development. United Nations publication. Sales no. E.05 II.D.19. New York and Geneva.

E-Commerce and Development Report 2004. United Nations publication. New York and Geneva.

E-Commerce and Development Report 2003. United Nations publication. Sales no. E.03.II.D.30. New York and Geneva.

E-Commerce and Development Report 2002. United Nations publication. New York and Geneva.

E-Commerce and Development Report 2001. United Nations publication. Sales no. E.01.II.D.30. New York and Geneva.

B. ICT Policy Reviews

ICT Policy Review of Egypt. United Nations publication. UNCTAD/DTL/STICT/2011/6. New York and Geneva.

C. Science, Technology and Innovation Policy Reviews

Science, Technology & Innovation Policy Review of the Dominican Republic. United Nations publication. UNCTAD/DTL/STICT/2012/1. New York and Geneva.

A Framework for Science, Technology and Innovation Policy Reviews. United Nations publication. UNCTAD/DTL/STICT/2011/7. New York and Geneva.

Science, Technology & Innovation Policy Review of El Salvador. United Nations publication. UNCTAD/DTL/STICT/2011/4. New York and Geneva.

Science, Technology and Innovation Policy Review of Peru. United Nations publication. UNCTAD/DTL/STICT/2010/2. New York and Geneva.

Science, Technology and Innovation Policy Review of Ghana. United Nations publication. UNCTAD/DTL/STICT/2009/8. New York and Geneva.

Science, Technology and Innovation Policy Review of Lesotho. United Nations publication. UNCTAD/DTL/ST-ICT/2009/7. New York and Geneva.

Science, Technology and Innovation Policy Review of Mauritania. United Nations publication. UNCTAD/DTL/STICT/2009/6. New York and Geneva.

Science, Technology and Innovation Policy Review of Angola. United Nations publication. UNCTAD/SDTE/ST-ICT/2008/1. New York and Geneva.

Science, Technology and Innovation Policy Review: the Islamic Republic of Iran. United Nations publication. UNCTAD/ITE/IPC/2005/7. New York and Geneva.

Investment and Innovation Policy Review of Ethiopia. United Nations publication. UNCTAD/ITE/IPC/Misc.4. New York and Geneva.

Science, Technology and Innovation Policy Review: Colombia. United Nations publication. Sales no. E.99.II.D.13. New York and Geneva.

Science, Technology and Innovation Policy Review: Jamaica. United Nations publication. Sales no. E.98.II.D.7. New York and Geneva.

D. Other publications

Mobile Money for Business Development in the East African Community: A Comparative Study of Existing Platforms and Regulations. UNCTAD/DTL/STICT/2012/2. New York and Geneva.

Implementing WSIS Outcomes: Experience to Date and Prospects for the Future. United Nations Commission on Science and Technology for Development. United Nations publication. UNCTAD/DTL/STICT/2011/3. New York and Geneva.

Water for Food: Innovative Water Management Technologies for Food Security and Poverty Alleviation. UNCTAD Current Studies on Science, Technology and Innovation. United Nations publication. UNCTAD/DTL/STICT/2011/2. New York and Geneva.

Measuring the Impacts of Information and Communication Technology for Development. UNCTAD Current Studies on Science, Technology and Innovation. United Nations publication. UNCTAD/DTL/STICT/2011/1. New York and Geneva.

Financing Mechanisms for Information and Communication Technologies for Development. UNCTAD Current Studies on Science, Technology and Innovation. United Nations publication. UNCTAD/DTL/STICT/2009/5. New York and Geneva.

Renewable Energy Technologies for Rural Development. UNCTAD Current Studies on Science, Technology and Innovation. United Nations publication. UNCTAD/DTL/STICT/2009/4. New York and Geneva.

Study on prospects for harmonizing cyberlegislation in Central America and the Caribbean. UNCTAD/DTL/ST-ICT/2009/3. New York and Geneva. (In English and Spanish)

Study on Prospects for Harmonizing Cyberlegislation in Latin America. UNCTAD publication. UNCTAD/DTL/STICT/2009/1. New York and Geneva. (In English and Spanish.)

Manual for the Production of Statistics on the Information Economy 2009 Revised Edition. United Nations publication. UNCTAD/SDTE/ECB/2007/2/REV.1. New York and Geneva.

WSIS Follow-up Report 2008. United Nations publication. UNCTAD/DTL/STICT/2008/1. New York and Geneva.

Measuring the Impact of ICT Use in Business: the Case of Manufacturing in Thailand. United Nations publication. Sales no. E.08.II.D.13. New York and Geneva.

World Information Society Report 2007: Beyond WSIS. United Nations and ITU publication. Geneva.

World Information Society Report 2006. United Nations and ITU publication. Geneva.

The Digital Divide: ICT Diffusion Index 2005. United Nations publication. New York and Geneva.

The Digital Divide: ICT Development Indices 2004. United Nations publication. New York and Geneva.

Africa's Technology Gap: Case Studies on Kenya, Ghana, Tanzania and Uganda. United Nations publication. UNCTAD/ITE/IPC/Misc.13. New York and Geneva.

The Biotechnology Promise: Capacity-Building for Participation of Developing Countries in the Bioeconomy. United Nations publication. UNCTAD/ITE/IPC/2004/2. New York and Geneva.

Information and Communication Technology Development Indices. United Nations publication. Sales no. E.03. II.D.14. New York and Geneva.

Investment and Technology Policies for Competitiveness: Review of Successful Country Experiences. United Nations publication. UNCTAD/ITE/IPC/2003/2. New York and Geneva.

Electronic Commerce and Music Business Development in Jamaica: A Portal to the New Economy? United Nations publication. Sales no. E.02.II.D.17. New York and Geneva.

Changing Dynamics of Global Computer Software and Services Industry: Implications for Developing Countries. United Nations publication. Sales no. E.02.II.D.3. New York and Geneva.

Partnerships and Networking in Science and Technology for Development. United Nations publication. Sales no. E.02.II.D.5. New York and Geneva.

Transfer of Technology for Successful Integration into the Global Economy: A Case Study of Embraer in Brazil. United Nations publication. UNCTAD/ITE/IPC/Misc.20. New York and Geneva.

Transfer of Technology for Successful Integration into the Global Economy: A Case Study of the South African Automotive Industry. United Nations publication. UNCTAD/ITE/IPC/Misc.21. New York and Geneva.

Transfer of Technology for the Successful Integration into the Global Economy: A Case Study of the Pharmaceutical Industry in India. United Nations publication. UNCTAD/ITE/IPC/Misc.22. New York and Geneva.

Coalition of Resources for Information and Communication Technologies. United Nations publication. UNCTAD/ITE/TEB/13. New York and Geneva.

Key Issues in Biotechnology. United Nations publication. UNCTAD/ITE/TEB/10. New York and Geneva.

An Assault on Poverty: Basic Human Needs, Science and Technology. Joint publication with IDRC. ISBN 0-88936-800-7. United Nations publication.

Compendium of International Arrangements on Transfer of Technology: Selected Instruments. United Nations publication. Sales no. E.01.II.D.28. New York and Geneva.

E. Publications by the Partnership on Measuring ICT for Development

Measuring the WSIS Targets - A statistical framework. ITU. Geneva.

Core ICT Indicators 2010. ITU. Geneva.

The Global Information Society: A Statistical View 2008. United Nations publication. Santiago.

Measuring ICT: The Global Status of ICT Indicators. Partnership on Measuring ICT for Development. United Nations ICT Task Force. New York.

READERSHIP SURVEY

Information Economy Report 2012: The Software Industry and Developing Countries

In order to improve the quality of this report and other publications of the Science, Technology and ICT Branch of UNCTAD, we welcome the views of our readers on this publication. It would be greatly appreciated if you would complete the following questionnaire and return it to:

ICT Analysis Section, Office E-7075
Science, Technology and ICT Branch
Division on Technology and Logistics
United Nations
Palais des Nations,
CH-1211, Geneva, Switzerland
Fax: 41 22 917 00 50
ICT4D@unctad.org

1. Name and address of respondent (optional)

....

....

....

2. Which of the following best describes your area of work?

Government ministry (please specify)	☐	Not-for-profit organization	☐
National statistics office	☐	Public enterprise	☐
Telecommunication regulatory authority	☐	Academic or research institution	☐
Private enterprise	☐	Media	☐
International organization	☐	Other (please specify)	☐

3. In which country do you work? ....

4. What is your assessment of the contents of this publication?

Excellent ☐
Good ☐
Adequate ☐
Poor ☐

5. How useful is this publication to your work?

Very useful ☐

Somewhat useful ☐

Irrelevant ☐

6. Please indicate the three things you liked best about this publication.

a) ....

b) ....

c) ....

7. Please indicate the three things you liked least about this publication.

a) ....

b) ....

c) ....

8. What additional aspects would you like future editions of this report to cover:

....

....

....

9. Other comments:

....

....

....

DATE DUE

DEMCO, INC. 38-2931